AN ADVENTURE ACROSS PERU

A MOTOTAXI RACE

AN
ADVENTURE ACROSS PERU

A MOTOTAXI RACE

NATHAN DONEEN

ThoughtBed Publishing

An Adventure Across Peru
A Mototaxi Race by Nathan Doneen

Copyright © 2018 by Nathan Doneen
www.nathandoneen.com

All rights reserved. No part of this book may be reproduced or transmitted in any form or by any means, electronic or mechanical, including photocopying, recording, or by any information storage and retrieval system, without permission in writing from the publisher.

Cover by Rob Allen
Editorial Considerations Provided by Emma Fell
Mototaxi Photograph courtesy of The Adventurists

ISBN 13: 978-1-948371-01-8 Kindle
ISBN 13: 978-1-948371-02-5 Print
LCCN: 2018904087

ThoughtBed Publishing

This is a work of narrative nonfiction. Dialogue and events herein have been recounted to the best of the author's memory. The author also acknowledges the difficult environment in which these memories were formed and apologizes in advance for any mistakes or recall error. The author trusts that as you read, you'll understand. Enjoy.

For the people of Peru...

...and the people of this planet.

Prologue

CINDY, "THE SLUT."

Cindy did not receive this title from me. Nor from my teammates. In fact, she had done nothing to warrant it. So it should be no surprise that, in this story, Cindy is the victim.

This is a difficult admission. You see, it was into our charge that Cindy was placed. It was us who were supposed to protect her. She had not volunteered to travel to the northwest coast of Peru, to a village of a few hundred people, where we were first acquainted. She had not requested we drive her a few hundred miles to the Sacred Valley in southeast Peru, which was our destination. And she certainly hadn't offered to be crammed into the back of a mototaxi. But that was exactly what she got, so Cindy's fate rested squarely on the shoulders of my team.

I don't mean to belittle her anguish, but Cindy was not in poor company. All of us had signed up for unbearable driving conditions, unpredictable mechanical failures, and unexpected cultural barriers at every step of the way. We were all looking for our own brand of misery. How else does one explain an international gathering with the purpose of elective suffering?

Besides her forced participation, what really set Cindy apart from the rest of us was her Barbie Doll proportions—which is to say her inhuman proportions. That's right: Cindy was a doll, imprisoned by plastic wrap on top of a quinceañera piñata. And even though she was inanimate, she had earned the title of Pink Fairy.

It was the Pink Fairy my team was awarded, and with it, the responsibility for Cindy. This was our additional task, our additional challenge.

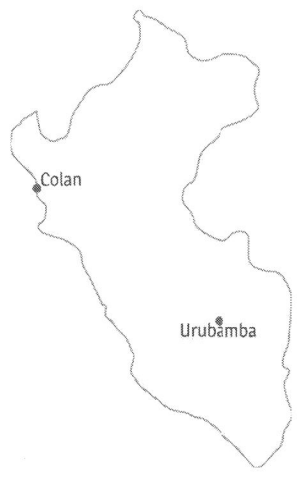

Chapter 1

Elective Ignorance

THE CELLS OF YOUR BODY routinely kill themselves. Stay calm—this is a good thing.

Old cells collect deficiencies, malfunction, and become diseased. To preserve the organism as a whole, they elect to die. Meanwhile, healthy cells divide in order to replace those lost. Given the varied stresses across cell types, different tissues are replaced at different rates. The lining of your small intestine will replace itself after just a few days; your stomach lining, after a week; your skin takes ten to thirty days; and the red blood cells circulating through your body will be replaced after four months—that's 100 million new red blood cells every minute.

How do we know these rates? During World War II, some very smart scientists developed the atomic bomb—you may have heard of it. After two detonations dropped the curtain on the Pacific theater, research was amped up, dragging the world into the Cold War and igniting an endless series of test detonations. Then came some very clever scientists who put these bombs to good, honest, morally undisputed use. Their research used the carbon-14 leftover from the nuclear explosions to determine the above tissue ages. The clever part: they didn't need more detonations.

Back to my point though: cells die. Not only do they die, but they're *supposed* to die. That most of us are ignorant of this process doesn't alter the outcome. In fact, I might argue that because it doesn't alter the outcome, most people would choose ignorance. That's not difficult to understand—that millions of these little pieces of me are dying every minute is not something I want to think about.

Perhaps that's why I wasn't fazed when Duncan, standing before the craziest group of people I've ever been a part of, made a case for ignorance.

At least when dealing with Peruvian Police.

"There's a phrase I want you all to memorize. I think you'll be surprised at how often it can get you out of trouble." When you've decided to race one of the worst pieces of machinery on the planet a few hundred miles across Peru, from Colan to Urubamba, a heaping pile of trouble is exactly what's waiting for you. "For all of you who don't speak Spanish—*and* for those who do—here it is: *'No fumar español'*–" Duncan chuckled, the two or three Spanish speakers in our group joining him. "–which means, 'I don't smoke Spanish.'"

The group burst with laughter.

"Saying 'I don't speak Spanish' is one thing. It is quite another to demonstrate it. What police officer wants to have a mime argument over a petty traffic infraction? Yes, it makes you look like a stupid Westerner, but you'd be surprised how many people have gotten out of a tight spot with that phrase. So please, commit it to memory."

Duncan went on to explain the guidelines of the race—the Mototaxi Junket—all of which centered on the theme of "Don't be an asshole." Then, after a few more anecdotes and some advice from our Peruvian liaisons, Duncan concluded the meeting.

I left, my mind already racing. Would we get lost? Stranded? Robbed? Would we spend a fortune to keep our engine running—all 150CCs? Would the desert permit us to cross it, or would we be desiccated? Would the mountains continue to stand tall, or would they prove to be a climbable divide? Would the jungle sprout our success, or would it leave us devoured in a humid and hasty decay?

My mind darted, but my body strolled. We made our way back to our hostel, not far from the hotel where the meeting had been. Nothing was far in Colan, a quiet beach town near the city of Piura. Sand buried the streets. Each step sunk into the road, cushioned and muted. There was no rush here; the sand wouldn't permit it.

At the hostel, a few teams had gathered on the oceanside deck. The table was covered with maps and beer bottles, the air filled with speculation on routes. The Scots paid extra attention—they hadn't even brought a map. That's because this wasn't a race in the traditional sense. The reason for speculating was because there was no course and, in fact, there was only one rule: "Get your mototaxi to the finish...no matter what." How we went about this was irrelevant. The whole purpose of using mototaxis was to make their second-rate quality, low dependability, and unpredictability contribute to the adventure.

The sun arced to the horizon, beer bottles emptied, and the tide came in, the extended surf polishing the stilts on which our hostel stood.

The next night we gathered again, and for a few minutes we all sat quiet. Not with fatigue from the last day of mototaxi test driving and tinkering or with the soreness from the soccer match against the locals. We were quiet in respect of what stood before us.

This stillness was a first for the group—a very diverse group. Possibly the only thing we all shared was the English language. The organization that hosted this race was a British charity, called The Adventurists. They have a unique approach to raising money. Organize a crazy event, draw in crazy participants, and have *them* raise the money.

I can't stress the crazy element enough—"Adventurists" is an apt name. With events like the Mongol Rally, the Rickshaw Run, and the Icarus Trophy, you can see how narrow a cross section of society this charity targets.

There were nearly fifty of us—about twenty teams—seated at a banquet table, the remnants of a feast laid before us. This was the Launch Party, the last opportunity we racers would have to bond before being thrown to the mercy of our taxis. Around the table were seated a number of Brits, the dominant demographic. Also represented were Australia, New Zealand, Romania, Scotland, South Africa, Switzerland, and the United States. But at that moment, we were engrossed with Peruvian culture.

After we had crammed our faces with the best Peruvian cuisine, to the groaning of stomachs and creaking of chair legs, and after everyone declined a fourth helping, a group of locals marched into the banquet room, wearing traditional clothing and carrying instruments. We fell silent for the performance.

Historically, the Spanish restructuring of the Incan culture had not been subtle. Since that colonial era, Peru's culture has been seen as a fusion of Incan and Spanish traditions. "Clash" may be a more appropriate descriptor though, as was demonstrated by the performers. The first dance was one of strict choreography, executed in time with plucked guitar strings that snapped out from strummed chords, paired with the clacking of the dancers' thick-soled shoes on the wood floor. Even the costumes were constrictive. That is not to say this dance wasn't beautiful or impressive, but it could not relate to the dance that followed. The indigenous customs flowed through the breathy music, through the loose and simple ornateness of the dress, and out through the dancers' relaxed and fluid limbs. The same musicians, the same dancers, the same small dance floor, all able to embody such disparate traditions. More impressive still was the performers' ability to transition between them without suffering the paradoxical nature of hosting both.

We were quiet. We were transfixed. We all sprung to our feet and beat our hands red at the conclusion, exchanging impressed glances and nods of approval. Many bows and toothy grins were returned before the dancers retreated out of the banquet room.

Duncan, less attractive and much less graceful, took the performers' place. As the company representative, Duncan was here to collect paperwork, hand out mototaxi keys, and see us off on our grand adventure. He gave us all the last-minute updates, the current standings in regards to money raised for charity, and then began the pre-race award ceremony.

These wouldn't be considered awards by most people—more like mockery. But in our group, mockery was a symbolic tip of the hat. If you weren't the punch line of any jokes, you were doing it wrong. So the awards were a good laugh before the race began.

Trophies included a toilet seat, a set of orange coveralls, and the Pink Fairy Award.

Awards were not random, but reflected the team's character. For instance, that toilet seat went to the team voted most likely to shit their pants while the coveralls went to the team voted most likely to attempt a roadside repair. So to understand the Pink Fairy Award, you need to understand my team.

I knew Scott from college. As an endurance runner, Scott had the following mentality: when in doubt, push through; if doubt persists, keep pushing. This is the kind of philosophy that translates to self-enabling. Not the type that leads to self-destruction, but to masochism. This might explain Scott's desire to become a polyglot. Our university was located in Washington state, but he had studied abroad in Morocco just to work on his French and Arabic. And after he registered for the race, he had turned his attention to Spanish. And that's not to mention the computer languages he knew as a programmer.

On campus, while Scott had been typing away in the computer lab, I had been in a formaldehyde-filled biology lab prodding the department's most treasured pickled specimen: a small shark with one side of its body cut away to reveal the internal organs. So how did Scott and I know each other? We had both worked at the campus rock climbing gym. But being on staff together still hadn't made us best friends. In fact, we never even saw each other after graduation.

So, surprise was the appropriate response when after two years of zero contact, I received an email from Scott. I clicked through the hyperlink he had sent and watched the three-minute video. My heart raced. I spent another two minutes on The Adventurist website before I sent Scott a reply.

Scott had asked several people to join this team before me. Almost all of them were enthusiastic, even eager to sign up. But, as is typical, all of them had an excuse. So Scott had changed tactics. Who was crazy enough to join him? Maybe the guy who pedaled a mountain bike more than 2700 miles from Canada to Mexico down the Continental Divide...alone.

The travel résumés of Scott and I stood in stark contrast to Andrew, a friend and coworker of Scott's. He had never been out-of-country. An Adventurist event seemed a difficult way to begin an experience abroad, so I had to hand it to the guy for signing up. And not just for signing up, but for driving the bandwagon straight into this race. Scott had mentioned the Mototaxi Junket to Andrew and after a little research, Andrew was ready to go, with or without Scott.

His gung-ho-ness and brilliance made Andrew a crucial member of the team and he was determined to be prepared. Months before the race, he and Scott had learned what engine would be powering our mototaxi. Andrew bought an old scooter with an equivalent engine and rebuilt it, just to get himself acquainted. Impressive. So was the toolkit he put together. And that's not to mention all the comforts of home Andrew installed on our mototaxi in the days leading up to the race: a GPS unit (complete with DC converter so we could run it off our mototaxi's battery), a throttle lock for those long straight stretches (think cruise control), and even extra padding for the driver's seat.

These things would be useful. But were they in the spirit of the race? The Adventurists organization encourages people to abandon modern comforts, to throw caution, and let the chips fall. We were supposed to get lost, be uncomfortable, and hate life. These luxuries would make reaching those objectives more difficult. It was because of this preparedness that we had won Cindy.

The Pink Fairy Award was the issuance of an additional challenge. Everyone thought we—team *Three Tired Travelers*— were most likely to cross the finish line with our limbs still attached, so we needed to be brought down a peg or two. As a result, Cindy was given to us with a task: deliver her to the finish line in pristine condition.

This would be difficult enough, but I was concerned about the hidden challenge lurking within our preparations. You can't be ready for the unknown, which was what waited for us outside the village of Colan. Would our preparedness give us a false sense of security? Would we be blindsided by the unpredictability of the race?

There was only one way to find out.

Chapter 2

Prohibition and Pisco

WITH CINDY and her piñata balanced in our hands, we strolled downstairs to continue the Launch Party in the main restaurant. Most of the Junketeers crowded around the cocktail menu designed just for the occasion. Available drinks were the Kick Starter, Sprocket Rocket, and Traffic Light Jello Shot, all of which were made with pisco, a high-proof spirit unique to Peru, like Scotch whiskey to Scotland. We had all acquired a taste for pisco in those few days and I can't estimate how many Pisco Sours had been ordered in Colan in that short period. In fact, I shouldn't.

In the days leading up to the race, the sale or distribution of alcohol was illegal. There was a government-mandated ban on alcohol for the duration of an election, which coincided with the start of our race. It was this ban that had pushed the start line to Colan, in fact. In previous years, the northern terminus of the race had been the city of Piura itself. The organizers couldn't risk depriving us of this liquid courage though, so they found a place that *would* serve us alcohol. It just happened to be 40 miles outside of Piura, in this coastal village.

The line to the bar was wide and slithered through the restaurant, bumping against tables and chairs. The legal issues of the night dragged out the wait. The restaurant staff wouldn't serve us beer in its bottle for fear we might wander into the streets and cross paths with someone of legal standing. That would have been an awkward conversation:

"Where'd you get that bottle of beer when there is a country-wide ban on alcohol?"

"Uhhh...no fumar español?"

Instead, the staff poured the beer into a glass. Does a glass of beer versus a bottle make any *gringo* less conspicuous in any Peruvian village? Hard to say, but the restaurant's choice was understandable. Given this was our last night though, there weren't many reservations among the racers, so the bar had run out of clean glasses. No bar-back had ever worked so hard. He ducked and dodged and wove through the crowd where he snatched nearly-empty glasses out of unsuspecting hands to stockpile at his sink. There, they got a quick rinse and polish before they were passed off to the bartender who skated back and forth across a pile of bottle caps between the beer fridge and the blender that made the Pisco Sours.

"Ay boys! Congratulations on the Pink Fairy!"

The Scots. We had been staying in the same hostel as this lot and they were a lively bunch. Lewis was an aspiring MMA fighter; Kane had fallen in love during our few days in Colan; and Shaun was determined to wear his kilt in the *traditional* fashion for the entire race (keep in mind, the driver straddles a seat).

Shaun nodded at our Pink Fairy. "She looks like a Cindy, huh?"

Yes...that's how Cindy got her name.

"Ay, she does." Lewis poked at her. "And that's a lovely green dress. It really matches her pink cowboy boots!" The Scots were among those to arrive at the bar before the glasses ran out. "You Americans really like those boots, huh? They match your guns!" They all raised their hands in the air, thumbs hammering down on invisible rounds that discharged through pointer-finger barrels. "Pew! Pew! Pew!" Their impression had not been influenced by the alcohol. They had been firing finger-rounds into the air every time they saw us over the past few days.

Scott stepped in. "How many times do we have to tell you guys? It's the *Texans* that have the guns."

Up walked Aaron and Josh (aka team *Duckface*), the sarcasm dripping from Aaron's words: "That's right. The *Texans* are here!"

Everything is bigger in Texas...at least that's the local mantra. In reality, it's the second biggest of the United States, but I'm sure most Texans would explain that it's the largest of the contiguous states. Guns are common there as are cowboy hats. It's also home of the Dallas Cowboys, who claim to be the most American team in the National Football League. How they can be more American than any other American team competing in an American league of an American sport is beyond me.

Texas is also very conservative. But in that sea of conservatism lies the liberal island of Austin, an environment well-suited to Josh and Aaron. Instead of bringing sidearms or ten-gallon hats on their Peruvian adventure, they packed a ten-pound bag of lollipops they could hand out to kids.

The Scots jumped back in. "In any case, a green dress with pink boots seems pretty slutty. Lucky for you boys you have Cindy 'the slut'...wish we'd have some female company along the way!"

Yes...that's how Cindy got her title.

"Anyways, it's time for a refill."

The Scots wandered back toward the bar while another team pushed toward us.

"Hey fellas, congrats on the award." The Australians, Barry and Gerald (aka team *Macho Picchu*), squeezed through the crowd toward us. They were some of the oldest racers, and my idols. They were middle-aged, but still pursuing their passions and dreams—in a fashion most unapologetic. And though representing Australia, Barry wasn't Australian originally. He began life in American where he became a pilot in the armed forces. He had participated in a military exchange program and served at a base in Australia. At the end of his time there, he had no desire to leave and has since called Australia home.

"So how do you boys plan on packing the doll?"

We glanced at each other. We had enough space and rope to tie her down, but she was on top of a piñata.

"Carefully?"

"I'm sure," Josh laughed.

"Hey, since we're all here." Aaron reached into his pocket and pulled out a few slips of paper. He passed one to Andrew and one to Gerald. "We made these *Peru Bingo* boards this morning. I got everything on there we were joking about. Josh and I had to make up a few more though."

We crowded around the papers and looked over the grid.

"'Rickety Bridge Crossing'?" Andrew asked. "How rickety are we talking?"

Josh shrugged. "The more dangerous the better."

Barry and Gerald looked up together. "'Picture with an AK47'?"

Aaron nodded. "Bonus points if you're the one holding it."

We laughed together over our *Peru Bingo* boards, a side game meant for just us three teams. Then it was time to catch up with the drinking crowd.

The plastic wrap encircling Cindy and her piñata crinkled under the jostling of the crowd as we forced our way to the bar line. Jan and Paddy queued up behind us. Another of the British teams, Jan and Paddy were also toward the upper end of the age spectrum. We had spent a fair amount of time with them, having taken a long day trip together into Paita for supplies.

Paddy and I had had many enlightening discussions, and with his accumulated wisdom he was able to help me figure out the existential angst I had been experiencing prior to receiving Scott's invitation. Little did Scott and Andrew know, but this race had liberated me from a job hunt, and the prospect of beginning the rest of my life.

"Paddy, have you heard from your friend yet?"

"Yes, finally. She made it to Lima, but she can't get to Piura until the day after tomorrow."

"Will you start with us tomorrow? Try to meet her somewhere?"

"We considered that, but there just aren't any good places past Piura for us to meet. Our plan is to start late and time it so that we pick her up from the airport. We'll be a day behind everyone. But who knows, maybe we'll catch up."

"We are all on mototaxis. There's probably a more-than-decent chance of that happening."

We racers maintained the line to the bar all night. The staff lost patience with their own rules and the problems they caused, so by midnight we were allowed to hold our own beer bottle. But the crowd-navigating bar back was posted at the door to ensure no bottles left and spilled the hotel's secret.

Team *Three Tired Travelers* played it tame at the Launch Party. What could be worse than a hangover on a mototaxi? After a long night of food, friends, cultural insights, and a lot of bullshitting, Scott, Andrew, and I headed back to the hostel to sleep away our last night in Colan.

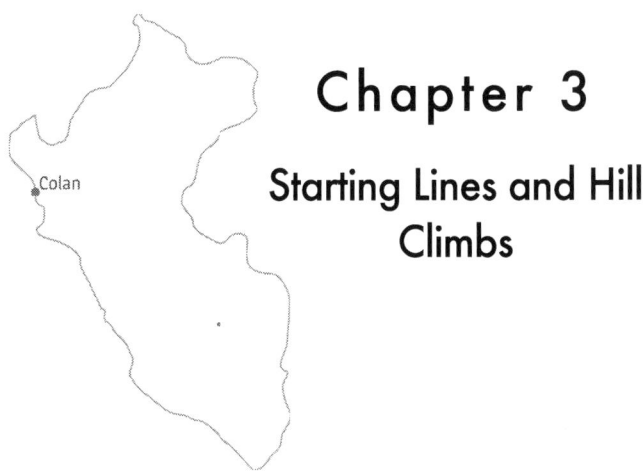

Chapter 3

Starting Lines and Hill Climbs

COOL EARTH.

This was the charity The Adventurists had partnered with and for which we had raised money. Given the massive amount of rainforest destroyed since the 1970s—and because the location of this event—it made sense to team up with Cool Earth.

Their model is to partner with villages within stretches of at-risk forest. Over a period of several years, Cool Earth creates an economic situation within a village that makes it beneficial for the villagers to conserve the rainforest. This approach concentrates the efforts of conservation within the rainforest itself.

At the starting line though, in the middle of the desert, the furthest thing from my mind was the rainforest. We woke early and helped our crew of local mechanics arrange the twenty mototaxis into two columns on Main Street, Colan. As a large Mototaxi Junket banner was strung across the head of the columns, locals began to congregate.

Mototaxis are common in Peru, but typically as transportation across short distances. Even mototaxi drivers—

the people who best understand the machine's capacities and limitations—thought driving a mototaxi nearly the length of Peru was insane. So it was no wonder that the locals had gathered. Who wouldn't want to say they had seen off the crazy *gringos*?

As the starting time approached, our fellow racers gathered too. Compression straps of luggage hummed through their buckles. Bungee cords groaned through their stretch, their hook ends squeaking against metallic frames. Blue tarps crackled as they enveloped luggage in the cargo bays, beneath the flapping of the mototaxi's own vinyl roof. Most teams attempted to start their engines. Some were even successful. Our mechanics ran to find the engines that emitted a death sputter with each kick of the starter—their solution was to free the floats inside the carburetor by rapping on the casing with a wrench. Meanwhile, suckers were unwrapped, their paper protection crumpled and stuffed away in the wake of Josh and Aaron, who were making the rounds with their too-heavy bag of lollipops. Zippers joined in the chorus, as last-minute items were either retrieved or stuffed away. This all happened to the flutter of camera shutters, their aim to capture it all.

Pete in particular had an eye for that sort of thing. He was the sole member of team *Rubber Duckies*, the third American team. Pete was in video production and worked on a popular NatGeo show. He had participated in the Mongol Rally a few years before, another Adventurist race from London to Mongolia. Now he was in Peru as the *only* one-man team of the race. His team name was also his traveling tradition: he handed out rubber duckies to kids everywhere he went and marked the location on a map. His world map was pretty dense with ducky markers. So of course, his yellow mototaxi was topped with a giant rubber ducky.

As the official start time approached, the local marching band appeared, as well as the mayor of Colan. It was only a five-piece band, but in such a small town, it was flattering. After the band finished, we crowded beneath the banner for a group picture, possibly the last picture of us alive. Then, we were ushered to a line in the sand behind the columns of mototaxis. We weren't allowed to start on our taxis because a proper race involves running. Spectators gathered at either end of the line, on the porch of a small store at one end and in the shade of a blank wall at the other. We racers did not dig our toes in for traction—the sand was endless. All was quiet as we crouched. The wind moved between us.

Duncan started the final count down. Before he got to "1," we all shot off the line. The sand was as thick in front of the line as it had been behind. It swallowed our feet, tripped us, slipped beneath shoes as we struggled to our mototaxis. Our fervor was uncommon in the relaxed setting, and us running to our mototaxis was as fast as anyone had ever moved in Colan.

Our taxi, Clifford, was near the front of the column. His bright red top, sides, and engine covers had reminded us of *Clifford the Big Red Dog.* The color was where the similarities stopped though because *our* Clifford was more disobedient and less predictable. That's why the electric starter failed under Andrew's thumb. Mototaxis started to fly past us as Andrew unfolded the kick-starter, and it took several attempts before the engine grabbed its spark and caught life. With Scott and I tucked away in the back and Cindy bungeed between the ribs of our mototaxi roof's frame, Andrew took us beneath the banner and down the sand street. We made a left turn off Main Street, our tracks the last indication that we had been in Colan and faced up with the hill we all feared.

In our three days of test driving, we hadn't had an opportunity to gauge our engine's power. We had all been in Clifford simultaneously, but not with any of our gear. And not on any grade. Now, fully loaded, Clifford was cursing us. And we hadn't even left the flat terrain yet. But with Colan at our backs, the hill was the only obstacle between us and the real initiation of the race.

As we approached the incline, we passed the Iglesia San Lucas, or the Church of Saint Lucas. Built by Spanish missionaries, it was the first Christian church on the shores of the South Pacific and is the oldest church in Peru. Its broad doors were closed, but only to keep out the sand. Was a prayer in order? Maybe, but we couldn't sacrifice our momentum. We flew past the church and began our ascent.

On the hill, Andrew moved down through the gears fast. Was it already a struggle? I may have been able to run up the hill faster. But no one was stranded on the side of the road, so maybe we would make...

"Is that a chain!"

We rolled past a snapped chain in the middle of the road, then past team *Macho Picchu*—Barry and Gerald—their mototaxi at a standstill. It was their transmission's drive chain. We climbed past them with a tinge of guilt. But this *was* a race, and it hadn't happened to us.

Scott and I leaned forward from our back seat, willing us up the hill. Another down shift. We were going to make it, right? My heart thrummed.

With a surge in both rpms and spirit, we crested the hill and found ourselves on the plateau that ran from ocean to mountains, covered with the barest of desert plants decorated with windblown garbage. Andrew shifted down again as we approached a set of *rompemuelles*, or "spring breakers." These speed bumps led to our first major decision: a T-junction. Most teams ahead of us turned right, as was our plan. A few turned left. We had two weeks to get our mototaxi to the finish line, and it would be that long before we were all this close again.

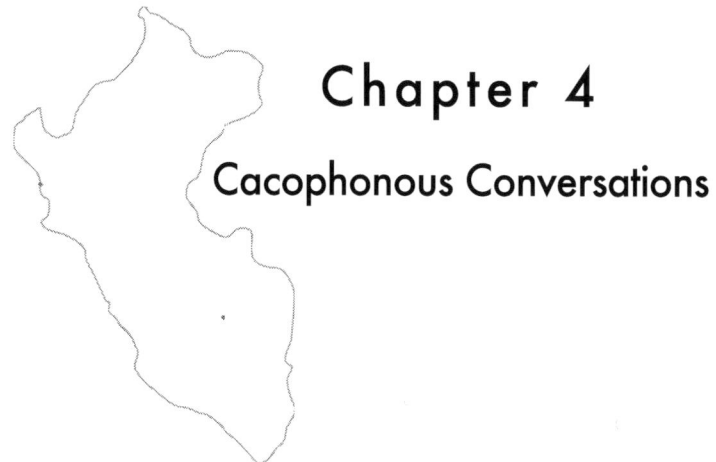

Chapter 4
Cacophonous Conversations

MOTOTAXIS are the supreme example of questionable engineering.

Not sure what a mototaxi is? Take a motorcycle. Now cut off the back half. Bolt the front half to a two-wheeled, rectangular frame complete with a small couch. On top of that, bolt another tubular frame fit with vinyl that extends over the couch and handlebars. Given the vinyl is usually red, yellow, or blue, it's not that hard to look at. But that's where the good news stops. The bad news starts when you bring up anything of importance.

Let's begin with the engine. It's almost a Honda. But rumor among the racers was the die-cast forms used to make this engine were those Honda had *rejected*. Great start. The manufactured product was a single cylinder, air-cooled, four-stroke engine. According to our mototaxi's registration, it was 150CCs, although most were actually 125CCs. And given how gutless it felt, we weren't too confident in the registration card's accuracy. Regardless, it was not a whole lot to work with. The transmission was a party too.

To be fair to our mototaxi, we never had any transmission problems—unless you count operator error. In America, the gearing configuration of motorcycle transmissions follows a general pattern: from neutral, you push the shifter (a lever operated by left foot) down to find first gear. A half step up brings you back to neutral. A full step up brings you to second gear. A full step up from second takes you to third and so on. This was not the case with the mototaxi. Neutral was found at the very top. And each successive gear was down a whole step on the transmission lever. No, this was not complicated. However, all three members of *Three Tired Travelers* had experience with motorcycles; all three were licensed in the U.S. to operate motorcycles; Scott and Andrew even owned motorcycles. That's a lot of muscle memory to overcome, which meant every gear change required us to actively think about shifting. When we didn't—which happened a lot—we tended to shift in the wrong direction. At least for the first few days.

Worse than the occasional handlebar header due to an accidental downshift, however, was our steering. The transmission was on the front half of the taxi—the motorcycle half. A series of chains transferred the transmission's energy to the rear—the sofa half. From an intermediate shaft mounted below the diamond-plate floor of our passenger bay, a chain ran to the left rear wheel.

That's correct, our three-wheel mototaxi was single-wheel drive. One could argue this made turning easier: wheels that lie in the same plane cover different distances through a turn. Having independent rear wheels would accommodate this difference (so would a rear differential, but that was asking for a lot). But that also meant our mototaxi pulled to the right.

This wasn't too bad on winding roads, where the frequency of turns forced you to swing the handlebars back and forth, to work different muscles, to allow perfusion of blood, and to concentrate on the road to a degree that drowned out the burning sensation of fatigue. On straight stretches though, my muscles seared to the surface. All the teams (except Pete, team

Rubber Duckies) had the option to rotate drivers and rest; but no one stopped when the mototaxi was still running. So we all did the best we could. My energy conservation technique was to press into the driver's backrest and lock my right arm, pinning the handlebars into a leftward veer. My arm was a tad long for this to be comfortable though, so I had to shift my weight to the left side of the seat and let the better part of one butt cheek hang free. A less efficient technique was to turn my left hand palm up and curl the left handgrip. I fought fatigue by switching between the two. Other people had similar techniques. One innovative team even fastened a length of cord to each end of their handlebars and ran it around their back. The operator could then lean back and trap the cord between him and the backrest, utilizing the friction to maintain a straight course. Whatever clever tricks we used were no match for the mototaxi though. We would all walk away with unsymmetrical muscle gains.

Another asymmetrical aspect of our mototaxi was braking power. Don't worry—all three wheels were fitted with brakes. Crappy drum brakes, but at least they all functioned. The two rear brakes were even linked so they braked together, more or less, which may have put the majority of the braking power in the rear. On a typical motorcycle, the front brake provides about 70% of the stopping power. This is because weight shifts forward as the bike slows. It's hard to say what the ratio was for our mototaxi though, especially since the shape of the thing didn't allow much forward shifting of weight. Really, these nuances were irrelevant, because the asymmetry lay not in the position, but rather in the origin of the braking power. On motorcycles, 100% of braking power comes from the bike itself. On our mototaxi, I'd estimate 10% originated from the anal sphincter pucker.

* * *

A few miles past the first junction, we veered off the pavement onto a dirt road to where a few other teams had stopped. This dirt track was a shortcut that bypassed Paita. As we exchanged high fives over the first few miles, a few teams zipped by without turning. How didn't they know about the shortcut? More high fives were exchanged to the accompaniment of laughter, and then we jumped back into our taxis...all but one team. Their gas tank had cracked and was leaking fuel. Colan was still the closest town, so they turned back. The rest of us pushed forward, down the dirt track.

The eroded washboards outmatched our shocks. The dusty surface outmatched our lungs. The scenery: dismal. It was the same flat desert, speckled with barren trees and opportunistic litter that clung to every pointy surface in sight: every thorn; every rock with an angular fracture; and every barb twisted up in the wire fencing between posts.

The surface's pockmarks and potholes were so varied that some routes were less abusive than others. As I drove, I tried to adhere to these tracks, to map out the mototaxi's spatial existence, to dodge washboards and swerve around craters. I was starting to get the hang of it, but before long we hit pavement again.

This much smoother road was the only link between Paita, a coastal city, and Piura, the region's capital. That meant traffic. And without traffic, Sue and Dorian—one of the British teams—wouldn't have gotten a tow. We were parked on the side of the road letting our engine cool (air was not an effective coolant when it was approaching 100°F) when they rolled past, leaning out the window of a truck to give a big wave, their taxi loaded on the truck's flatbed. Another pang of guilt, but also another celebration that the misfortune was *theirs*.

In Piura, Scott took the helm for our first urban experience. It was wild. The streets were packed with motorcycles, cars, mototaxis, tuk-tuks, trucks—no space was wasted. Though intimidating, this was a reflection on the skill of Peruvian drivers. Driving was not something all Peruvians could afford. This meant, as far as we could tell, that almost everyone that drove made it a profession. Whether a chauffeur, a truck driver, or a mototaxi driver, most people at the wheel made their money there. This was something we could not appreciate until we were in the heart of traffic, surrounded by skilled drivers.

Horns blasted. Up and down the street, numerous vehicles contributed to this cacophony. But there was a discernible meaning in the chaos because in Peru, horns are different from their North American brethren. In the USA, horns make heads turn. You might honk at someone if they take too long to accelerate off the line when the light clicks green, or if someone cuts you off, or if you're just a flat out prick.

In Peru, nobody flinches at the sound. Horns are lighter, less voluminous, almost comedic in their apparent ineffectiveness to communicate. But just the opposite is true. The horn, rather than drawing attention from everyone, is meant to grab the attention only of those in its immediate vicinity. Like this, a lot of people can blast their horns without drowning each other out, thus maintaining effective communication. And yes, these horns *are* used to communicate. Peruvians do use their horns to call each other pricks, or to bark at pedestrians in crosswalks, or to tell the guy in front to pick up the pace; but it's more likely they'll give two quick blasts to say "I'm in your blind spot" or "I'm going to pass now" or "Hey guys, I know it's crowded in your lane, but I need to get over, so watch out." The communication between Peruvian drivers is amazing, and admirable. This was something we could not appreciate until we came to Piura's major crossroads.

And by "major," I mean we were shitting our pants.

We were not fluent in the elegant Peruvian dialect of horn blasts. And this ignorance was apparent at this intersection, because everyone was chatting. No horns said, "The light's green!" or "Heads up, I'm running the red light!" That's because this was an uncontrolled intersection; no traffic lights, no traffic officers, not even a red octagonal *Para* sign. How "major" could an uncontrolled intersection be? There were two painted lanes for each direction of travel for each of the two intersecting roads. But remember: no wasted space. These two painted lanes translated to three lanes of traffic in each direction.

This was not as simple as scaling up the ethics encountered at your typical four-way stop. People were going straight, left, right—all at the same time. No one stopped. Mototaxis, cars, pickups, trucks, busses—to an outsider, it was insanity. An aerial view of the intersection would have revealed the order of the procession, but from where we sat, it was anything but orderly. It was the horn chatter that governed things. People blasted, "Excuse me," "I'm slipping in front of you," "You go first," and—my favorite—"I'm committed!" Scott, following suit, edged into the intersection and weaved through the various travel vectors, approximating a path that would have been outlined with bright white hash marks had it been an American intersection. Together, Scott and Clifford used the horn to say, "On your left" and "Sorry, we don't have a clue what we're doing!" Wanna-be polyglot? Scott's translation skills had transcended language and—to the relief of our pants—transected that intersection.

With the nexus of chaos and ignorance behind us, the three car-widths of traffic in a space only two lanes wide was less intimidating. The mototaxi brakes squealed and it reoriented toward a gas station—our first refuel.

"Scott! Well done, man! You did great."

"Yeah, that was intense. And my right arm is killing me!"

We refueled, filled our jerrycan, and foiled a young attendant's efforts to steal the Captain America Shield from the front of our mototaxi. I took the controls from Scott, and we hit the road again. We would follow the 1B all the way to the city of Olmos, where we planned to end the day.

But first, I had to get us out of Piura.

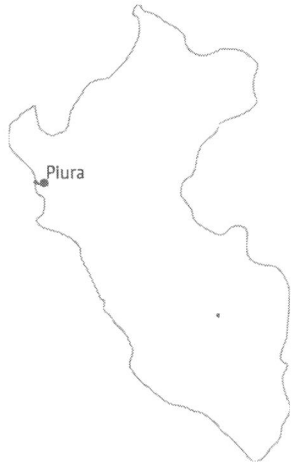

Chapter 5

Braking Power

HAD TRAFFIC BECOME MORE CONGESTED? Was this Piura's rush hour? Or had my roots caught up to me? My childhood was spent in the country, lost amidst wide open spaces. My perception of traffic was not typical.

Regardless of *how* congested it was, it *was* congested. My country-boy moves were not aggressive enough for this fast-paced environment, and the other drivers capitalized on it. Their horns squawked "Watch it, amigo," "Look at this joker," and "Thanks for the space, *gringo*!" Discomfort morphed into humiliation which increased the octane rating of the fuel that fed my fire. I made my lane changes faster, took advantage of gaps, and tapped out retorts on Clifford's horn. Roots run deep though, and my country passivity tried to take the wheel on occasion. This caused us to get stuck in the slow lane, to give pause at the sight of pedestrians, and to explore our mototaxi's maneuverability. Mototaxi maneuverability? Explore how?

Another taxi came up on our left. As it drew ahead of us, a pedestrian on our right hailed a ride. The mototaxi swerved into the gap ahead of us, taking up position to swoop down on the fare. I turned to check my blind spot.

From my teammates in the back seat came a collective groan. A dusty squeal emanated from the braking taxi ahead.

The texturized rubber of the left handgrip folded under the pressure of my gloved hand. My fingers slipped from the clutch lever and curled around the bar. With this solid grasp, I threw my torso off the right side of the bike—my left leg hooked on the seat—and wrenched back on the left handgrip. The handlebars obeyed what the weight of my upper body commanded. Clifford swerved left. The brake squeal faded as the mototaxi ahead of us halted. Our front tire made the turn with room to spare. But remember, Clifford was triangular—avoiding a collision with our front half didn't mean our back half wasn't doomed.

My trunk still hanging off the right side of the seat, I was already in position to see if we would make it. Still willing the taxi to the left, I looked back over my shoulder. Our right rear hub, the widest protrusion of our back end, approached the stopped taxi. Scott, on the right side of our taxi's couch, leaned forward, eyes tracking the hub. Andrew leaned across the seat, gaze directed over the back seat, past our luggage, and through the spokes of the wheel. It was the making of a traffic accident. The hub inched closer. None of us could pry our eyes away. Closer now. This hypnosis exploded seconds into minutes into hours. The hub was right there now.

"Whoa!" The groan behind me transformed and confirmed what I had seen. Our hub had missed the halted taxi.

I heaved my body back to an upright posture centered on the seat, allowed the handlebars to straighten out, and the mototaxi to resume its rightward pull.

"Nathan, did you see that? We weren't even an inch from that mototaxi!"

Oh…I saw it. And it did not have the appropriate effect. Instead of breaking my confidence, it gave me a sense of security. That was so close, it didn't qualify as a near miss; it was an act of God. At least an act of the Mototaxi Junket gods, and they had smiled upon us. We were untouchable. I rolled on the throttle, made aggressive lane changes, embraced the crowded lanes by rubbing hubs with other taxis, and used Clifford's horn to say, "Here I am!"

We ducked and dodged and dived through traffic. This approach served us well...until I committed a cardinal sin: I attempted to pass on the right.

I had been enjoying the adrenaline drip that came with the constant maneuvering. And my arms had been enjoying the consistent turning, the most effective way to combat the mototaxi's pull. But I soon became overzealous. We caught a pair of slow mototaxis moving in tandem, occupying both the left and center lanes. I moved to the right lane. If I overtook the pair, all the left lane real estate ahead of them would be mine. Before I began to pass them though, the rear corners of the car ahead of me lit up red. Yes, a full framed, paneled, heavy, dense car—it stopped. My foot stomped on the rear brake pedal. My hand squeezed from the front brake lever whatever life it had left. Then, in the midst of a full-body flex, a flinch at the coming impact, I discovered the source of that extra 10% of braking power.

My sphincter wrapped around the strands of fate, became entangled in the ethereal strings with which that cosmic fabric called space-time is woven. How else do you explain what became the shortest stop of the entire race? And it was short enough. We matched the car's full stop, with half a foot to spare between us.

My body relaxed and released the now-knotted cosmic fabric, allowing space to shrink back down and time to catch back up. I turned to the back seat. "I think it's time to get out of this town. How about you guys?" We laughed, and as the car sped off again, so did we.

My confidence returned to a manageable level and we escaped Piura without further incident. The blacktop tapered, traffic thinned, and structures shrank in size and frequency. As we returned to the desert, the highway stretched out ahead of us to reveal subtle hills rolling away from the coast.

* * *

Somewhere outside Piura, we spotted a familiar silhouette. A mototaxi sat on top of the upcoming hill, off the side of the road. There was no population center nearby, so there wasn't a need for mototaxis. These had to be Junketeers. Our slow uphill approach provided ample time to speculate who it was. Blue-topped? That narrowed it down. One…two people? That narrowed it down further. Was that a bag of Dum Dums in the back?

We pulled off the road, behind the parked taxi. Lounging in their vinyl shade were Josh and Aaron, team *Duckface*. I cut our engine. It was a good opportunity to shed some heat. They abandoned their shade and walked over.

"Hey, guys," I said. "Broke down?"

These were mototaxis after all. And we already knew of three teams that had suffered mechanical failures. But the way Josh and Aaron had been kicked back on their sofa, the lollipops in their mouths, the nonchalant glance at each other—none of it corresponded to a breakdown.

Josh pulled the sucker from his mouth. "Nope, just letting her cool down."

"Yeah, we've done that a few times too," Andrew said. "Hopefully these things will cool down faster the further we get from this desert."

Aaron leaned his folded arms against the frame of our canopy and ducked his head into the shade. He spoke through his sucker. "Have you guys noticed that your engine is sluggish, or weak? Anything like that?"

I looked back at Scott and Andrew. With these engines, "sluggish" and "weak" came stock. Did he mean in addition to the pitiful standards under which we were forced to operate?

"The only thing I've noticed is it loses power as it overheats," I said. "Apart from that though, it seems to run fine."

Aaron removed the sucker from his mouth. "Yeah, ours gets weak too when it's hot. But it seems pretty bad even when it's cool."

I turned to Andrew, our resident mechanic. Everyone else turned too. Prompted by the collective stare, Andrew offered,

"Maybe the idle is low? Or the carb is dirty?" He shrugged. "It's hard to say."

Josh spoke this time. "Yeah, we didn't know what to think of it either. It doesn't seem to be a big deal anyway." He popped the candy back into his mouth. "Apart from that, it's still running ok."

Running is the mototaxi definition of "ok." Even not-running could be ok in the right circumstances. In Paita, many mototaxi operators cut their engines on long downhills to save fuel. A single cylinder engine doesn't burn much fuel, especially over distances as short as Paita's hills top to bottom. These drivers displayed a level of efficiency consciousness I had not encountered before. We were less concerned with efficiency. Since leaving Piura, our throttle had been wide open. This was a race, and fuel efficiency was not factored into the final standings.

It was midafternoon, and Olmos was still a ways off. We decided to caravan with Josh and Aaron, a relief for all involved. Companionship was one remedy for the anxiousness of uncertainty, and in this race, nothing was certain. Once our engine cooled, we hit the road again.

After we got moving, it became clear that Josh and Aaron's concern had been legitimate. Following them was a chore. We had to hold back on the uphills to keep from tailgating. We held back on the downhills as well, to create more space between us. Overall, our taxi was faster, despite the fact we were three people while they were two, a weight discrepancy that should have made *us* more sluggish.

We passed them.

If our proximity to their rear bumper couldn't push them faster, maybe the fading of ours into the distance could pull them along. We stayed true to our agreement though and kept them in sight. Then the straight, open stretch of road veered, then ducked and dodged and wove itself into the groves of trees scattered across the desert.

The brown and gray vegetation became thick, tall, and grew up to the crumbling edges of the roadway. Seeing the Texans was impossible. We continued, as though they were right with us. The cheap vinyl of our back seat squeaked every time I turned to glance behind us. There was no way they could have caught us, but I was compelled to look anyway. What if something happened? What if we thought we had to turn back? Would we? Before I could consider the answers to these questions, we stopped to cool the engine again. Five minutes later, they came around the bend, the noise of their engine silencing my thoughts. They pulled behind us and killed the taxi.

"We see what you mean about being sluggish. You guys should be faster."

"Yeah, we noticed too." Aaron worked his right shoulder in circles. "You guys don't need to wait for us. We don't want to slow you down."

We *Three Tired Travelers* looked at each other, a unanimous decision made in silence. " We can finish the day together. Our engine overheats a lot anyway. When we stop, we'll just wait for you to catch up."

"Sounds good."

The next few hours progressed in the same fashion. We would lose them, pull off the road, and relax until they caught us. Lose sight, cool the engine, and hang out. Pull away, stop, wait. The only break in the repetition was a ridge on the eastern horizon. With each iteration of the pattern, it stood closer.

As the sun dipped behind us and the bleached landscape began to darken, Duncan's words echoed through the ether: "Don't be an asshole." One of the Junket guidelines was "no driving at night." But this was a recommendation only meant to reduce the chance of participant pain, suffering, and/or death (reduce, not eliminate). We were still on the desert's open road, so had the advantage of high visibility to reduce our chances of an accident. A disadvantage, though: the dropping temperature.

Scott and I sat on our sofa, heads ducked, arms wrapped around torsos. Andrew had the engine and the continual leftward corrective steering for warmth. Scott and I looked at each other. We both nodded. It was time to add some layers. Besides, our engine had been loving the cool night air so it had been a while since we had stopped, meaning it had been a while since we had last seen Aaron and Josh.

Scott leaned forward and shouted above the engine, "Andrew, look for a place to stop!"

Andrew nodded.

Scott sat back, and the chills on my skin intensified at the prospect of warm clothes…or at least full sleeves. But the road continued to disappear beneath us, the whine of the engine steady, the sunlight also vanishing.

Scott and I squeezed ourselves now, trying to trap our bodies' warmth. It wouldn't be long before we were hugging each other. Scott leaned forward again to shout and pull Andrew out of his trance state—the guy was in the zone. He was focused on covering miles and finding Olmos. But at this pace, it would be a long time before the Texans found us.

We rounded a bend and ahead of us were lights. Not many, but the first since nightfall. It was the village of Virrey, which wasn't much more than a cluster of houses, a scattering of cars, and an abundance of empty space. We slowed, and Andrew pulled Clifford into a line of parked cars.

Scott and I had jumped out before we had come to a full stop. We pulled at the rope and tarp that covered the rear cargo rack. Scott donned his sweater while I dug for mine. It must have been at the bottom of my backpack—I hadn't thought I would need it in the desert. As my hand squeezed past the brick of a first aid kit, Scott walked away, throwing in a few high knees. It could not have been easy for a long-distance runner to be sedentary all day in the back of a mototaxi. There it was! My fingers snapped around the fleece and I yanked out my sweatshirt.

"Nathan!" Scott trotted around the adjacent car. "There's a bike over there."

So? The bicycle was a global concept, one better understood in lesser-developed countries. Bicycles are, after all, the most efficient mode of transportation humans have conceived. Scott's brow furrowed at my complete indifference.

He continued to paint the picture he had left at a single brush stroke: "It's a tandem. Loaded with bags. It has an Australian flag."

Chapter 6

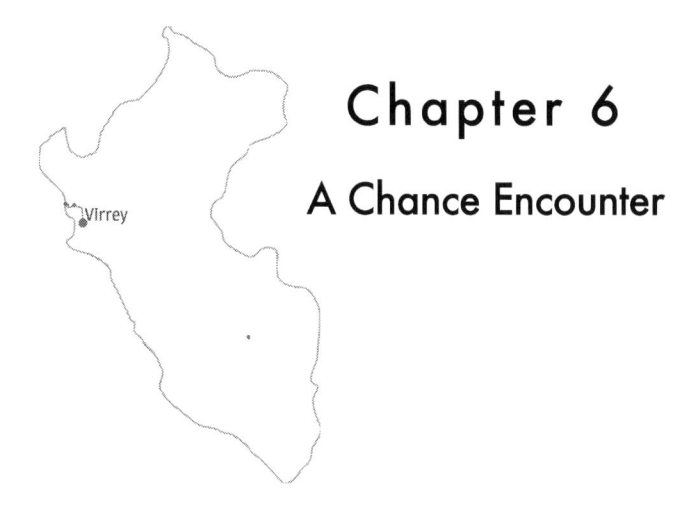

A Chance Encounter

PAST THE VW BUG parked next to our mototaxi, a flagpole stuck up. As I made my way around the back of the Bug, a breeze teased the tattered end of the banner showing off the royal blue base and a few white stars. Past the chipped yellow paint of the Bug's trunk, a bicycle was revealed. A damn nice bicycle. Instead of the stereotypical tandem that has both riders in the pedals-under-hips-under-shoulders set up, the front wheel was smaller than the back, a seat mounted above it with a set of pedals extended out in the front like a joust. This put the front cyclist in a reclined position. The rear cyclist sat in the usual fashion and had control of the handlebars which seemed to be cabled to the front wheel. It was difficult to tell, partly because it was dark, partly because this bike was loaded with so…much…stuff.

A set of beautiful panniers hung from the left and right sides on the front and back, all puffed out like marshmallows toasted in the desert heat. Helmets rested against the panniers, hung from their clasps; a bundle of tarps was wedged between the rear wheel and seat; flip-flops hung from whatever straps were available; wide brim hats dangled from the handlebars next to drying towels; water bottles were stuffed into various nooks and crannies. There was even a large spare tire lassoed around the rear seat post. These cyclists were well-settled into their steed. They were the real thing. I turned to Scott and Andrew. Did they realize what we were looking at?

Scott pointed over my shoulder. "Looks like a restaurant. They're probably inside."

I turned. Light spilled from a wide door. "We have to go say 'hi.'"

Andrew glanced at our own steed. "Aaron and Josh will be able to see the mototaxi. They'll probably come looking for us."

"Then let's head in."

We stepped onto the cement porch and through the door.

The porch's cement stretched into the restaurant, and served as the stage for the plastic chairs which corralled plain wooden tables covered in checkered tablecloths—the slick vinyl variety easy to wipe down. Concrete posts supported a frame of long, slender branches stripped of their bark, revealing the mottled brown patterns of the grain, to which the roof of corrugated tin was fixed. The walls were either bare concrete or wooden panels painted white. Lights near the ceiling dangled from their copper wiring, the sheave of insulation cracked.

Beneath a set of these lights sat a couple, a few empty plates on their table, eyes fixed on each other.

Would we be intruding? Would they be welcoming? A heat rose in my face, along with an uncertainty. A few other diners eyed us, sure to give us away before we could retreat. It may as well be us that made our presence known. I took another step forward.

"Do you two belong to the bike outside?"

Both sat up and looked. Our eyes all locked on each other, a long moment of silence passing.

Then the woman yelled. "English speakers? Please sit! Join us!"

We dragged some chairs from an adjacent table and introduced ourselves. Brenden and Emma—in their late thirties—were on a grand tour. A few minutes after we explained the Mototaxi Junket, in walked Josh and Aaron. We ordered dinner and—as any fated encounter of travelers requires—a round of beers.

The Aussie's trip had started several years before, with the planning stages while they were employed at an international school in Japan. The physical trip had kicked off from Whistler, British Columbia, 16 months before. This was not far from our native Washington State, which was an incomprehensible distance from Virrey, Peru. Incomprehensible to us, that is; Brenden and Emma could probably recall every inch. Bremma ("a name that preceded the whole 'Brangelina' thing") had biked more than 9,300 miles (15,000 km). Sixteen months? No wonder.

Brenden and I spoke a lot about touring, me picking his brain about some of the more technical stuff while he threw in tales of the road. I told some stories from my own bicycle tour, but there was no comparison. The trip I had taken was a warm-up compared to what Brenden and Emma were doing.

They had cycled the West Coast of the United States, traversed Mexico, took a sailing detour in the Caribbean (during which they cycled the length of a few islands), continued down through Central America, crossed from Panama to Columbia, cycled south through Ecuador, and then into Peru. They had more than a few stories to tell.

My favorite was about their handlebars. It had been summer when they pedaled the West Coast of the U.S.; Mexico had been flat out hot; and so had Central America. Brenden had been a sweat spring in the first year of their ride. His position was on the rear of the tandem, so he operated the handlebars. Often, sweat would run down his arms, to his hands, and onto the handlebars. Given the curve of the bars, the sweat would run down to the handlebar clamp.

There's a chemical reaction called a reduction/oxidation reaction—redox for short—which is a transfer of electrons between the molecular species involved. Some clever scientists (natural philosophers in their own time) segregated the two parts of this reaction: the reduction half and oxidation half. By doing this, they could manage the flow of electrons. This flow is where our battery technology comes from. Car batteries, smoke detector batteries, watch batteries, nickel-cadmiums (NiCad), nickel-metal-hydride (NiMH), and lithium-ion (Li-ion) batteries—all harness the redox reaction. It's even used in the hydrogen fuel cells NASA engineered into manned spacecrafts. The hydrogen and oxygen that reacted to produce electricity formed water as a byproduct, which became the astronauts' drinking water. Used in this way, redox reactions can be quite productive. But this reaction is still spontaneous, one that will happen of its own accord.

Sweating is a process of evaporative cooling. And sweat is salty. That's because your body has no cellular water pump. Instead, your body manipulates some other chemical principles and pumps salt. This creates a condition in which the water moves itself, following the salt to the surface of your skin. Your cells try to recover these salts, but some are lost in the process.

For example, some of Brenden's salts were dissolved in his sweat, which ran down his arms to the handlebars, and down the handlebars to their handlebar clamp. That the bars were a different metal than the clamp was a disastrous detail. The salt water formed an electrolytic bridge between the metals, which began the transfer of electrons.

Iron commonly falls victim to the redox reaction and is oxidized to iron oxide—rust. Rusted iron, despite its rich color, is thin and brittle. It chips away in the lightest breeze and crumbles under the softest touch. Over the first year of their trip, Bremma's handlebars were oxidized. One day, Brenden went to make a turn. A handlebar snapped clean off. The bike continued straight while Brenden held the bar, attached to the bike only by the various brake and gear cables.

They had to hitch a ride to the next town. Their hosts there were friends with the owner of the local bike shop. Because Bremma's tandem was specialized, so was the shape of the handlebars. They had anticipated ordering the bars from the UK and waiting for them to be shipped across the pond. But the shop owner had the equipment to manufacture new handlebars, ones that would resist the electrolytic corrosion the old bars fell prey to. Little time was lost. Brenden just had to swap out the old bars for the new.

This was just one of many such stories, all documented on their blog. This website was their compromise. In the planning stages, Emma had not been thrilled with the idea of pedaling for a year. But she saw Brenden's passion. She agreed to the trip on the condition that they document their trip and raise money for charity.

Emma not wanting to tour? But she was straight cyclist to the core. That's because after the first few weeks, Emma fell in love with the lifestyle. That was why their year-long trip was now in its sixteenth month. And after all that time, they still rode with purpose, raising money for the World Bicycle Relief charity.

We asked for the address of their website. Prepared, Emma pulled out a rubber stamp. After she had stamped a page in my own journal, she didn't hand it back. She stared at something on the page opposite their website URL.

"What's this quote?"

It was something Duncan had recited before the race, a Tim Cahill quote: "An adventure is never an adventure when it happens. An adventure is simply physical and emotional discomfort recollected in tranquility."

Emma's response was very Australian. "Well that's the biggest load of shit I've ever heard."

We argued for the next 30 minutes over the meaning and merit of the quote. In its context, it was meant to demonstrate that an experience, though difficult or even awful at the time, can be looked back upon as a fond memory. This was relevant to us Junketeers. We had been anticipating breakdowns, navigation errors, and language barriers. If we could get to the finish though, that would all change. Every breakdown would become an uproar, every wrong turn a chance to see the unimaginable, every mimed conversation a bond forged in a way most unconventional.

"Sure, sure," Emma nodded. "That sounds nice and all, but I'm perfectly capable of realizing I'm in the midst of an adventure, even when things have gone to absolute shit. And I don't need hindsight to remember that fact."

"It's true," Bren nodded. "In some of our worst moments, when I was completely stressed—or even scared—Emma was just laughing and taking pictures." He chuckled and shot a wink toward Emma. "It can be quite annoying at times."

It seemed Emma's default behavior was to welcome a challenge rather than be victimized by it, and I couldn't help but be jealous. Is it better to resist an experience and demonstrate fondness only after the fact, or to go into an experience excited? If embracing difficulties could actually alter present circumstances and reveal their better potential, shouldn't we feel obligated to do so?

Viewing the world through this perspective was a skill Emma had admittedly developed during their 16-month tour. Was this a skill that could be developed after only three weeks?

We had embraced challenge by being part of the Mototaxi Junket. Problems were inevitable. But after our first day—which had been not only smooth, but delightful—what problems were there to anticipate?

We slipped into the relaxed setting of a group of strangers turned friends, eating and drinking and talking. Nothing in Olmos could match the time we were having in this small town, so we ordered another round.

When it got late, Scott spoke with the owner and arranged for us to sleep in the restaurant. As we pushed the tables aside, we Junketeers decided this would qualify for the "Sleep in a Stranger's House" square of *Peru Bingo*, and laughed about it, sure we had one more square than Barry and Gerald. Then, as we all unrolled our sleeping bags and prepared for sleep, Emma rocked our worlds with several horrible renditions of American pop songs. Not until we all laid down—lights out, doors secured—did her true voice came out.

She sang a song of her own imagining, the downy melody wrapping around me until sleep snuck up. My eyelids grew heavy, and before I traded the outer darkness for the inner, one last thought flittered through my mind: yes, this *is* an adventure.

* * *

The morning light pried my eyes open. The concrete pushed through my sleeping pad and poked my shoulder blades. Things were in motion, the day at its start. But I laid, one hand gripping my abdomen, a fixtureless glass lightbulb above me, its pendular motion a reminder. One day in and we were already behind schedule. Now I was also behind on sleep.

During the night, I had been torn from sleep by the blare of the restaurant's television, a 60-inch flat screen mounted to the wall. Remember that election which had inspired an alcohol ban? By coincidence, our race had started the same day the polls closed. So while we had been crossing the region, its population had been gripped with constant updates of vote counts. All day, the banners had flowed along the bottom of the news network's broadcast reading "this guy was winning…until we counted some more votes…now that guy is winning." Then, while we slept, the tallies were finalized and the results announced.

Our host couldn't wait another five hours to find out who had won, so in the dead of night had brought the TV to life. We all laid and endured, hoping sleep would take us again. It didn't and what felt like hours later, Andrew wandered across the restaurant to turn the TV off. What had happened to the owner? I hadn't cared. The silence and darkness had been a relief.

Still, sleep had not returned. On my back again, my semi-conscious mind had begun to work out why I was still awake. My eyes snapped open. Something was wrong. There had been a small ball of fire in the pit of my stomach. Its searing action was subtle, but this was an ember at the start of its life, determined to spark a bigger flame. With a sigh, I had rolled to my side, hoping sleep would bring relief.

On the floor flooded with daylight though, in the middle of a concrete hug, counting the minutes with the swinging light bulb above me, I was forced to accept the blunt truth: sleep had not quenched that ember. I stumbled from my sleeping bag and wandered to the bathroom in the back of the restaurant.

Glass windows aren't popular in Peru. Not in the desert anyway, where the daily forecast is drought. Instead, the rectangular holes in the wall were just that—holes. They were often up high to vent hot air. That's where this window was. Was it really a window though? It was small, maybe six inches high by twelve across. The size kept out the blaze of sunlight, but this was too small. It couldn't even catch a breeze.

I needed that air circulation. Peruvian plumbing wasn't held to the same standards as in other countries. Toilet paper could clog things up and cause some serious problems, so social convention was to dispose of toilet paper in the trash bin next to the toilet. You can imagine how things smelled. Though, in this particular bathroom, the trash bin was not the primary source of the stench. I was.

What had started the night before as a small ball of fire had grown. Every time I woke up, the pain had reached lower and lower, coursing through my small intestine, my large intestine, and—by the next morning—my colon. That was what dragged me from my sleeping bag—I was desperate to ease my bowels.

Food poisoning is never fun. In a foreign country, it's even less amusing. When racing a mototaxi, it's inconceivable. I had been to the toilet three times since waking up. I hadn't even packed my sleeping bag yet. I stood and made another contribution to the trash can, then held down the flush lever to make sure everything would go down. My stool was becoming less and less solid—a feat since it had *started* as diarrhea.

I burst through the door, the fresh air sapping the sweat away while I walked back to the front of house. My solo relay race between the mototaxi and bathroom had not gone unnoticed though.

"Nathan, you ok?" Scott paused the punching of his sleeping bag into its stuff sack.

"Yeah, just some stomach problems." It was called traveler's diarrhea for a reason. Never mind that I had had zero trouble during our first five days in Peru. And apart from being inconvenient, wasn't Montezuma's Revenge supposed to be painful? It had to be. How else could I explain the pulsating, intense, abdominal pain?

"Aaron got a message from Gerald. It sounds like the Aussies will be in Olmos for a while. Josh and Aaron are going to take off soon and get ahead of us since we're faster." He cinched down his stuff sack. "You almost ready to head out?"

"Yeah, just need to repack."

Scott slid the sack into his backpack. "Sweet man! I'll start loading the mototaxi. Andrew's already out there giving him a once-over."

"Sounds great."

That was a lie. Anything that took me more than thirty feet from a toilet did not sound great. But this was a race. I squeezed my things back into my bag, and at the very top left my supply of toilet paper.

Outside, Bren and Emma crammed down some calories, their fuel for the day, while we Junketeers loaded our mototaxis. After a few pictures (some featuring Cindy, the Pink Fairy), Aaron and Josh took off toward Olmos. It was still early, bright but overcast. And the early start would help make up the miles we had lost the night before.

Our bags were packed, Cindy was re-secured, and the mototaxi had passed Andrew's inspection. After we exchanged our last hugs, handshakes, and well wishes, Scott and I crammed into the back of Clifford while Andrew kicked the engine to life.

Back on the road, it wasn't long before we caught Josh and Aaron. That's because it wasn't long before we came to our first big hill. The desert we had been crossing was one large, flat lowland. Apart from some rolling terrain, there had not been any climbing. But the ridge that had sat on the eastern horizon the whole day previous had snuck up on us in the dark and now loomed ahead.

We started to climb.

Josh and Aaron's taxi was struggling. As we made to pass them, Scott jumped from the back of ours. By "jump," I mean he stepped out of the back given our slow pace. Then he jogged up to Josh and Aaron's taxi, seized the frame, and began to push. Andrew and I crawled past them, Scott's quads pumping, a big smile on his face. It was probably the best his legs had felt in days and with their help, Josh and Aaron's taxi made it past the steepest section of the climb. As they sped up, Scott did a bobsled jump into the back with Josh.

They slowed again at the top—on purpose this time—so Scott could hop out and climb back in with us. As a two-mototaxi caravan, we started our descent down the far side of the ridge. My cheeks elevated at the prospect, an emotional reaction developed during my bicycle tour, zigzagging through the Rocky Mountains following the Continental Divide. On my mountain bike, I had earned every inch of gained elevation—it was not until the descent that gravity changed sides and had pulled me along for free. It was similar in a mototaxi. Every inch of elevation gained was by the sheer power of hope and prayer, as well as a stiff wrist on the throttle. Once we crested, our spirits soared. Gravity favored us now. We didn't even need a running engine. How could descending be anything but enjoyable?

The factor that ruined our descent: the view.

To the east, another ridge loomed, obscured by the clouds. It dwarfed the one we had just crossed. We gained miles, and the tires pulled Olmos closer. Despite having one of our daily goals in reach, my mind was elsewhere. We should have driven through the night—the darkness would have spared me my realization. What had looked like clouds was in fact the next ridgeline. The grayness of morning had played a trick on my eyes. After a few more miles, another bank of clouds transformed into another thick mass of rock. Several more miles, and the clouds that had remained also turned to rock. They morphed again and again. The Andes stretched to the stars, and our mototaxi trembled at the sight. Or was that just a section of bumpy road? An argument could be made for either case.

Scott and I exchanged a look—one that hid a cringe—now that we better understood the immensity of our task. Andrew's throttle wrist had pulled us away from Aaron and Josh again, so we cruised the last few miles into Olmos alone. We would wait for them in town while we searched for Barry and Gerald.

Chapter 7
Dusty Streets and Aqueducts

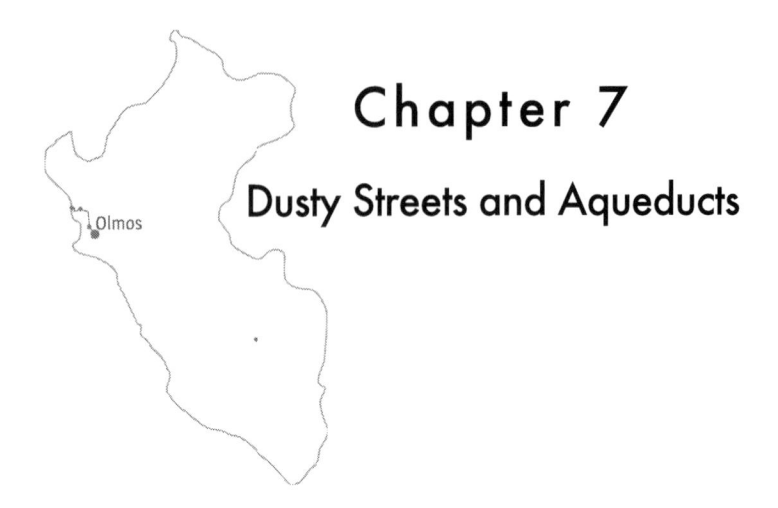

COSTA, SIERRA, Y SELVA. That's coast, highland, and jungle, the three domains of Peru. However, Peru's coastal lowlands can also be described as deserts.

The Pacific's Humboldt Current is one of the world's most notable upwellings of deep ocean water. This current flows along Chile and Peru, providing nutrients that allow these waters to teem with aquatic life.

On the coastal lowlands however, the Humboldt actually lowers productivity. This water chills the marine air, preventing any coastal precipitation that might originate from the west. Meanwhile, the Andes mountain range—*la sierra*—is a barrier to coastal rain that might originate from the east.

Together, the ocean and mountains create an uneven distribution of water across Peru. The coast gets 10 inches of rain annually; the Andes, between 40 and 160; and some eastern jungles receive over 400 inches of rain.

Given their abundance of water, the jungles and mountain valleys are Peru's most productive areas. Unfortunately, the Andes separate these areas from the large cities of the coast and also from the country's international ports. This greatly impacts Peru's exports.

One solution to this economic conundrum would be to move water from the inundated, unpopulated, secluded east side of Peru to the drought-stricken, populous, connected west.

Peruvians reached the same conclusion more than 80 years ago, which was when they first initiated a water relocation project. The goal was to tunnel beneath the Andes to create an aqueduct. Water from the constantly flooded Huancabamaba River—which drains to the Atlantic—would be channeled into the Olmos river, which drains to the Pacific. The relocated water would be used to irrigate the Olmos Valley of the Lambayeque Region. After 80 years, the project was finally completed. In the spring of 2014 the flow of trans-Andean water was initiated.

This project was an engineering feat, the end result being an aqueduct ranked as the second deepest tunnel in the world. It has altered these two watersheds, hampering destructive floods in one and providing water for agriculture in the other.

The addition of two billion cubic meters of water to the region was not apparent, however, as we navigated the dusty streets of Olmos. Granted, the irrigation channels had been filled only weeks before. There was still a lot of development to come.

We left the highway and penetrated to the heart of town. High buildings (as in more than one story) flanked the road and channeled us further into Olmos, encroaching on the street so that the available space narrowed until we burst into the *Plaza de Armas*.

Palm trees. The tall, bushy greenery demanded attention. Their vitality leaked into the environment, as though in a watercolor. Other small trees and large shrubs added to the lush color of life, which clashed with the white sidewalks that circumscribed and traversed the square. Opposite the oasis, and the most prominent structure in the town square, was the church, the Parroquia Santo Domingo de Guzman. Its height made it visible to the entire town, beckoning all to its doors.

But the gentle shades of pink, orange, and brown stucco made its height less imposing.

We circled the square and exited the city center on the adjacent street. There had been no sign of Barry and Gerald on our way in. Maybe this street would offer a clue. On our way back to the highway, the road opened up, buildings shortened, and a breeze tousled the road dust. Ahead of us, standing on the side of the road, were Barry and Gerald.

Though the mototaxi had several drawbacks, one great advantage was the geometry of its frame. You could lift a rear wheel and tip the frame until it came to rest on the front wheel, opposing rear wheel, and the protruding corner of the diamond plated passenger's foot plate. A mototaxi was its own tripod; no jack required. Of course, this triangular base was so narrow a gust of air could return all wheels to the ground in a hurry, a consideration to make before crawling more than six inches under it. This was the current position of Barry and Gerald's mototaxi. A mechanic sat on his stool beneath it, tapping with his wrench on a sprocket to tension the drive chain. Barry and Gerald stood back, half watching as they bantered. We turned off the road and nosed up behind their taxi. Scott gave a beep that said, "Good morning!"

"Hey, boys! You made it!"

Scott dismounted and began the ceremonial handshake that existed between Junketeers, one that celebrated the fact we were all still alive. But instead of clasping hands, I stumbled from the back, clutching my gut.

Scott said, "You guys are getting a late start. We didn't think we would catch you before you left."

"Yeah, we were assholes last night," Gerald said.

"Assholes?"

"We drove through the night. Got to town pretty late."

Barry jumped in. "And it was crazy."

Andrew and I exchanged a glance. "Crazy?"

"Everyone was out waiting to hear the election results, so it was crowded. Took us a while to find a hostel."

"Found it just in time too," Gerald added. "There was a lot of celebrating…with gunfire."

"Yeah, two people died last night." Our team dropped three jaws and raised six eyebrows. Barry and Gerald both nodded.

"What happened?"

"Not everyone was happy with the results, and things got…" The alcohol ban had been lifted when the polls closed. "…out of hand."

"Dang." We turned toward a shout from the mechanic. He was shaking the pain from his hand.

"So how was your boys' first day?"

Scott and Andrew began recounting events since we had last seen Barry and Gerald outside of Colan, their chain on the ground. I focused on my bowels. The morning's bout of diarrhea had not cleaned things out. There was still a burning sensation in my gut. And my bowels were…shaky. Not shaky as in unstable, but as in quivering. My interior muscles pulsed, surged, vibrated. Was that normal?

"Nathan, you're awfully quiet this morning."

I was jarred back to reality. "Yeah, I'm not feeling great."

"Still adjusting to the Peruvian cuisine?"

"Well, I was fine in Colan, so I think it was just something I ate last night."

"There's a great market just down the street there," Barry pointed back toward the square. "Lots of great fruit. That might settle things. It will at least go down easy."

I glanced at my teammates. We had not had any food yet and we all wanted to eat before we left Olmos. We nodded in agreement.

"Any idea how long you guys will be here?"

The mechanic's short stool scraped against the ground as it was yanked from underneath the mototaxi. With minimal effort, the mechanic pulled the mototaxi out of the air and settled it back onto all three wheels. The sight should have been framed in the pages of a comic book, the small mechanic throwing around that much weight as though it was nothing. In any case, it was a sign of progress.

"We'll probably get going soon."

"What was wrong with your taxi?" Andrew asked. As our official mechanic, he was thrilled to have made it through day one with no major problems. But now was a good opportunity to glean some useful mechanical information.

Barry and Gerald just smiled. "Nothing. Figured we would just take it to a mechanic every day and make sure it's in good enough shape to get to the next mechanic."

We had discussed doing something similar. But in the interest of time—and a little bit of money—we had decided to perform the more routine maintenance ourselves.

"You aren't worried about wasting time?" Andrew said.

"Well, it might take time to find a mechanic and let him go through the taxi," Barry said, "but it's a hell of a lot faster than breaking down in the middle of nowhere and trying to fix things ourselves or find a tow."

"These guys know what they're doing better than we ever could," Gerald said with a nod to the mechanic, who was sitting on his haunches, his wrench now tapping the carburetor to free the floats inside. "We might have the next one rebuild our carb. Maybe you guys should do the same."

In past Junkets, teams had rebuilt or even replaced their engines to make the finish line. Though cheap compared to the U.S., these mechanical bills were still steep to a few twenty-somethings with college debt. And I wasn't even employed.

Scott gave a non-committal, "We'll think about it," before we said our goodbyes and good lucks. We crawled back under the vinyl of our mototaxi and edged back into the vehicular flow. Once he spotted a gap in oncoming traffic, Scott made an aggressive U-turn, a maneuver any Peruvian driver would've been proud of. As we passed the Aussies again, Scott tapped out through the horn: "Don't be an asshole!"

Chapter 8
Bathroom Ethics

THE SOLUTION TO POLLUTION IS DILUTION.

This cute mantra is the bane of the environmentalist. At a glance, it seems true enough. But deeper scrutiny reveals logical flaws.

I was enrolled in a geology class when the Deepwater Horizon oil rig exploded and sank, leaving its well uncapped and uncontrolled. According to the British Petroleum press release, oil was "escaping" from this well and every effort would be made to "protect marine and coastal environments from its effects."

When our class reconvened, the well had been gushing oil for several days. It had already been dubbed a disaster. The incident had little to do with igneous rock, but our professor took up the topic as though it was our purpose. After he broke down the system shortcomings and the failed backups, we talked possible solutions. What could be done? What could stop the leak? What could contain the oil? How were these deleterious effects to be minimized?

One precocious student raised her hand, the mantra in mind.

"But isn't dilution the solution to pollution? There's always that if nothing else works, right?"

My professor, his 6'6" frame leaned against the whiteboard at the head of the classroom—no doubt wiping up some remnant dry-erase ink with his blue jeans—lowered the oversized mug of hot coffee from his mouth and locked eyes with her, his gaze magnified by the black, square-framed glasses propped on the bridge of his nose.

"How do you dilute the ocean?"

A pop, pop, pop filled the room. It was the water molecules that broke from the surface of our professor's coffee, wisps of steam whisked away by his slow exhalation, a measured breath for the massacre that lay before him. A few thousand neural circuits—the mantra's physical form—withered in the realization of our own cognitive dissonance. With a single question, this one man altered the thinking in a group of undergraduates.

Dilute the ocean? With what? In this case, dilution was not a solution. But what if that reasoning was extended? What if a lake had been polluted, or a river? Those were likely connected to the ocean. The environmentalist recognizes the interconnectedness of our global systems. Pollution in one part—though entrenched, segregated, out of sight and out of mind—is pollution in the whole system. The solution to pollution is *not* dilution; the solution is not polluting. Duncan had said it best: "Don't be an asshole."

The Deepwater Horizon incident worsened. Over 87 days, the well discharged an estimated 4.9 million barrels of oil into the Gulf of Mexico. It was the most devastating oil spill in U.S. history.

In Olmos, I was the agent of my own environmental disaster. It was like grasping an old, four-lobed faucet handle, the cool steel slick with condensation. It was like the plumbing was under pressure, such that water burst from the tap. It was like a bucket had been slipped under that faucet, and the forced stream punctured the placid surface of still water beneath it. This was exactly what I heard. Instead of a faucet though, I was the source of the forced stream. My placid receptacle was a toilet.

We had made it back to the square, but my bowels had been imploding. Desperate for a bathroom, Andrew and I set out. The market forgotten, we walked to a few establishments and asked for *el baño*. Finally, someone obliged.

I navigated a maze of tables and plastic chairs. In the back of the building, I shuffled into the bathroom. Clutching at my bowels, which made an extra loud cry of desperation at their proximity to relief, I managed to resist until I was turned and my pants were dropped. The sound was like a faucet, powerful and consistent. My elbows on my knees, my face in my hands, I hunched in defense at the auditory horrors. The flow turned to spurts. My head shook. How much fluid was I losing?

The spurts stopped. I straightened my back, sighed. This was not good. What had it been about my dinner the night before? Was the chicken undercooked? Had the salad vegetables been rinsed in contaminated water? And why was I the only sick one?

No reason revealed itself, but I continued to ponder, an eye fixed on the door, not quite big enough for its frame. I wasn't afraid of what lay outside that rectangular border of light, but what did not: a toilet. That said a lot about my bowels. The bathroom was the size of a broom closet. Water pooled at one end; the want of a wastebasket left used strips of paper scattered across the floor; and the wall's tan paint, even under a dim incandescent bulb, couldn't hide the smears of body fluids and feces. My last bathroom had only a tiny window—this one wasn't ventilated at all. And I didn't want to leave?

My intestines wriggled, squirmed, and produced a second showing. This discharge was more liquid than the first. The gushing splashes resonated in the toilet bowl, amplifying the sound that came from between my thighs. My body slouched, a victim to itself.

What was happening? My bowels were not imploding; they were exploding. Maybe a microbe had been introduced into my gut, one my body wanted nothing to do with. The solution: a flood. If the floodwaters of the Huancabamba River could move sediments from the Andes to the mouth of the Amazon in the Atlantic, why couldn't my body do the same? Why couldn't I flood the mountainous region of my bowels and discharge these unwanted microbes at the mouth of my… I guess that's where this metaphor ends.

The flood concept stirred something in my mind, something a geology professor had killed years before: the solution to pollution is dilution. That was my body's tactic. Flush these microbes out, dilute them, divide and then conquer the remainders.

Toilet paper in hand, I began to clean up. I worked slow, in case another bowel movement came along. My first piece of soiled toilet paper in hand, I paused. The plumbing couldn't handle it, but there was no receptacle. My eyes flittered along the wall, stripe to stripe, then down to the floor. My hesitation shrank alongside my desire to be in that closet. I dropped my own shit-strip to the floor. Then another. And another. I contributed until I was clean. My feet took my weight again as I rose, circulation returning to my legs. One hand pulled up my pants while the other clutched my thinner roll of toilet paper. Both hands full, I had to leave my pride on the floor.

Physical relief was better than pride though, and my emotional state was improving. I slung my backpack onto my shoulder as I turned back to the toilet and pressed the flush lever. I was halfway to the door and fresh air when I heard it: nothing. I stepped back and pushed down the lever again. No flush; just a low hiss. How had I not noticed it? It was the subtle sound of water sneaking into and then right back out of the toilet's reservoir.

My pride still wrapped up in the paper on the floor, guilt now compelled me. I pulled off the tank's cold porcelain lid.

The typical toilet is simple in design. Water flows through a valve and into the reservoir. When the water reaches a specific level, a float closes the valve. The flush lever is connected to a large flap at the bottom, so when pressed, the flap opens. Then the water rushes from the reservoir into the bowl.

Maybe the link between the lever and flap was the problem. The flap not closing would explain the perpetual flow of water and the lack of a flush. I set the porcelain lid down and peered into the back. What I found was a deteriorated seal on the flap. It was crisp, flaking away, missing in spots. There was no fix. I replaced the lid, the obvious question in mind: leave it? My guilt was eroding under the flow of sensory input: the fecal color theme, the aroma of excrement and mold, the dankness of the pool in the corner. Leave it? What choice did I have?

Another twinge. Not in my bowels, but my brain. A microburst of electricity to justify abandonment: the solution to pollution. Water still flowed through the reservoir, into the bowl, and down the sewer line. Eventually, enough water would trickle through that toilet to erase any trace of my deposit. I turned again and popped the door out of its frame. I met sunlight, fresh oxygen, and dry air to wick away the sweat of straining. I walked back to the front of the establishment, refusing to estimate how much time a proper dilution would take.

Andrew was sat at a table, an Inca Kola in hand. I raised an eyebrow at the beverage. Though delicious, it wasn't something that could settle a stomach—too much sugar. Andrew was also feeling a bit queasy, so why had he bought it?

He answered my eyebrow. "They let us use the toilet. Figured we should buy something."

I nodded. A new toilet made more sense than an Inca Kola, but Andrew was right. How had I not come to the same conclusion? Had my manners decayed along with my guilt? Or was I just ready to leave that place behind, fearing I would be blamed for the toilet? Other people were just not a concern.

The glass bottle was still nearly full, so I sat. I was glad for Andrew's company. He was representing foreigners far better than me—my representation was shit. Andrew offered me the soda. I hadn't consumed any fluids since the night before, so I tried a swig. It was a rich drink. It hadn't passed from lips to tongue before my body refused. I forced down what little was in my mouth, but passed on a second attempt. It was too rich for Andrew, too. We walked out, the Inca Kola left on the table. Ungratefulness was not the impression we wanted to leave. But given what else I had left, we knew there would be no invitation to return anyway.

Andrew and I crossed the square, heading back to where we had left Scott. My condition was deteriorating. Andrew said so. Not with words, but with subtle glances from the corners of his eyes. He was checking on me. He even offered to find food for me. That was bold—he spoke less Spanish than I did.

"No, Andrew." I blurted. "I think it just needs to pass. Thanks though."

"Can you handle being on the mototaxi?"

Would it be better to stay in Olmos? Would my condition allow me to ride in a mototaxi all day, not to mention operate one?

"Yeah, I can handle it. I'll probably be miserable wherever I'm at. We may as well make some progress." A spasm struck my gut, tickling the pain receptors. I laid a single hand across my stomach. "We'll see about driving though. I'm pretty sure I couldn't handle city traffic right now."

He nodded. "Worst case scenario, Scott and I take turns. It's not a big deal."

"Thanks, Andrew."

We abandoned the sidewalk and crossed the street between the park and church. In typical Scott fashion, he was chatting up the locals and making friends. Pretty good for a guy who studied Spanish for just five months…in his spare time.

Inspired by the increasing pressure and irritability inside my gut, I crawled into the back of the mototaxi. Several car lengths ahead of me, people made their way up the steps and into the church. I chuckled. Maybe I should ask for forgiveness too. Another spasm shot through my gut. Or was my repentance just beginning?

Chapter 9
Hand Jam Heterosis

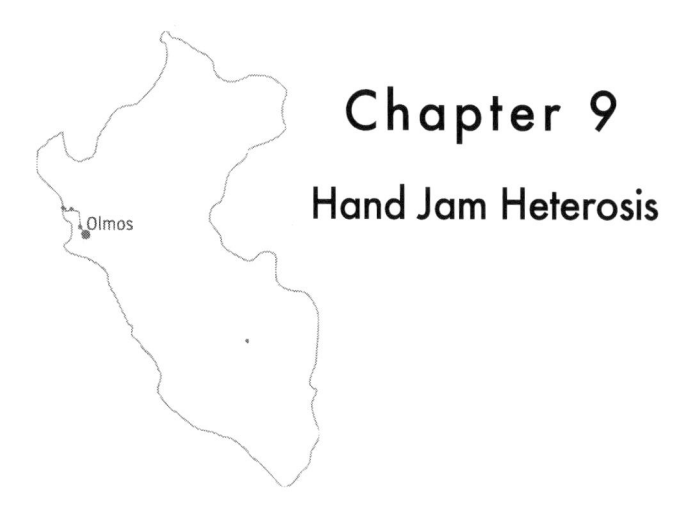

ON OUR WAY OUT OF TOWN, we spotted Josh and Aaron. They were at the same mechanic's shop that Barry and Gerald had visited. We pulled in again to check on them. They had made it to town fine, but we officially disbanded our caravan due to the difference between our top speeds. We planned to meet up again that night though, in our target destination: Bagua Grande.

We made one last stop at a gas station to top off Clifford's tank and to empty my bowels. With elbows on knees and hands cupping chin, the scourge of my bowels was exported from my body. This stop was more pleasant than the previous because this bathroom was something special. The brickwork high on the wall allowed air to circulate and natural light to flood the room; a nice tin wastebasket sat to the right of the toilet, and—because I had tested it before sitting down—I took comfort in the flushing capacity of this toilet. If I was going to be forced into a toilet tour of Peru, I had better learn to appreciate some of the little things.

This appreciation ended at the bathroom door.

Dehydration set in. So did irritability. And the churning of my gut had become constant. Fortunately, the rhythmic pounding of the road rumbling through the mototaxi's shocks was of some comfort. The driving of my teammates, however, was not.

I morphed into a physics conundrum, equal and opposite. Outwardly, my behavior was acceptable, even nice at times. But inwardly, my thoughts were aggressive, critical, and reminiscent of a 5-year-old's tantrum.

Things were intolerable. Why was the shifting so sloppy? Even when the lever was pressed in the right direction, our rpms were all wrong. God forbid I wasn't paying attention during a downshift lest I fly right out of the passenger bay and land in front of the taxi to be run over by the one powered wheel. And what was with the speed bumps? Why did we keep hitting them at full speed? Was I the only one who saw them?

I pulled out my notebook. Though I thought it might help me ignore my gut, it was primarily an attempt to alleviate some stress. I scribbled out my complaints in the pages, my scrawl capturing the roughness of the road and of my attitude.

Really, it was fortunate our mototaxi was zipping along. And the countryside was amazing, which would explain why Scott and Andrew were so entranced and how those dang *rompemuelles*—spring breakers—snuck up on us. But my gut dominated; negative thoughts percolated; I grew callous. My journal captured a list of predicted mechanical failures we would suffer due to the driving styles of my teammates. The only omitted prediction was the International Space Station falling from the sky—the road became too bumpy for writing before I had got to that one.

Inspired by my own pity party, the mototaxi's engine threw one as well. Just as we began the climb toward our first major pass, the engine lost power, then faltered. Clifford lurched to the side of the road, to a wide gravel pullout, before the engine finally gave out.

The four-stroke cycle echoed in my ears, but diminished and allowed the crunch of settling gravel to enter, the space between pops filled with a breeze.

"How you feeling, Nathan?"

I rested my arms on my knees.

"Shitty," I drawled. "Speaking of which…"

I stepped from the back seat, grabbed my toilet paper, and set off to search for a quiet place in the bushes. Scott grabbed his camera and took off up a trail, trying to gain a vantage point above the road. Andrew left the taxi as well, stretching his legs on the wide shoulder. I found a spot, as cozy as any, and relaxed the tension of my abdomen with a sigh. Then I sank to a squat.

Back at the mototaxi, I threw my thinning toilet paper roll back into my bag, the used bits discarded in the bushes. There was very little hesitation or guilt this time; it was biodegradable.

"Any better?"

"No." I sighed.

Scott slipped his camera back into its bag. "Well, just give it some time. It'll pass."

"Yeah, if I don't die first." I had not consumed anything that day. Apart from losing a large volume of water through my colon, we were still in the desert, where the heat inspires sweat and siphons moisture straight from your lungs.

Andrew swept his hand around the engine.

"I think it's cool enough. You guys ready?"

"Yeah." Scott pushed his bag under the cargo hold's big blue tarp. "Do you want to drive, Andrew?"

"Actually," I jumped in, "do you guys mind if I drive?"

Apart from the congealed negativity, writing had provided some physical relief. Maybe driving would be a good distraction, too. Maybe it would wrench my mind out of that negative place and throw me to the open road, twisting into the mountains, climbing for our first pass. Maybe I needed to test my own skills before critiquing my teammates'.

Scott and Andrew exchanged an optimistic glance.

"Yeah, man. If you're up for it."

I pulled on my gloves, mounted, and we were off.

My arms pressed and pulled the handlebars; my trunk leaned sideways off the seat; my spine braced against the seat back while my right hand rolled the throttle grip back and forth and my left hand squeezed and squeezed and squeezed the clutch lever. My thighs clenched the seat on the sharper corners, and my eyes flicked from the road ahead to my mirrors and the road behind. Our mototaxi occupied the whole lane when we could, lessening the severity of the turns and hugging the banked roadway. But when traffic meant to overtake us, we flirted with the road's edge and—at times—the long fall below.

Progress may have been slow, but it was steady. And the physical exertion was a welcome distraction. My gut still made its presence known, but it wasn't the same pain. This pain let me take in the surroundings. The greenery increased as we climbed higher and passed through small villages, collections of five to ten houses that hosted as many families.

Most houses had the same base layer of commercial white overlaid with a name and logo in red and blue—a political advertisement. Why were there so many in these rural areas, though? There weren't exactly a lot of voters around. Were people that invested in their political system, or were competing parties bribing homeowner's with a new paint job, the one condition being the party got to decide what the paint was? A fresh coat of paint on your house every few years? Sounded good. Or was that assumption too pessimistic?

In any case, the paint's crisp edges clashed with the environment, where all the different shades of green blurred together, conserving the variety of the view while making it impossible to pick out any specific border or boundary contained within it.

Just 5 miles from the top of our climb, the engine quaked, a beat from its rhythmic existence misplaced. It was too hot. I downshifted (pulling up on the gear selector) and rolled back on the throttle. Maintaining high rpms made it difficult for the engine to die. So I opened up the throttle until we found a suitable spot.

We pulled onto a wide shoulder between the road and a few houses. Several small faces appeared. Some from around corners, only the tops of their head visible; some from doorways, their bodies concealed by the home's dark interior; but all eyes took us in, the *gringos* with a mototaxi—a sight few Peruvians ever experience. Curiosity dragged some of the children from their hiding places, in want of a closer look.

I paced through the gravel and fresh blood perfused my legs. Large inhale. Large exhale. My pain was in check and my attitude was improved. An adult emerged through one of the doors, also pulled by disbelief. The man greeted us and Scott explained the Mototaxi Junket—or he tried, anyway. Confusion took hold of the Peruvian. Not just in his face, but in the synchronized sag of his eyebrows, chin, and shoulders. I would learn to recognize this confusion, and I saw it in every such conversation, which all unfolded the same.

You're traveling from Piura to Urubamba? Of course, but why by mototaxi? Why not fly? Or bus? Given the mototaxi's ubiquity, almost everyone had ridden in one, so there was a cultural understanding of this machine. It was regarded as useful, but wholly unreliable. There was a reason we could find a mototaxi mechanic in a village of fifty people, and there was a reason he could sustain himself financially. So why drive a mototaxi from Piura to Urubamba? Why, if we had the means to get their faster, in more comfort?

Charity. When Scott explained this, our journey made more sense. But why a mototaxi? That question remained, and for a reason. The problems we could experience were no mystery to the locals, because these were problems the locals would avoid.

In the West, we've reached a point of complacency. We seek out or create problems in order to experience the satisfaction that comes from creating a resolution. The day-to-day life of rural Peruvians was already filled with problems. For them, encountering complications was a passive process; for us, we've had to make it an active one.

These differences make traveling rich though. Our motives may have been a mystery, but our actions were not. People were impressed with our objective, were grateful that we wanted to preserve the rainforest, and were thrilled to interact with us.

Our engine cool, it was time to leave. I resumed my place on the front rather than switching as we had done on previous breaks. With only 5 miles to the top, I was determined to finish the climb.

Not far past the village, the grade mellowed and the lower incline let me gain another gear. The next thing I knew, we neared the top, summited, then started back down. Rather than stop to commemorate, gravity urged us on, and on the descent, the mototaxi climbed to speeds we had not known it was capable of.

* * *

Heterosis is a genetics term that describes the tendency of crossbred individuals to have traits similar to their parents', but of a superior quality. You can see this in dogs, where mixed breed pups suffer from fewer medical conditions than their purebred parents. Heterosis is also demonstrated by proprietary cash crops, which typically produce yields higher than either of the parent varieties. The concept of heterosis is also known as hybrid vigor.

Hybrid vigor: this embodies the notion that combining two differing sets of genetic material enhances the success of both. But why limit this to genetics, or biology for that matter?

Not long after we began our descent, I tried to reinvent the idea of hybrid vigor. I veered across the oncoming lane and pulled onto a shoulder. Our engine was hot again, as were the brakes, but it was really my bowels that had demanded the stop.

I dismounted and scanned the panorama. When we had crossed the pass, we had also crossed a climatic divide. The lush green of the climb had become a barren brown on the descent. Was this due to water availability? Or maybe seasonal variability? Whatever…where was I going to shit?

The road cut into the mountainside, so flat ground was sparse. And there was little vegetation to shield the pride I had reacquired on the ascent. Game plan? A few hundred yards down the road was a bush, on the outside of a turn. It was worth a look. On the walk though, my perspective shifted and the shrub transformed into a treetop. I left the pavement and found its roots anchoring the trunk below a rock wall that propped up the outside edge of the road. The ground was steep—difficult squatting conditions. But it was private. And shaded. And this rock wall—it had potential.

Remember that climbing gym where Scott and I met? One rock climbing technique I learned there—hand jamming—utilizes the different widths of distinct finger positions to lock one's hand inside a fissure. So, perched on top of ground that was quite precarious (even for a standing man), my eyes swept across the mortarless wall and identified several promising cracks.

Heterosis? How about hybrid invigorated skill sets? With one hand jammed into the rock wall, I leaned back into my squat, poking my back end out to relieve myself. I had combined an extreme sport technique with the action of popping-a-squat, establishing myself as an extreme defecator. Hybrid vigor? I'll let you be the judge.

Before you decide though, you should know that whatever vigor the maneuver provided may have been diminished by the complications of wiping. The squished roll of toilet paper refused to be manipulated by my free hand and threatened to roll into the ravine below every time I bobbled it. In that time, my thighs started to burn while the stones that clasped my hand began to tear skin. But I managed. With my pride still intact, and my confidence bolstered, I re-emerged onto the road.

There, I realized I had contaminated the one shady spot. The sun reminded me of this on every step of the return walk. The landscape had absorbed the sun's energy all day, reached capacity, and now emitted that heat itself. A drop of sweat rolled down my nose—more of my body's valuable water, lost. My feet were heavy, my breathing rapid, and a weak vertigo jostled my brain. Why the strange sensations? My feet moved of their own volition, my eyes fixed on Andrew and Scott sheltered in the mototaxi's shade. Was this just the heat intensifying my dehydration? I glanced west to gauge the distance between sun and horizon. The mountains, without their green sheath of diversity, displayed their serrations. Incredible. The ridge was vast, its peaks steep. I glanced back down to my feet, heavier with the magnitude of earth in mind; but they still trudged. It was amazing they kept on at all, especially given how tall the mountains...

It clicked. We were still close to the top. Was it the elevation getting to me, the lower availability of oxygen? Doesn't hypoxemia compound the effects of dehydration? Or is it the other way around? Regardless, I needed to descend.

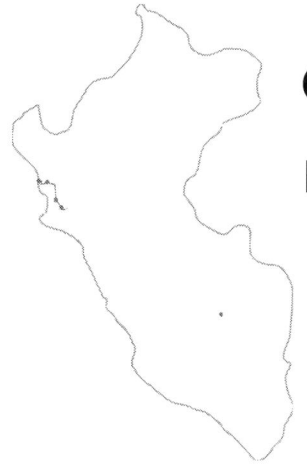

Chapter 10

Roadside Romans

MY NEW SYMPTOMS made me give up driving for the luxurious sofa. A good thing, since what had been a dull, persistent pain on the ascent morphed into sporadic, stabbing pain as we descended.

At times, I had no abdominal discomfort. But those moments were interrupted at the sharp point of agony's jabs. I closed my eyes and flexed my whole body to keep from squirming. Then my abdomen would relax, the invisible wounds healed by a miracle—only to be torn open again. After a few repetitions of this cycle, I left my eyes closed. Maybe I could sleep. That would pass the time, maybe even speed the passing of this illness. Sleep didn't come though.

Our descent continued. We made another stop to cool our engine. I wandered off to relieve myself, yet again. Yes—another account. Hearing about my bowel movements must be getting old, but experience the despair I did, a despair created by the repetition. And be happy *you* aren't getting a rash.

It was on another exposed slope, covered in boulders that offered decent footing options. I hugged my knees, my squat facing me away from the slope and toward the view, the browns and tans of desiccation. My discharge hit the baked hillside and ran down between my feet. I leaned over further, to look behind me. My discharge was now clear, clear enough to bottle and pawn off as purified water. That couldn't be good.

I cinched down my belt and scrambled back up the hill.

At the mototaxi, I laid in the shade—water bottle in hand—the pointed gravel under my back a distraction from the needles in my gut. If my body's effort to flush my bowels was so thorough that I was shitting pure water, how much more water could I afford to lose? None? My lips rested on the brim of the open bottle, but my stomach wasn't enticed. I tried to force a sip. My body fought me the whole way and won.

My water bottle still full, I looked out at the landscape, the Huancabamaba River channel. How was it so dry? Wasn't this the watershed meant to provide the Olmos River valley with enough water to irrigate a desert landscape? Maybe we had passed Limón Dam while my eyes had been closed. If we were now downstream from the dam, then the flow here would be highly regulated. It was a shame I couldn't regulate my own floodgates.

We pressed lower into the watershed, and things turned green. The color was provided by the grasses and shrubs; it wasn't lush jungle, but it was a welcome change. Even more welcome were the mototaxis parked on the side of the road.

The Scottish flag hung from the rear taxi. We parked behind it. The second taxi belonged to one of the British teams. Shaun, our kilted friend, strutted over and leaned against our mototaxi.

"How you boys doing?"

"Hanging in there," Scott answered. "No major problems yet."

My stomach churned.

"Yeah," Shaun nodded to the lead taxi. "Their clutch cable gave out. It's been quite the ordeal getting it back to working." The taxi in question fired up. The other Junketeers backed away, tools in hands, covered in the grime of the road. The taxi took off down the road—a test drive.

Andrew asked, "Have you guys seen anyone else?"

"Apart from you blokes, just the Aussies. They came by not too long ago. Said they were headed for Bagua Grande. We're hoping to get there before tonight, too."

"So are we," Scott said.

The newly-repaired mototaxi came back towards us, our Scottish friend Kane at the wheel, giving a thumbs up. The mototaxi pulled back into its spot and my stomach groaned.

"Well, we've been going at it together. Really helped when that cable went. You boys want to join…till we make Bagua Grande, anyway?"

We gave a half-understood glance to each other. Caravanning with Josh and Aaron had been great for their company, but worrying about two mototaxis wasn't ideal. We weren't about to take partial responsibility for three.

Scott stepped up. "We'll join for a while. But if we get separated, let's not worry about it."

Shaun glanced over his shoulder. The other guys pushed their packed tools into their cargo racks.

"Let's get going then!"

Scott started the engine and pulled onto the road, at the head of our caravan. We gained some distance before the others pulled back onto the road, but we had them in sight. The road paralleled the river, tracing its northern bank. Across a bridge, the road climbed from the river and floodplain in search of the more interesting curves and subtle gyrations of the valley wall.

Within a mile of this change, the two other taxis caught up. Another mile, and they passed us. A third, and we had lost sight of them. Funny…and ironic. We had not committed to the caravan so we wouldn't be weighed down. But now it was they who capitalized on that noncommittal clause. What was not funny was how easy it was for them to pass us. Both mototaxis had zipped by, no problem.

Of course, not all the taxis would have the same top speed. But back at Colan, during our grand departure, we had kept pace with everyone, including the Scots. Now they could blow by us. What had changed?

The dull red of the gear indicator's electronic readout flicked through the gears faster than our single piston. The numbers jumped up on the descents, mimicking our speed. On the climbs, they dropped. Using a lower gear was fine, but wasn't Scott using a gear lower than I had used on our climb over the pass? Or was I crazy? After 10 more miles, it was undeniable: our engine's rpms were dropping. Clifford was losing power.

I leaned toward Andrew. He leaned back.

"I think something's wrong," I shouted through the wind.

He pursed his lips, then nodded. We both sat back, unsure of what we could do.

The miles continued to roll under us, but at a decelerating rate. One hill betrayed our mototaxi's secret though. There was a pause in the engine's song as Scott dropped into second. Andrew and I looked at each other again. Third gear should have been sufficient. He leaned and shouted to Scott.

"Find a place to pull over."

• • •

Vegetation encroached on the road, eating at the pavement's edges. The further downstream, the more luxuriant the valley became—it was a mile before we found a small rocky shoulder to park on.

"Did you notice a loss of power, Scott?" Andrew looked up at Scott from the knee he had taken to do a quick visual inspection of the engine.

"Uhhh…I'm not sure. I've been too focused on the steering to notice."

I looked up from my hunched position on the side opposite Andrew. "We've been paying attention to the gears. Based on that alone, we've been losing power."

Scott nodded and turned to the road that lay behind us, as though searching for an explanation in the memories that he had left physically rooted to the environment.

"Could it just be overheating again?"

Andrew shrugged. "Could be any number of things. I'm thinking fuel though. We should have the carb cleaned in the next town."

"I agree." I popped off the red side panel that concealed the upper half of the engine. Also behind it was the line that ran from the fuel tank to the carburetor. We had spliced in an inline fuel filter—ingenious right? "Do we have another fuel filter?"

Andrew shook his head.

"Well, we can let it cool," Scott said, "since we're stopped. Maybe that'll help."

We nodded.

"We'll have a mechanic in Bagua Grande look at it," Andrew said. "In the meantime, we can change the oil. That will cool things down faster."

An image of dark viscous liquid running from a drain stirred something within me.

"Can you guys handle it? I'm going to grab my toilet paper and step into the woods."

"Of course."

After another squat session, I stepped back out of the roadside vegetation. Andrew was pouring an amber liquid back into the engine. It was so clean, so fresh, so tranquil in the steady pour that it was difficult to tell if that amber arc was even flowing. When would I be able to replace my fluids? When would I feel that refreshment?

Andrew passed the emptied blue plastic container to Scott. He poured the spent oil from the catch tray back into it, this arc blackened by the last day and a half.

"Dark," was all I managed. Andrew's eyebrows shrugged.

Scott capped the container and looked up at us. "Should we leave it?"

Peru's rural garbage disposal system was underdeveloped. People piled garbage along the road every few miles. It was one of these piles we were parked next to.

I shrugged. "When in Rome, right?"

We repacked and took to the road, our blue plastic quart of used oil perched upright on the roadside, an icon of our hypocrisy and of our endeavor's paradoxical nature. We had raised money for an environmentalist effort, but still bought new gear and equipment for the trip; still lined up flights to

Peru; still entered an event that required the consumption of fossil fuels. Then we leave a quart of used oil on the side of the road. Very environmentally-conscious of us. And our justification: the locals do it.

When in Rome, do as the Romans do? Please, locate the Roman Empire on any modern-day map.

Should destructive behavior be justified because it's a cultural norm? Should the slashing and incinerating of rainforest, the spilling of oil onto beaches, and the dumping of plastic into the oceans be acceptable? Don't we answer this question with every filled tank of gas? With every plastic bag we take from the grocery store? With every cell phone—laden with heavy metals—that we throw away?

Don't we answer this question with every blue plastic quart of used oil we abandon roadside? It's no secret what's down this path, and unless we want to go the way of the Caesars, we should consider a new direction.

"How's it compare!?" Andrew's yell jolted my attention back to the mototaxi. He was leaning forward to project his voice.

"Better," Scott shouted back.

My eyes tracked the flicking of the gear indicator. The mototaxi was performing better, but only marginally.

There was a break in our tree tunnel, a window onto the landscape. The valley was falling into shadow. Hopefully we would make Bagua Grande before nightfall.

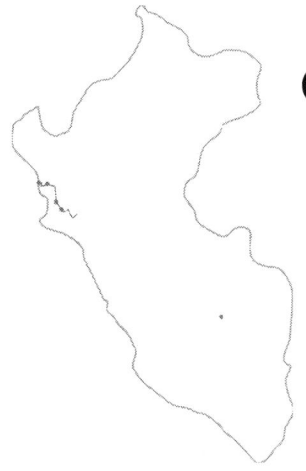

Chapter 11
Lost Composure

I HAD ADDED A LAYER. After that chilly ride in the desert, I kept my sweater accessible from the back seat. The sun had left the valley, and the ambient light that poured in over the peaks was also fading.

I yelled to Andrew over the engine, "How long would it take to clean the carb?"

He pursed his lips, gave a sideways glance at the engine. He turned back. "An hour?"

Our mototaxi's performance was decaying. You can usually attribute loss of engine output to one of two factors: fuel or air. I learned that during my childhood on the farm. During my first year operating a combine harvester (a John Deere 6622 Titan II), the engine had sputtered and died in the middle of a hill climb. I had panicked and freewheeled down the hill, backward. In that case, the loss of power had been an air problem—the engine air filter was so packed with dirt that the engine had suffocated. In the case of our mototaxi though, I was betting on fuel.

I shouted back to Andrew, "Could you do it in the dark?"

His eyebrows raised.

"Wouldn't want to." He trimmed syllables in the engine's noise. "Some small parts."

Bagua Grande was a long way off. At our current rate, it would be very late when we got there...*if* we got there. May as well face the problem now and bring our speed back up. But I wasn't about to take apart the carburetor—that was beyond my skills. And with Andrew backing down too, there wasn't much to do.

Air? Or fuel? Fuel or air? Maybe the problem was more technical, but if it was, I didn't know enough to help. So, air or fuel? This was a single-cylinder, four stroke engine—how could air be the problem? It had to be the fuel. And it was too big a problem to ignore. I worked backward from the carb, all the way to the tank. The first day of the race was the first time we had filled the gas tank to the brim. These mototaxis were owned by The Adventurists organization itself. They had probably sat unused since the last race. When was that? Six months ago? Maybe there had been some condensation in the tank. That would have made a redox reaction possible, corroding the inside. Maybe when we filled the tank we had mobilized that corrosion.

"Andrew!" I followed his lead and dumped the spare words. "No extra fuel filter?" He shook his head to confirm what he had said earlier.

Corrosion—that could mean sediment in the fuel. If the filter had caught enough of it, that could impede the fuel flow. That was it. We just needed to ditch the filter.

Shit.

We could run without a filter just fine. Most mototaxis did. But we had cut our fuel line to splice in the filter. If we removed it, the tubing between tank and carb would be too short. Whatever. It didn't need to be pretty, just functional—and only for half a day. This was doable.

I hit Andrew on the shoulder and shouted, "Got a plan." Projecting forward now. "Scott!" He did a limbo lean to hear better. "Pull over!"

I liberated our tools from beneath the tarp of our rear cargo hold, the makeshift rope and bungee netting undone and limp, the guys next to me while I relayed what I had gone over in my head. I passed the toolkit to Andrew and continued to dig.

"Nathan," Scott interrupted. "We cut the fuel line. We can't go back to a direct feed. The tubing is too short."

I stood. "Not with this."

I held up our water filter kit, which included several feet of clear plastic tubing.

"The tubes are different sizes, but I'm pretty sure we can squeeze our fuel line inside the water filter tubing. We can just use a few inches to splice the fuel line back together."

Scott and Andrew exchanged a shoulder shrug. "Sounds good."

The urge to urinate came out of nowhere.

I tossed the filter kit to Scott. "Can you guys start pulling stuff apart? I really need to pee."

"Yeah." Scott made for the front.

"I'm going to grab a headlamp," Andrew said.

Andrew took my place rummaging through our gear while I walked away. I made it ten feet before I met the wall of trees and shrubs that bordered the grassy gravel shoulder we had parked on. The vegetation was dense. Only shadows and the dark were visible past this wall. And near the equator, twilight is shorter than at higher latitudes, so the night was advancing on our gravel patch as well.

My fly undone, I started to void my bladder. More water lost? Great. At least I was upright and relaxed rather than in a squat, straining against...

I lost control. My fate-tangling sphincter no longer had the strength to dam the flow. It burst. Fluids were draining from my front and my back. My belt and fly already undone, my hands flew to my hips, thumbs hooking waistbands so I could tug everything off and away from the flood waters as I fell into a squat.

So much for that relaxed, upright stance. Fluids spurted, like water from the classic hand pump so often used in the Old

West to draw water from the ground. This well, though, was poisoned.

There was no denying it: I was a mess. I called out. "Hey, can one of you bring me some toilet paper?"

Twilight was gone. The last shreds of light revealed only the outline of my hand before my face; dark concealed the color and texture. One of the headlamps next to the engine rose into the air. It floated to the back of the mototaxi, where it directed its attention into our bags. A moment, and it popped back up. It made a single broad sweep across the shoulder until it crossed me. It clicked off, but the footsteps belonging to the lamp approached. The feet stopped just short of me. Andrew's voice: "You ok?"

"Yeah." He held out a box of towelettes. I had to lean onto one foot to reach it. He couldn't help it—his eyes were averted. "Just tired of this."

"Hang in there." The footsteps retreated. I yanked a moist towelette from the box as a light clicked on back by the taxi.

One good thing about the diarrhea was that, at this point, voiding my bowels meant draining them of water. So whatever had made it into my clothes had not made a huge mess. But it did make me desperate for a shower.

Sanitized and less wet, I rejoined the mechanical efforts. The piece of tubing we cut from our filtration kit was a perfect splice. But while I squatted next to Clifford's engine to feed the tube to the other side, a glint caught my eye. Our throttle cable. It was disjoined from its attachment to the carburetor. The nut was too loose to provide any tension. This reduced the range of motion in the throttle control.

What the hell? How had Scott not noticed? His hand had been on the throttle all afternoon. And why hadn't Andrew spotted this during his once-over when we changed the oil? I'm the one covered in his own shit...so why was I doing all the thinking?

I had no appreciation for my teammates. Not for the kindness they had shown me since becoming sick. And not for the kindness they had demonstrated by inviting me. Why was I even there? I didn't know Scott *that* well. I had only met Andrew a few months before. Shitting myself on the side of some rural road and then having to fix a mototaxi in the aftermath wasn't what I had expected from this trip.

The nut tight and cable tensioned, I flopped onto the sofa and let Scott and Andrew gather and pack our tools. My pulse thrummed in my ears, behind closed eyes as the tarp crinkled and ropes cinched behind me.

Back on the road, the mototaxi ran better. Good thing, since we were yet again the assholes Duncan had warned us not to be, driving in the dark. Even though all of the lights worked (blinkers, high and low beam headlights, and passenger bay markers), we were hard to spot on the windy road. So I also held a cyclist's light out the back of the taxi, the LED's red pulse synchronized with my abdominal throbbing.

Chapter 12

Mechanical Improv

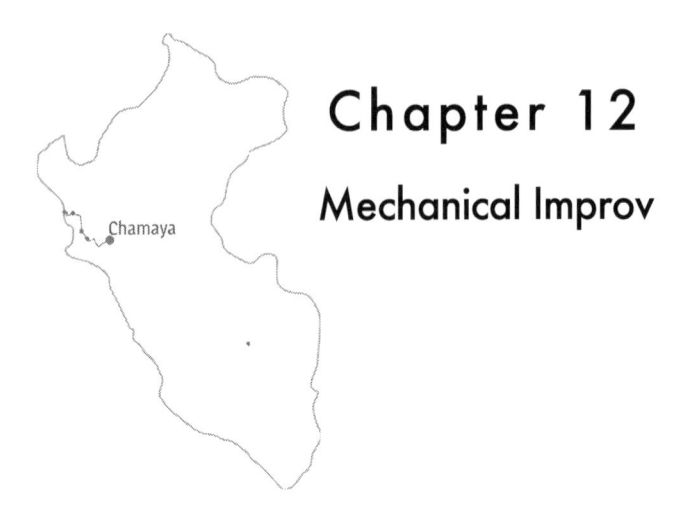

"'AN ADVENTURE is never an adventure when it happens.' Well, Emma, in light of today–" I sat on the bed of our hostel room, alone. I had pulled out my camera to record a confessional. "–I have to say I agree. Today was hell. I can't wait to look back on this experience with any sort of fondness." My eyes wandered across the room, while I searched for scraps of that conversation with Emma. "Sure, I *know* this is an adventure. But that's not how it feels." I turned the camera off.

Clifford's performance boost had been short-lived. We had barely made it the 12 miles to the next town—Chamaya—where we stopped to weigh our options. Chamaya was a small town extending in parallel to the major roads that intersected there. Given its size, there had been a case to press on. But I had begged Scott to find a place for us to stay.

Scott had stepped into an internet cafe to ask about lodgings. Lucky for us, above the cafe were rooms for rent. The cafe even had a garage-style door large enough for our mototaxi to fit through, and after negotiating with the owner, we pushed Clifford inside for the night.

Upstairs, we found our room and the communal bathroom. It was another closet-sized bathroom, but this one had a shower head and drain too. I could touch all four walls while sitting on the toilet. So I laundered my clothes while sitting, then began my shower before I even stood up.

I was refreshed by the cold water, and enough of my negativity had been washed away by the water to reveal some of my buried motivation. I pulled out my camera. Doing something adventurous while having a good time is a lot different than being adventurous while in a miserable state. Emotions have a way of trumping reason and logic. It was a perspective Emma and I had missed, and one I would not forget.

Andrew and Scott had gone to explore the town and find dinner. My camera packed again, I forced a sip of water then crawled into bed. The hostel was like a chimney, and our room was near the top, the only window small and high on the wall, too high to lean out or to hope for the feel of a breeze. That's why I had skipped drying after my shower. I had hoped to conserve some water by supplementing my sweat.

I drifted in and out of consciousness until Andrew and Scott returned, and with a sports drink I had requested. Along with the water, my body had lost a lot of electrolytes. This beverage teemed with them. But it went down as well as the water had. The full bottle sat on the nightstand until morning.

* * *

We woke early. Our mototaxi had to be out of the internet cafe before it opened. While we pushed Clifford back to the street, we debated Cindy.

The Pink Fairy Award had been bestowed upon us to mock our preparation and handicap our team. Wouldn't it be an even greater mockery if we finished with Cindy in pristine condition? That had been our goal. But her piñata base was big—it took up a lot of space. To preserve its condition, we had bungeed her between the ribs of the roof's frame. It was ingenious…until we picked up speed. The wind whipped the plastic packaging, driving us to madness. Two days of flapping had been enough to change our minds about this packing scheme.

"What about making sure nothing happens to her?"

"We can still do that, but why the piñata base? It's massive, and annoying."

"And the plastic wrap is starting to tear."

"It only took two days for this damage to appear. What's another ten or twelve going to do? May as well ditch it now if it's going to be ruined anyway."

"So ditch the base and keep Cindy?"

"Yeah, we'll wrap her up in the plastic and throw her in the back. Agreed?"

We all nodded.

Then came the important debate: find a mechanic here or take our chances on the road to Bagua Grande?

We needed to at least ask around for a mechanic. How would the mototaxi cover the 25 miles to Bagua Grande? During the last 12 to Chamaya, it had run only on our desperation—and that was in short supply at the start of the day. But mechanics probably were, too. No doubt there would be more—and better experienced—mechanics in Bagua Grande.

Why not both?

Scott asked around. After fifteen minutes, we learned there was no official mechanic in town. Strange. But one guy had a friend that knew a guy who lived just up the hill. Good enough!

We parked in the driveway while our guide (baffled by our task) knocked on the wood door of a small house. It opened. A few minutes later, a man wearing nothing but bright yellow basketball shorts and a backwards maroon baseball cap appeared. His wardrobe may not have fit the part, but the basket of tools in his hands did.

Scott described our problem as best as he could and the two men set to work. After fifteen minutes, yellow-shorts waved us closer, one half of the carburetor in each hand. We all stepped around him and leaned in.

"Damn." We had been right to find a mechanic. Sediment sat in the bottom of the fuel chamber. The mechanic ran a finger along the side, leaving a metallic wake in the foreign, brown coating.

Yellow-shorts dumped the remnant fuel and wiped out the carb. With the halves atop a piece of cardboard, he strolled back to his house. He returned with a bicycle tire pump to blast the foreign material out of the jets. Much pumping was done, and much rinsing with gasoline.

With everything clean, reassembly began. But there was a problem: the seal between the fuel and air halves of the carburetor was stretched. The O-ring didn't fit into its manufactured groove. The mechanic battled with it, tried to make it work. It was the only option—he had no replacement. After the O-ring jumped from its groove a dozen times, he sat back, kneeling on the cardboard. He stared at the halves in each hand and the crazy-shaped O-ring looped around his pinky finger. Was he thinking or praying? Whichever, it had brought inspiration. He stood and marched back to his house again. This time he returned with an automotive silicone.

He squeezed a bead from the tube and scraped it into the groove. He set the O-ring onto the silicone and tamped it down with his finger. This time it stayed. He pressed the halves back together to our congratulations and grateful head nodding.

The reassembly complete, we returned to the hostel to grab our stuff. Andrew and I tore Cindy from her piñata prison while Scott loaded our bags. After a second guilt-ridden debate, we left the piñata on the sidewalk. It was another piece of trash perched against the building and the only evidence of Cindy's kidnapping as we drove off with her body wrapped in plastic and shoved in the back.

Five-minute karma.

We made it a half mile before the engine suffered a sputtery death that no amount of kicking could remedy. Well, at least we knew where the local, impromptu mechanic lived. We turned the mototaxi and started to push it back to town. The road was exposed, the morning sun hot. To walk, to push the taxi, to be active instead of sedentary felt so good after the misery that had been the day before. But sweat beaded behind the weight of the taxi and beneath the rays of the sun. It was another contribution to my water deficit. After five minutes, we were jogging and I lost the strength required to push the mototaxi further. With my hands wrapped around the tubular frame, it started to drag me.

Scott threw me a glance from the other corner, then tossed me his camera. "Trail us and get a shot of us pushing." He gave me the perfect excuse and let me save face. I fell back and clicked on the camera.

Then my brain clicked.

While I had been "disposing" of the piñata, Andrew had mentioned that the choke cable had been detached. The mechanic hadn't reconnected it—no big deal. But what if the choke was on? The purpose of the choke is to reduce the amount of air in the air–fuel mixture entering the cylinder. This is used when the engine is cold. Once warm though, the choke needs to be turned off so the engine doesn't flood. Our engine had run for half a mile before it sputtered out. Couldn't that be explained by the choke?

I yelled to Scott, but he and Andrew had already pushed the mototaxi far ahead. They didn't respond to my yells, at least not before they disappeared around a bend in the road. The heat chased me all the way back to town until I reached the sanctuary of tree shade. I ambled back up the small hill to the mechanic's. I grabbed my water bottle from the taxi and collapsed onto a bench of simple wooden planks. I rested there while he and the boys took the mototaxi for a test drive.

After a few minutes, they pulled back into the driveway. It *had* been the choke. With a final farewell from our mechanic, we hit the road again, and stayed there, tracing the river up through its valley until we reached Bagua Grande.

Chapter 13

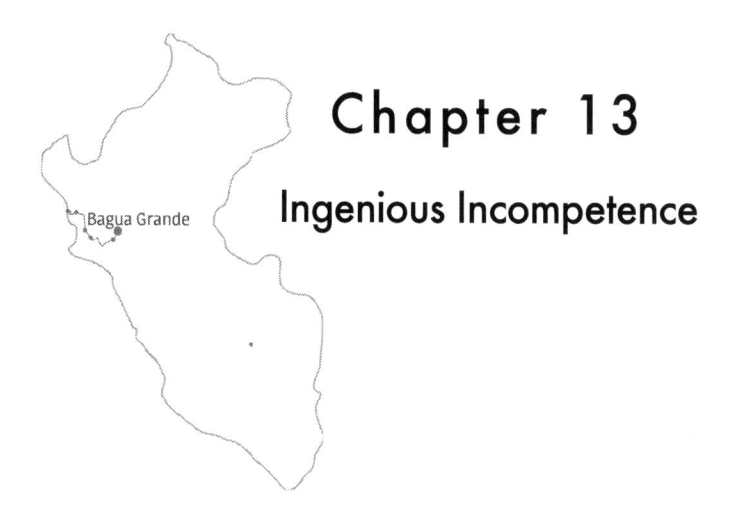

Ingenious Incompetence

BAGUA GRANDE is a modest city of 50,000 people and serves as the capital of the Utcubamba Province. It was in Bagua Grande where I found some relief. Yes, I found another decent toilet; but the real milestone was eating...sort of.

We found a restaurant on the corner of a busy intersection, both street-side walls open to the sidewalk to funnel in customers and breeze alike. There was a large chalkboard menu mounted in the back, above a kitchen. I left it to Scott to order. It's a Peruvian custom to serve soup with most meals. Scott and Andrew had not understood this the night before when they had gone to eat. Their soup finished, they left before the main dish was served. Now aware of the error, they were more excited about the options on the menu.

The Spanish word for broth is *caldo*. It's an essential word when deciding on food, because there are a number of broths to be found in Peru. *Caldo de maize, caldo de pollo, caldo de gallina, caldo de carne, caldo de* etc. I had a meat variety served with a half-submerged hunk of fleshy bone. I didn't eat my main dish or anything solid from the soup, but I did finish the broth. It was the first real sustenance I had consumed in the past 36 hours.

Invigorated and motivated, I drove. Given how well the mototaxi had run that morning (after the choke incident), we skipped the mechanic in Bagua Grande and continued up the Utcubamba River valley, further into the mountains.

There, fat drops fell. Cold, fat drops. We had already been stopped by our hot engine when the rain began and we rushed to yank on our waterproof gear. The river we had been following had gotten smaller and smaller, and its valley more and more narrow. At times, the topography was more reminiscent of a gorge than a valley, steep-walled and barren, except where plants had wedged themselves into cracks between layers of gray and pink rock. Ready for our first rain, we took off again.

Half a mile down the road, the pavement dark with moisture snapped back to a bone dry and barren gray. Mountain weather—we had heard changes could be abrupt. Our waterproof layers were shed before they were even allowed to function.

The lack of rain was still fortunate though, because Clifford started to struggle again. He didn't like climbing. The road arced up, becoming steeper with every inch we progressed, to the point that it was steeper than anything we had climbed thus far. Were we stopping more than usual? Was the grade the reason the engine was overheating so much? Hard to say. We were getting close to Pedro Ruiz though, so we kept pushing.

Further and further we went, higher and higher we climbed. At one point, the valley was so narrow that the roadway had been carved into the rock wall of the gorge. It was like driving through a stretch of subway tunnel where it intersected a station, one side missing through which light flooded the tube. Only on this stretch, the platform was far below us, cascading in the opposite direction. Then, as if to balance the gorge, the road crossed a bridge and into another open-faced cave.

The road was surreal, a bizarre form of concealment that allowed us to sneak into the mountains, into a landscape still so rich and green that humans were the outsiders and natural processes were still the dominant force.

Our rail-line surfaced as the gorge opened. The valley walls pulled back slightly like a set of stalled stage curtains. We had to climb up and peek around one of the valley walls to find what was hiding backstage: Pedro Ruiz.

Confined by the valley, the town was spread thin, never more than a few structures wide. Most of the town was a single line of buildings that flanked either side of the road in the classic sandwich arrangement: structure–street–structure. It was when the buildings faded away ahead of us and the town petered back to jungle that we realized we had gone through downtown. We pulled into a parking lot, the mototaxi our first topic of discussion.

Engine performance over the last day and a half had been as predictable as my bowels—and as pleasant. And just as I had grown tired of my bowels, we all were fed up with our engine. So it was off to another mechanic.

We double-backed and found one on the main street. He was a legitimate mechanic, with a business front and a large selection of spare parts, the most prominent of which hung from a street-facing wall. The smaller, more mundane, less shiny parts were filed away in the shelves behind a large counter. Like all mototaxi mechanics, he pulled out his short stool and set to work.

We were sitting on the sidewalk, me still at the mercy of stabbing pains, when the mechanic whistled and waved us over. We crossed to the far side of the taxi, where he sat. He extended his arms, half of the carb in each hand. Another "damn" escaped my lips. What had been mechanical ingenuity that morning was now the incompetence of an amateur.

The ill-fitting O-ring was still in place, but its adhesive was not. It had worked its way into the carb where it mixed with the gas—a liquid in which it was soluble—so that the silicone broke apart into tiny droplets that turned the gas cloudy. Some fragments remained clumped together and floated, their sunken brethren no doubt clogging things up. That explained the difficult climb.

The mechanic looked up at us, shaking his head and explaining how dumb that had been. He dumped the gas and wiped out the carb. Then came the wire brush. Next was the air to clean the jets. This mechanic had an air compressor though, which packed a higher pressure than the morning's bike pump. The carb clean and almost reassembled, he disappeared into his shelves. He emerged with a new O-ring. The fit was perfect.

Less confident in Clifford's health, and impressed with our current mechanic, we discussed if we should have him do anything else. We came up with a laundry list, most of which he shook his head at.

"What's he saying, Scott?"

"It sounds like none of these fixes are necessary."

The mechanic jumped back in, his speech so fast that I was hoping for a set of verbal *rompemuelles*.

"He can do this stuff if we want him to, but he doesn't see the point."

Mototaxi mechanics are interesting, as well as their philosophy. Everywhere, the general rule was don't fix what isn't broken. I had already learned this from my father—he's the type eager to fix things. So I had no problem with our mechanic's opinion.

"Yeah, he says replacing the drive chain might put extra strain on the transfer chain. New brakes have to be broken in, and they aren't great on downhills anyway."

The mechanic kicked our rear wheel and gave a chuckle. The tire was worn, the tread's pattern faded to the texture of eggshell at the middle. He spoke again.

"Yeah, he says this tire will get us past Urubamba, that we don't need a new one."

"Well then, that settles it."

We huddled and pooled our money. Paying bills was a challenge. It wasn't that we couldn't afford it, or that we didn't have enough cash; rather, the bills we did have weren't small enough. Large bills were commonly counterfeit. If people were confident they could spot a fake, they would accept them. But many people weren't confident, so were reluctant to accept them. And of course, banks, ATMs, and exchanges love dishing out the large bills. So with our small bills and coins brought to the exact amount, Scott broke the huddle and paid the mechanic.

Our carburetor was clean again—a relief. But visiting multiple mechanics in the same day was unnerving.

"Hey!" said Andrew, looking over my shoulder.

I turned. Coming up the road was another mototaxi. Mounted on the top was an oversized rubber ducky.

"Pete!" we all said together.

We waved like madmen as Pete drove by. My waving was more akin to a starved and half-crippled madman, but our collective effort had been enough. Pete turned around.

Since we were all still alive, we decided to get a celebratory meal together at a nearby restaurant. It was more *caldo* for me. The staple ingredient was hominy. The mushy grain lacked the flavor and texture my mouth and stomach could appreciate. It was nowhere near as satisfying as my earlier *caldo*, and I only managed to get down half. The murky surface cringed back at me as I herded the hominy with my spoon. Could I afford to not finish it? Whatever fluids I had gained earlier in the day had been lost in my pre-dinner bathroom visit. My bowels couldn't hold anything. Neither could my mind.

My attention flickered between the soup and the conversation. Scott, Andrew, and Pete exchange tales of the road. I wanted to participate, but my enthusiasm was buried beneath my knotted gut and self-pity.

"Hey!" Scott pointed through the restaurant's open facade. A mototaxi passed by, the driver in…orange coveralls? The passengers too?

"The Kiwis!"

Scott and Pete chased them down. Andrew and I stayed. It wouldn't do us any good to have the restaurant staff think we had skipped the bill. I sipped at my water. This was a taste I had taken for granted. Maybe one day I would again. Then this would all be a story to tell. We already had so many, as did Pete. And this was only day three? What stories laid ahead of us, just waiting to be lived and recollected?

"Andrew! Nathan!" Scott trotted back into the restaurant, Pete on his heels. "We caught the Kiwis!" Pessimism and fatigue tightened the corner of my right eye. Scott beamed. "They are staying here tonight. They found a hotel online." My eye relaxed. "And get this: it has reviews."

What hotel, in the Andes, off the periphery of the beaten track, had reviews?

"It is pretty late," Andrew said. He turned to me. "What do you think?"

Another hominy-flavored gut gurgle.

"May as well get a room," I said.

"Awesome!" Scott turned to Pete. "Pete? You going to stay too?"

Pete nodded. "Yeah, I'm going to try to find an internet cafe too."

"Let's get moving then."

We left the restaurant and clambered back under our mototaxi roofs. Scott triggered the engine and flipped the lights on. Another quick sunset. The town shrank in the darkness as the last stage lights were blocked by the valley's closing curtains. Three blocks up and we were at the hotel. Rooms had two beds each. We rented two rooms for the night, perfect for the four of us. And there was an added bonus: private bathrooms. Just the mention of *agua caliente* dissolved the contempt I had for my condition, and the indifference I had for my teammates. A hot shower? I hugged Scott.

Chapter 14

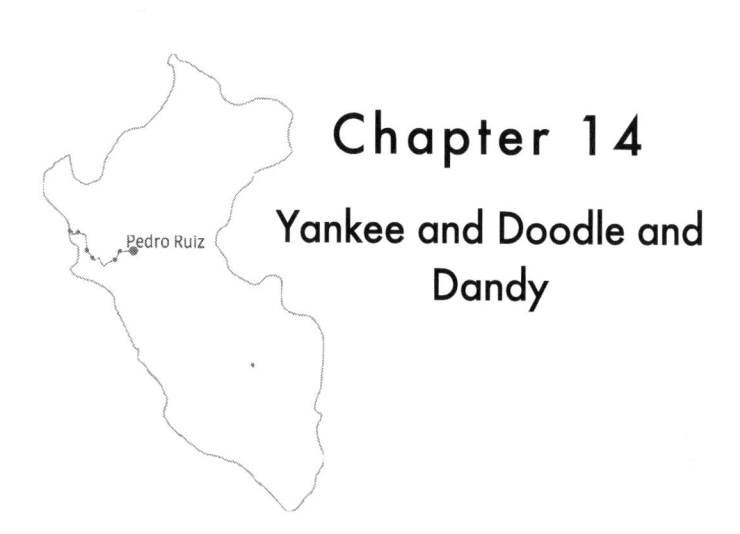

Yankee and Doodle and Dandy

CALIENTE: SPANISH FOR "HOT." Though advertised as a hot shower, a more appropriate claim would have been *agua no muy fría,* or "not so cold water." Still, it was one of the best showers of my life.

That water, there was a reason it was only not-so-cold. Like most Peruvian hotels untouched by a mass of *gringo* tourists from the West, this one was not plumbed with hot water. But the bathrooms had been retrofitted with a shower head that had an integrated heating element.

I had anticipated an immediate shower, so after I christened the toilet I was not that thorough in my cleanup. My cheeks had already been rubbed raw, so I conserved some toilet paper and stepped into the shower extra filthy. I reached for the valve of salvation, the one that would cleanse me of my digestive system's sins, but my hand was stilled. Not by the appearance of a messenger or some other holy apparition; not by divine intervention or some other remote will; but by a gray tube that ran out of the ceiling and into a small breaker box next to the shower's plumbing. The box had been painted to the wall—not glued or screwed, but painted. And the small gauge wires with the loose wrap of electrical tape that emerged from the box—they disappeared into the shower head. Electricity and water mix right? Isn't it just that sometimes people get the recipe wrong?

I turned the tap. If the flow of water was too slow, the circuit broke. So for five minutes, I alternated between adjusting the flow density and resetting the breaker. I bounced, rocked, and gyrated under the water's thermal awkwardness, and twitched, pulsed, and ticked with the electric current that flowed through my fingers. But the water was too fast to be heated before it rained down. It did take the edge off though, and for those next five minutes I put my bar of soap to work.

The drain looked awful. Water spiraled and concentrated the filth: the dust of the road, my residual fecal debris, my general negativity and loathing, all down the drain. Salvation. I dried, then collapsed into bed.

* * *

"¿Mas plano o mas montaña?" Garbled Spanish: my attempt at communication and a sure sign of an attitude turn-around.

Her reply was too fast for comprehension. We stood outside the hotel, next to the mototaxi, a map of Peru in my hands. The night before, while I utilized the "suicide shower," there had been some route discussion between Scott, Pete, and the Kiwis. Pedro Ruiz was at a major crossroads. From here, we could head south and remain in the Andes. Or we could continue east and find the fringe of Peru's northeastern jungles, which we could follow south.

The Kiwis were headed east, as was Pete. Our original plan had been to turn south, but in our minds was planted a seed of doubt. Clifford's climbing abilities had not been inspiring. That wasn't going to change on the mountainous route. But we had also conspired with Josh and Aaron. They thought we would go south, and had planned to do the same. If we suffered any substantial delay—which felt inevitable—they might catch us. Going south meant a better chance of seeing them again. And on top of that, going east felt like a betrayal. How could we convince the Texans to go south, into the mountains, with a piece of junk while we ambled across the broad river valleys to the east? All of us torn on our direction, I turned to local knowledge.

The hotel owner gave me a moment to digest what she had said. It hadn't sunk in. I leaned towards her, eyebrows raised, map still outstretched.

Her mouth broke into a toothy smile. She pointed south. "Muchas montañas. Montañas grandes." She turned and pointed east. "Montañas." She traced the jagged Andean peaks in midair until they tapered off and, finger moving horizontal, she said, "Plano."

"Yo entiendo," I nodded, my own smile appearing. East would be flatter. But was it really the better route? Scott had explained to the owner the night before what we were doing and where we were headed. Good thing she had the context, because I didn't have to prompt her before asking, "¿Tu prefieres?"

After more tongue tumbling, missing vocabulary, and gesticulating, she conveyed that both routes were very beautiful. If we went south, we could even find a popular waterfall. But that road had several climbs, several passes, several descents; that made the easterly route more favorable for a mototaxi.

"¡Muchas gracias!" The exchange had been a struggle for both of us, but communication is flexible. With just some scraps of Spanish, we had had a whole conversation. Much had been conveyed by tone, facial expressions, and our hands. The giant road map had helped too. Both of us thrilled with our accomplishment, we hugged. I bent at the waist so she could get her arms around my back. She took advantage of the height adjustment and planted a kiss on both my cheeks.

Laughter escaped me. I was taken aback and flattered all at once. The heat rose in my face and it must have been the most color I had shown in days. I returned to my full height—a little taller than before—as Pete came out of the hotel lobby.

I told him what the owner had told me, which confirmed his decision to head east. Then he produced a rubber ducky and presented it to the owner. The middle-aged woman returned to her youth and squealed. She clasped the duck between both hands and peaked at it inside her laced fingers, as if afraid it might fly away. Then she threw one arm around each of us and pulled us into another doubled over embrace. Doubly doubled over. She must have been the first person in Pedro Ruiz to hug two *gringos* at once.

She walked back inside, flaunting her new pet to Scott and Andrew as they emerged. I told them what the owner had recommended, then reiterated everything else we knew about the two routes. I made the case to go east. Abandoning the route on which we might find Aaron and Josh didn't feel right. But they might learn the same things we had and make the same decision. At least, I hoped so.

Andrew cinched down the tarp on our cargo rack. "So…east?" He looked at me.

I turned to Scott. "East?"

He looked back at both of us. "East."

It was incredible. If the shower had been shocking, the drive was stunning.

The morning was gray as we left Pedro Ruiz. The clouds did not reach down into the valleys, but had remained overcast. At the edge of town, the road began to climb. And climb. And climb. We slithered up the mountain, topographic undulations forcing us to play hide and seek with the road ahead. Carved into the hillside, it was narrow by necessity, the green vegetation encroaching on one side and empty space on the other.

Even on such a treacherous road, the level of communication between drivers was such that they passed each other with confidence. Lead drivers used their blinkers to signal when it was safe to pass, and would-be passers waited for that signal.

After an hour of passing and being passed, we stopped to let the engine cool. From our spot perched on a shoulder (one of the few), the valley stretched out before us, the floor falling away. In the distance, a ribbon laid across the hill, curls we had followed forty-five minutes earlier. Yet there it was, set into the ridge where the valley terminated, so close. It was several hundred—if not thousands—of feet below us, but we may as well have thrown rocks at it, thinking we could get them to the far side, where the bank was cut so steep the green turned to pink like a fresh wound that the constant water erosion wouldn't let heal.

We all reached for our cameras. Even Cindy made it into a few pictures, posing on top of a rock. She was not very graceful, but what could we do? She just wasn't that flexible. It was when we were manipulating the joints she did have that we discovered her wearing a second outfit under the dress: a blouse and blue jeans.

More surprising than her hidden wardrobe was what she did while we posed her: she started singing. Yes, she had a music box in her abdomen. And was that...*Yankee Doodle*?

As a modern nursery rhyme, the origins of this song are oft overlooked. From the pre–Revolutionary War era (the war in which the North American colonies won their independence from the King of England), it was sung by officers of the British military to mock colonial soldiers, the supposed Yankee Doodle Dandies. "Yankee" was a nickname for the colonials (which has lived on as the official mascot of one of New York's pro baseball teams). The origins of "doodle" aren't as clear, but my favorite interpretation is that it's synonymous with "fool". And—best for last—"dandy": young men adopting feminine mannerisms and ornate attire. But wait! There's more. "Dandy" was a term Englishman happily applied to their fellows, those that managed to follow this fashion. That this term made it into the lyrics implies that the English did not mock the Americans' desire to be dandies, but their inability to achieve even *that* level of sophistication. There you have it. Yankee Doodle Dandy: American wanna-be cross-dressing fools.

Well England, need I remind you how your red-coat regulars did against a ragtag army of American wanna-be cross-dressing fools? It's no wonder why this song is sung with patriotic fervor; what better way to rub it in the faces of the Brits?

So why was Cindy singing this song in Peru? That was beyond us. Cindy was just full of surprises. But there was something symbolic in it. Really, the song is about owning your shortcomings to disempower your opposition. It felt prerequisite to the race that we own up to the fact that life had been easy—maybe not for any one individual, but culturally. In the West, it seems we have become complacent. What better way was there to disempower the challenges of the race than to acknowledge that fact, to set ourselves on a path that guaranteed the destruction of that complacency?

After singing along to a few verses and having a good laugh about it, we tossed Cindy in the back and hopped back on the mototaxi. Our climb continued, and we now passed through the occasional village, where half of every building was supported by stilts to undermine the topography. We got a good look at the stilts because every village was flanked by *rompemuelles* large enough to bottom out our suspension, even at a snail's pace.

At the top of the climb, we reached the village of Pomacochas, settled on the banks of a lake by the same name. Again, this place represented the clash of cultures. Pomacochas is the Hispanic variant of the Quechua word *Pumaqucha*, or Puma Lake. Quechua was the language of the Incas and is still spoken in Peru. It was another language Scott had studied before our trip, but because it has no written form, it had been a challenge.

Along the banks of Puma Lake, the landscape stretched out. Instead of the constant grade of our morning, the road arced up and around ridges, dipped through low valleys, and hopped narrow rivers. When basins opened up, so did the vegetation, offering us a view. Plots of farmland checkered wavy valley floors, which were occasionally cut by the meander of an alpine stream. The air was fresh, brisk, and we all had pulled on an extra layer.

The road crossed into a national park. Signs marked an overlook and on the wide shoulder was a handful of cars, a familiar mototaxi among them.

We parked and made the short hike to a gazebo. The view swayed toward the Atlantic, weaving through each successive ridge stacked to the horizon. Parallel valleys terminated into one narrow basin, the single line of sight that outstretched the view found in any other direction. A roof of clouds capped the tallest peaks, and the spotted breaks in the cover served as mobile skylights driven by the wind, broadcasting light across the landscape as if reflected from a disco ball. The forest was vibrant, and danced with sunlight, the green hues shifting with waves of light. The song of insects shifted too, next to a constant accompaniment of birdsong. My lungs took one large breath, and out came a sigh. My limbs tingled.

Set up on a fence, at the edge of the clearing, was Pete and his camera.

"Hey, guys! Still going strong?"

"You bet! How about you? Exhausted from navigating all those turns? We've already switched a few times."

Pete gave a subtle shrug. "I'm still doing alright. Better than the Kiwis, anyways. They're behind us now. Their mototaxi was getting worked on in one of those towns. I'm guessing they broke down." He turned back toward the view, and our eyes followed his. "The light is great right now, the way the clouds are shifting. There was even some rain in one of the valleys a few minutes ago. At one point the sun came in and lit up the fall streaks."

We leaned against the fence next to Pete.

After getting our fill, we made our way back down the trail. On her way up was a woman talking on her cell phone. She came to a full stop when she saw us, turned as we passed, and—red and quick-lipped—jabbered into her phone. The only word I discerned was "*gringos.*" We just smiled.

Chapter 15

Menu Nuance

THE MOTOTAXI was under a sun skylight now. As we shed a layer, Andrew asked, "Nathan, you want to drive?"

I was working my way back to an equal share of driving. Even though I had driven a lot less, Scott and Andrew didn't force it upon me. Their reasoning: I had been sick. But I had seen their faces—they didn't want to give up time at the handlebars, either. It was fun.

Curves were my thing though. The curvier, the better.

From the overlook, the view down had been as impressive as the view out. Its main feature was the road, cutting back and forth through the vegetation, making wild switchbacks down the ridge. The number and frequency of curves made it difficult to tell which segment of visible road connected to which. It looked as if the surveyors had plotted this course with a map and can of Silly String.

"Hell yes, I want to drive." I gloved up and mounted.

We pulled out, tailed by Pete, and the road descended. The skylights continued to shift above us while I shifted my weight back and forth across the mototaxi saddle, the curves reflected in my motion, in the muscular movements required to overcome the mototaxi's centrifugal force and lack of precision steering. The road swerved right, my torso fell left. A hairpin back to the left, my body jumped to forward right. I couldn't stop smiling. Not even when it rained and the front tire sent back a parabolic arc of water to soak me. It was refreshing, an impromptu coolant for the engine and me, both worked hard by the turns and the grade. Past steep drop-offs with clear views and through tunnels of leaves misted with insects, the road swung from macro to micro as much as from left to right. But always down. After being spun through the switchbacks, the curves mellowed into subtle wobbles, and—too soon—they fell flat to the valley floor.

We crossed the valley's river on a robust bridge, the steel painted a bright orange that popped among the greens and yellows of the surroundings. Sensing the stretch had concluded, I stopped to cool the engine, the brakes, and my arms. Of course, the burn in my left arm was more intense, it having had to steer against the mototaxi's tendency to pull right.

Pete soon caught us, and we decided to grab lunch together. Still riding my high, I returned to the back seat. As we pulled out of our parking spot, I glanced back up the hillside, still smiling. Scott and Andrew weren't enthusiastic about curvy roads? Lucky for me.

* * *

"Scott…what's *gallina*?"

"I'm not sure. But it's not chicken."

Piloting the mototaxi on that epic descent had worked up my appetite—its first appearance in days. But just the idea of chicken made me cringe. Not a voluntary "maybe-I-shouldn't-eat-that" cringe, but a tongue-swelling, throat-sealing, stomach-knotting, refusing-to-secrete-stomach-acid type of cringe.

After we had crossed into the San Martin district, we spotted a roadhouse. We walked into an empty establishment, apart from the chickens that scattered from ankle height to take cover beneath the chairs and tables. The walls were covered in a strange combination of full-sized posters. Half were naked women (think 1980s Playboy—thanks, dad), each in a pose approaching sultry, but not surpassing it. Alongside these were pictures of babies, in cute baby clothes with cute baby smiles in their cute baby poses. Also strewn across the wall were a few puppy posters. These felt especially out of place. Given how many feral dogs we had seen, I wasn't even sure if Peru had that man's-best-friend mythos. And maybe the strangest: a pale-skinned, blond-haired Jesus, arms outstretched on two or three different posters. The one thing the wall was lacking: a menu.

In small restaurants, only one—maybe two—dishes were prepared. So whatever was cooking was what you got. My stomach churned at the lack of options. The last roadside restaurant had not treated me well. I wasn't about to let this place disrupt my recovery progress.

A woman appeared from the back. I stepped towards Scott, tipping my head to his ear. "Scott, please no chicken. My stomach can't handle that." He nodded, then spoke with the woman. As was typical, I caught single words: *pollo* (chicken); *enfermo* (sick); *alérgico* (allergic). The woman nodded.

"No es pollo," she said. "Es gallina."

Scott nodded his approval and asked for *quatro*, his hand tracing the circle we stood in. The woman nodded and disappeared into the back.

"Scott?" I stepped forward again. "What's *gallina*?"

Scott turned around. "I'm not sure. But it's not chicken." He shrugged. "She said it wasn't *pollo*. Pete...you know?"

Pete's Spanish wasn't on par with Scott's, but it was decent. He had been managing fine on his own. "I remember hearing it before, but I can't remember what it is."

Scott shrugged. "I guess we'll find out."

We took a table. The chickens acclimatized to our presence and pecked at the feed near our feet. A few minutes later, our lunch appeared: a large plate of rice, beans, and—you guessed it—chicken.

Quick review! *Pollo* means chicken. But if you need to be more specific, *gallo* means rooster; *gallina* means hen.

"No pollo," she had said. "Es gallina."

Wonderful.

I ate, but without touching that chicken. The rice and beans were plenty for my shrunken stomach. And if they weren't, I didn't notice—the smell of chicken had shriveled my appetite.

Andrew also played it safe and avoided his hen. Scott and Pete showed no reservations.

After our meal, we stood around the mototaxis and had that all-too-familiar conversation. We decided not to wait for each other should we get separated, a decision influenced by the appearance of the Kiwis flying past as we ate. It had reignited our spark, and we all remembered this was a race.

We said our goodbyes to Pete. Scott took the helm and guided us back to the road, team *Rubber Duckies* still at the roadhouse behind us. Little did we know, we would see Pete again...soon.

Chapter 16

Intersecting Vectors

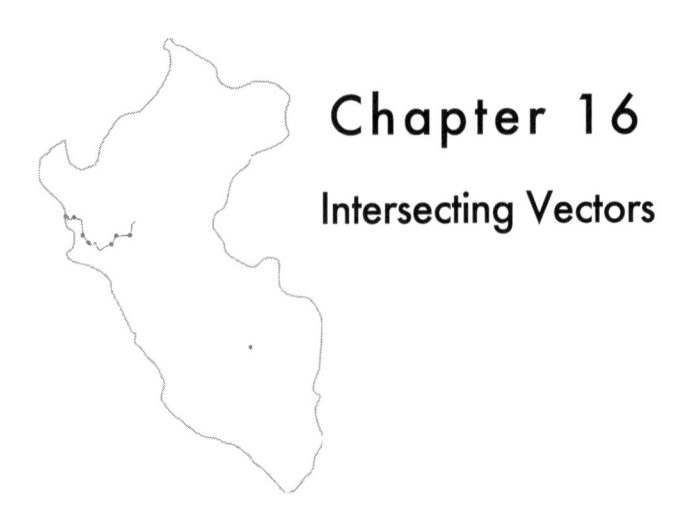

A BLAST RANG OUT BEHIND US.

My eyes shot to Andrew. He had already turned to me. Our eyes met for a split second, confusion between us. Then we grabbed the back of the sofa and wrenched our bodies around.

Several car lengths back was a semi-truck and trailer. Gray smoke poured from the trailer's left side, from the wheels on the inside of the road. A blowout. In the smoke, a dark mass pulsed, in rhythm with the truck's speed. The shredding tire was rolling off its rim and with each rotation of the wheel the distended rubber flapped more wildly. Within the first ten turns of the wheel, the rubber came off. The driver didn't even have a chance to slow down.

Andrew and I were so focused on the events behind us that we had given no thought to oncoming traffic. There hadn't been any. But at the pinnacle of rubbery discharge, that precise instant the rim threw the tire, a motorcycle—traveling in the opposite direction—appeared.

The tattered tire was in motion, vicious and cyclonic. Its trajectory looked to intersect that of the motorcyclist. Did he have any idea what was about to happen? Smoke rolled out from under the trailer, distracting, obstructing. He wouldn't know to look for a chunk of rubber flying for him. How could he know he would need to dodge one?

The paths intersected. The projectile was true to its target. The man was struck by the rubber.

At that exact moment, the motorcycle and its operator vanished into the trailer's cloud of smoke.

"Holy shit!"

The rubber reappeared, spinning along the far side of the road, its momentum altered.

"What's going on, guys?" Scott called back.

We ignored him. We didn't have an answer. We were still waiting to see the outcome.

A break in the smoke. The motorcycle was still up, the operator's feet still poised on the pegs, while his hands had a death grip on the bars—he was caught in the dreaded wobble. The bike gyrated between his legs, too far left, too far right, too far left, too far right, like a spinning top about to topple.

After five fast wobbles, the bike's pendular motion began to decay. The next wobble was smaller. The next, smaller still. Then the smallest. And then, the bike was upright, balanced, in equilibrium.

"Yeeaahhhh!"

The motorcyclist looked back over his shoulder, staring down death.

"What's happening?!"

Scott was lost. An explosion from behind us, expletives from Andrew and me, followed a moment later by cheering.

The motorcyclist disappearing down the road, Andrew and I sat again, our bodies forward, but still facing each other.

"Holy shit, dude!" I yelled through my smile.

"I know!" He yelled back.

Then a thought crossed my mind. My smile fell and eyes dilated.

"Holy shit, dude!"

Andrew didn't reply, but he must've had the same thought. He yelled to Scott. "Pull over!"

We covered another quarter mile before Scott pulled off the road, on the outskirts of another town.

He killed the engine and turned around. "What happened?"

Andrew and I were in the midst of our own discussion.

"What do you think? Should we go back?"

"I don't know. Do you think he was that close to the semi?"

"I'm not sure. I feel like he was pretty close behind us. The semi could've passed him, could have been right in front of him."

Scott interjected. "What are you guys talking about?"

We turned to Scott. "Pete."

What if Pete had been close to the semi? What if he had been dodging rubber fragments too? Or worse, what if he hadn't managed to dodge them? We decided to wait five minutes. Then we would turn around. In the meantime, we gave Scott an explanation.

The tire exploding, the rubber fragmenting, and then colliding with the motorcyclist, who not only hadn't died but hadn't even hit the ground. The whole thing was amazing—not only that it had happened, but that we had witnessed it. But the telling was not something we could enjoy. Not yet.

As the five-minute mark approached, we eyed each other between glances back down the road. It was time to make a move. But then—to our relief—Pete appeared.

I sighed another, "Holy shit, dude."

He pulled in behind us.

He had missed the whole thing.

He had passed some chunks of tire in the road and then a semi-truck pulled off to the side—but that was it. So Andrew and I told the tale again, with much more fervor and enthusiasm this time around, and with a lot more laughter.

It was the first time I was happy with our mototaxi's tricycle conformation. Those three points of contact with the road meant no balance problems.

Compared to that incident, the remainder of the drive to Moyobamba was tame. There were no near misses. There weren't even any stressful climbs. In fact, the road was as flat as the farmland it cut through.

In Moyobamba, we found a hotel off one of the main streets. Of the places we had stayed thus far, this one was the most posh. We got a room with two beds and a private bathroom. Again, they claimed hot water, but I knew what they really meant.

On our way out the door, the owner advised us to be back before dark, that the neighborhood could be dangerous at night. He even had a garage down the street where we could store the mototaxi. Motivated to get things done, we took off.

First up was Clifford's oil change. We found an automotive vendor and a low-trafficked street. This time we used two old coke bottles from the side of the road to hold the spent oil— the color was a spot-on match. We left the bottles with a mound of paper and loose debris held down by discarded construction materials. The pile sat on a corner, obstructing the sidewalk in two directions of travel. Another guilt twinge.

We ventured back, looking for food along the way, but the lunch still filled our minds and stomachs. It was after dark before we located the garage and had to convince the attendant that we were guests at the hotel and that the owner had sent us. She couldn't be blamed for questioning us. Three *gringos* with a mototaxi was suspicious.

After a short, quick walk back to our room, we snacked on whatever food we had in our bags, showered, and reviewed our map. I camped on the floor, happy to forfeit a bed. The day had been an epic turn around, for my health and spirit. From the conversation in mangled Spanish, to an epic segment of road, and the amazing incident involving the semi and motorcyclist, the day had delivered on all fronts.

Chapter 17

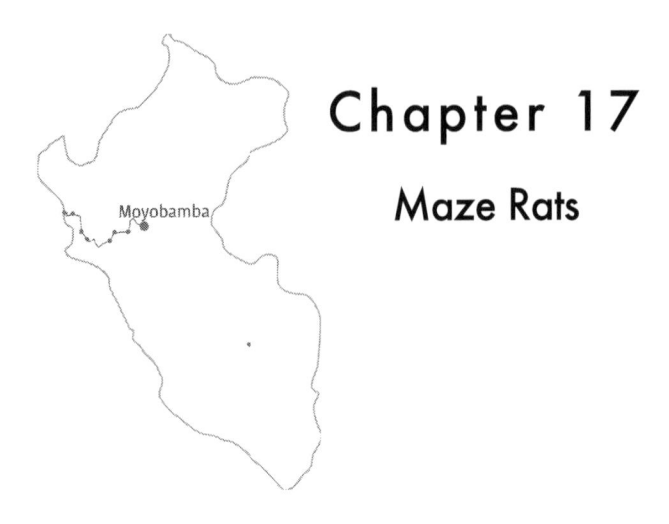

Maze Rats

THE BIOLOGIST AND ESSAYIST LEWIS THOMAS once wrote that "...disease usually results from inconclusive negotiations for symbiosis..."

Our germ theory of disease is based on the notion of microbes—nasty little critters—trying to invade our bodies at every chance. That perception is not correct though. The world abounds with microbes, most with no interest in us. In fact, our bodies are covered in microbes. Your skin, your mouth, your intestines, your genitals—microbes everywhere! So to say microbes are the problem would be a horribly inaccurate simplification. In fact, our own body is the cause of many of our disease symptoms. In his essay, Thomas goes on to say that our immune response is more dangerous to us than most of the organisms it responds to.

A good example of this is food poisoning. The food we eat is digested in the gastrointestinal tract. To aid in this digestion is a whole smorgasbord of bacteria. But if an outsider is introduced and discovered, an immune response is mounted. Part of this response is an overproduction of cytokines. These molecules travel to the brain and trigger a cognitive shift towards sickness behavior: that's the nausea, dizziness, fatigue, body aches, etc. that come with being sick. This sometimes includes vomiting as well.

The immune system of Scott—the only one of our team to eat the *gallina*—replicated this process. So he spent a large portion of the night puking. Of course, I lay on the floor near the bathroom. The splashing was reminiscent of my own toilet tour, but the chest convulsions and gagging reminded me of what I had been spared. Extreme diarrhea and dehydration? Maybe I had lucked out.

That next morning, we all dragged. It solidified our decision to skip a hot spring detour. We had reached a consensus the night before by counting the days we had left to get to the finish line. It was the best choice, but not everyone had been satisfied with it. In our current state though, it was the choice most appealing to all. "Hot Springs" was a *Peru Bingo* square that would have to wait.

Pressed for time, we packed as fast as our fatigue allowed. After a stop at the nearest bakery, we hit the road again, headed for Tarapoto.

As we left Moyobamba, the only color to be seen was the bright green of my jacket and rinsed red of Clifford's vinyl canopy. The rain had drained all color from the sky, leaving a dull reflection of the gray streets below. Outside the city though, a fragment of the spectrum was restored: the variety of greens we had seen the past two days.

We continued east along another long, flat stretch. The air began to hug us, heavier than it had been in the mountains. The jungle contributes to its own humidity, a result of so many plants losing water vapor through their leaves. But the day's cloud cover should have limited that. This moisture was likely evaporating rain. Regardless, it felt like the forest had exhaled and wrapped us in its breath.

I stopped us at a village gas station. All of us battling our immune systems, we took turns in the bathroom. Our varied bodily responses made us delay another *Peru Bingo* square: "The Naked Mile." We didn't want to imagine the bodily fluids any of us might leave on the seat after driving the taxi in the buff. We did wonder, however, if this square had been inspired by a particular Scotsman and his kilt.

While I waited for my turn, I did a quick accounting of my nutrition during the race—the balance sheet made me gnaw on some bread. Its texture was foreign. The flakes of crust sucked up my mouth's moisture. But I salivated in response and the added enzymes broke down the carbohydrates into smaller sugars that tickled my taste buds. Why hadn't we thought to visit a bakery earlier?

Swallowing was forced. Not because of nausea, but because the muscles had been sedentary for days. It was work.

Andrew took us back out. The clouds dissipated, but the humidity clung to the earth. The forest canopy hosted islands of brown: groups of a dozen wooden homes topped with a thatched or corrugated tin roof. Then we passed large fields, flooded, feeding water to the soil and the atmosphere. The closer to Tarapoto, the less consistent the forest canopy and the more persistent the agricultural clearings.

Clifford's horn had also lost some musculature. In the countryside, most of our communications had been "¡Hola!" Now, in Tarapoto, Clifford was hoarse with blasting, "I'm already occupying this space;" "No, don't merge into my back seat;" and "Holy shit, think thin!"

Tarapoto—the City of Palms—is a commercial hub of northern Peru, and though Moyobamba is the region's capital, Tarapoto is its largest city.

Maybe that's why the streets were so narrow. At times, I could've touched the buildings on either side of the road simultaneously. Ok…that was a gross exaggeration, but I'm sure those streets were smaller in my memory than either Andrew's or Scott's. That's because I drove.

On the outskirts of the city, streets had been much wider, buildings much shorter. There was traffic, but not enough to inspire claustrophobia. This was where we began the search for a mechanic. Apart from wanting the usual carb cleaning, the transmission chain was slack. It was a fix we could manage, but why risk its integrity or the time if we were headed to a mechanic anyway?

I dropped Andrew and Scott to run back down a one-way street to check out a shop that looked promising. I circled the block and found them outside, waving me into the shop, which was nothing more than a simple patch of grass shaded by a tarp. The mechanic was a large man, tall and well-built. That doesn't make much sense in hindsight given the size of every Peruvian we had encountered. Maybe my memory of his physical appearance has been skewed by his personality.

The mechanic squatted and lifted the mototaxi from its wheels to the convenient tripod stance. With a crescent wrench, he loosened a single bolt, and with a single stroke hammered the shaft on which the sprocket was fixed. This tightened the chain from the transmission; but now the chain to the rear wheel threatened to drag on the ground. He tightened the bolt and dropped the taxi back to the ground. Before the rear suspension stopped bobbing, the mechanic's hand reached out, open and palm up.

Some gestures need no translation.

We glanced at each other. This was not a battle worth fighting. Forget the carb. Scott handed over the coins and we pushed the mototaxi back onto the street.

"Well, that was a success."

"Maybe we'll find better mechanics downtown."

"I'd settle for friendlier."

"Let's head that way then. Still a lot of ground to cover today."

We plunged into the city.

Our search for an ATM took us into the center of Tarapoto. We were rats trapped in a maze, a maze that overflowed with rats, all who knew where they were going. The narrow roads did most of the navigating, funneling us down one-way streets, trapping us in traffic four mototaxis across where only three could fit, and delaying us with red traffic lights perched halfway up intimidating inclines that threatened to stall our engine.

Finding the square was a relief, but parking was not allowed. We dropped Andrew off and took to the roads again to circle around. This circle turned into a blocky zigzag that crossed itself several times—even when we made a second lap. Before we started the third, Scott spotted Andrew and we pulled into the no-parking zone in front of the bank. We got some looks from the armed guards surrounding the armored trucks. I pulled back into traffic in a hurry.

One goal accomplished. Time for the second: find a mechanic. They were probably on the main road, but where was that? We had all lost our sense of direction in the maze. But we had driven uphill to get to the square, so downhill was as good as any direction. After a lot of shouted "left"s and "right"s from the back seat, a lot of missed turns, and multiple laps in more than one roundabout while we argued which way to go, I pulled over.

"Guys!" I killed the engine and turned on them. "Let me explain my backseat driving policy." I paused, trying to keep calm. "Don't do it."

We were on the edge of a major roundabout. We must have been close to mechanics' row. Scott had been asking other drivers for directions while we were in slow-moving traffic and at red lights. Most drivers were excited to help the *gringo* trio. But traffic hadn't been slow enough and lights hadn't been long enough for us to get all the information.

I took a few deep breaths. The midday sun was hot, but so was the caramel-colored clay anchored in the deteriorating pavement patchwork of the streets. It glowed. Did it reflect the sun's entire spectrum? On busier streets, dirt was kicked up by traffic and the air itself was aglow, the flames held at bay by the humidity.

This sucked. Where were the country roads with no traffic? Where were the beautiful views that left us in silence? Where were the curves that made me smile? "Either of you want to take over?"

"You're doing great, Nathan," Scott said.

"Agreed," Andrew nodded.

We *were* still alive. "It's just stressful. No offense, but you guys shouting where to go isn't helping." They nodded. "Scott, can you try to get actual directions? This wouldn't be as bad if we knew where we were going."

"I'll see what I can find out."

He walked to the far side of the roundabout, to a shop with a group of mototaxis parked outside. I fished my water bottle from underneath the sofa, actually motivated to drink. It was warm and collecting the aerosolized clay stirred up from the road.

Mid-drink, a mototaxi died on the road in front of me. It hadn't coasted to a stop before the driver jumped up and down on the kick-starter. He stopped to say something to the fare in his back seat. Then he hopped off and pushed the taxi toward the gas station on the edge of the roundabout. Was this guy going to lose his fare? Over what, an empty gas tank?

I jogged over and pushed on the opposite side. The fare eyed me with raised eyebrows and a hint of a smile. At the pump, the driver scowled at me before turning his back. With no words spoken, not even a smile exchanged, I walked away.

My leg flew over our mototaxi seat and I snatched my water bottle again. Why was he so ungrateful? Sure, he was frustrated. But that look he gave me—why was he angry at me?

"Guys!" Scott ran up. "We aren't far. This place over here fits mototaxis with custom tops. They said all the good mechanics are just a little further up this street."

We pulled back into the roundabout. I claimed karmic justice over the ungrateful operator who was still parked at the gas pump, kicking the starter, his back seat empty.

Chapter 18

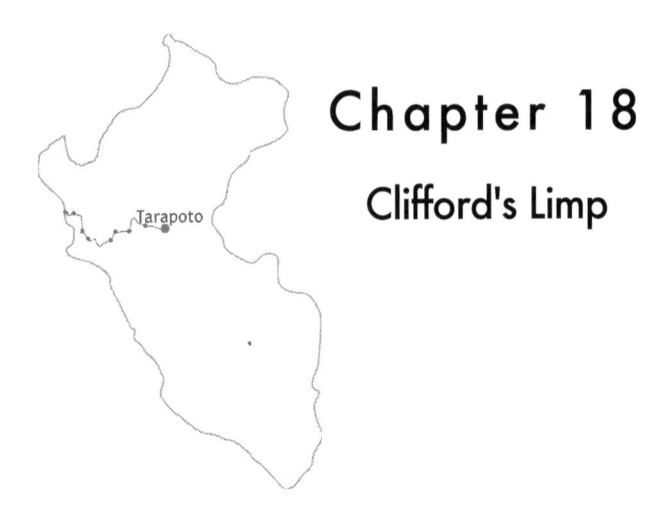

Clifford's Limp

THE DOPPLER EFFECT is the change in wave frequency due to the observer moving relative to the wave source. That sounded technical—how about a demonstration? When a massive truck drives toward you, the pitch of the sound is higher. Once the truck passes, the pitch is lower.

Most people have some memory of this, whether a car, truck, or train, whether experienced in real life or through the media. Maybe a reason it's so memorable is the increasing volume that comes with it. As the source gets closer, the sound gets louder. So as that truck approaches you, yes, the pitch is high, but with it the sound gets louder and louder until...

I jolted awake. The pitch fell and faded—a passing truck. Only five days in and I'm sleeping in the back of the mototaxi. What a testament to human adaptability.

The stress of the morning had helped. Tarapoto had been exhausting. It was a relief to find a good mechanic and sit in the shade while he did work on Clifford—good work too. I didn't understand most of what he did, but with great speed and efficiency, he had torn apart and reassembled half of the taxi. Back on the road, we could tell.

Scott drove us out of Tarapoto, south on the 5N highway. The heat, potato chip purchase, and fatigue mixed with the gentle rocking of the mototaxi put me to sleep. It was a short nap though, a good thing given the scenery.

The road made a short climb, rounded a hill, and dropped toward the banks of the Huallaga River. Jungle channeled the flat, brown waters through the landscape, a placid appearance that was deceptive. The Huallaga River, part of the Amazon River Basin, runs for 700 miles and is mostly unnavigable due to a series of gorges and rapids. Here though, it lazed through the landscape, a pattern the road mimicked.

Lazy were my feelings too, leaned back on our couch, taking in the view. Even though we were headed up the valley, the grade was so low that there was no real climbing, just some rolling hills. But there was something behind us that was not lazy—another mototaxi.

We yelled over the engine.

"Junket team?"

"Why else would a mototaxi be out here?"

The blue taxi caught us and its occupants were revealed: one of the two-man British teams. We waved and cheered out the back before they accelerated and made to pass us. They pulled even with us and we all pumped our fists in the air and gave thumbs up, hollering encouragement to each other the whole time. Then they accelerated and pulled in front of us. After a few minutes, they disappeared among the crests and troughs of the rolling landscape.

Another team! One we hadn't even seen since Colan. And were they cruising! Envy tugged at my mind. To be only two men would make things easier. Less weight, faster speeds. The envy then morphed into guilt. I was man number three.

Andrew yelled from next to me on the couch, "Nathan, you feel that?"

"Yeah. I thought I felt it back near Tarapoto but wasn't sure." We both tuned into the mototaxi's rhythm to confirm our suspicions.

"Stop? Check it out?"

"Engine's probably hot anyway."

We pulled onto a nice paved shoulder nestled between two hills, the river on our left, the sun moving to our right.

Scott dismounted and turned. "Do you guys feel that?"

"That wobble?" I nodded my head. "Yeah, Clifford is limping."

"I didn't feel it earlier," Scott thought out loud.

Andrew spoke up. "I think it's the hills. It's more obvious going downhill. Maybe because we're going faster."

Scott nodded. "What do you think it is?"

Andrew was already pulling out his tools. "Well, the mechanic shifted the left wheel assembly back to tighten the chain. I don't think he did the same to the right, so the wheels might not be sitting even."

Andrew loosened a few bolts and—while Scott and I lifted the frame—persuaded the wheel to inch back with a hammer. The bolts tight and the engine cooler, it was time to see if things were improved.

Andrew mounted the taxi, fired up the engine, dropped the transmission into gear, and eased off the clutch. The engine died.

Weird. We were on flat ground. Clifford didn't need that much throttle to get moving.

Andrew fired up the engine again. More throttle this time as he eased off the clutch. Phrump. It died again.

He turned around. "Well?"

Scott and I shrugged. "More gas this time?"

A third try, the throttle opened further than necessary. A third failure.

A pause. Then Andrew chuckled and dismounted. Scott and I gave each other the same look. What did he know that we didn't? Andrew walked to the back and unpacked the tools again. Scott and I followed.

"You figure it out?"

With a flick of the wrist, Andrew unrolled the tool pouch across the back of the mototaxi. "The brake," he said, sliding a wrench from its sleeve. "We pushed the wheel assembly backward. But we didn't adjust the rod connected to the brake. The brake is engaged right now."

Simple problem, simple solution. Andrew loosened the nuts and spun them down the linkage rod. With Scott on the brake lever, we tested it, tightened it, and took our places again.

Takeoff was successful this time. The ride was smooth and the wobble gone. Hopefully it hadn't been what rocked me to sleep earlier, otherwise I might miss it.

Villages became more frequent and more of the land had been developed for agriculture, the crops in different stages of their growth cycles. It seemed most fields were tilled, sown, flooded, harvested, drained, and then burned. The flooding of the fields called to mind the iconic rice paddies of rural China. But Peru has its own iconic crop, and though we didn't expect to see any fields, this particular valley was well known for it.

The sun was on its way to the horizon when I took control of the mototaxi again. An afternoon traversing the flat farmlands had been restful, rejuvenating. Now though, the road led away from the main river valley and up a smaller valley into the Andean foothills. The road meandered, flowed around the base of some hills, over the tops of others, tracing the lines that separated jungle from farmland.

It was golden hour in the patchwork landscape. Yellow crops weren't just dry, but crisp. Orange tree trunks weren't just sturdy, but columnar. Red flower petals weren't just vibrant, but blushing. The landscape emanated the energy it had absorbed all day, with the subtle details that were its own signature.

I flipped on our marker lights and headlight. The road's curves straightened out as the sunlight failed and just as we reached our destination, Juanjuí.

Andrew paid for ritzy accommodations that night: a room with three beds, a bathroom with hot water, and air conditioning. Was he feeling generous? Or was he desperate for us to sleep? At that point, those were the same thing.

We parked the mototaxi in the hotel's lot and stowed our bags in the room before taking to the streets. Our stomachs had all been compromised in one way or another in the days previous, so we were hesitant to choose a restaurant for dinner. Instead, we found a small corner market.

We wandered the aisles, trying to translate some packaging while finding food items with American equivalents. We filled a small basket. Together, it was a bland spread that wouldn't do much for our palates. But priority went to our stomachs. We returned to the hotel to eat and shower.

My dinner consisted of canned tuna mixed with *papitas* (small, French-fry-shaped potato chips) sandwiched inside fresh dinner rolls. The protein/salt combo wrapped in fluffy carbohydrates hit the spot.

"Nathan," Scott said emerging from the bathroom, "you're up!"

Our shower had two separate water taps: one hot, one cold. The taps turned under my hand, one more than the other. I had become familiar with cold water and hot water had been fading from my body's memory. Bit by bit, I tightened the hot tap, searching for the perfect temperature: less than lukewarm. I sighed familiarity at the coolness and smiled at the cold's edge. It was dulled by its warm counterpart, but still sharp enough to scrape away the filth.

The last to shower, I emerged from the bathroom hoping we were all ready to pass out. We were, and so was our air conditioner, blowing cool air to remove the restlessness from our sleep.

Chapter 19

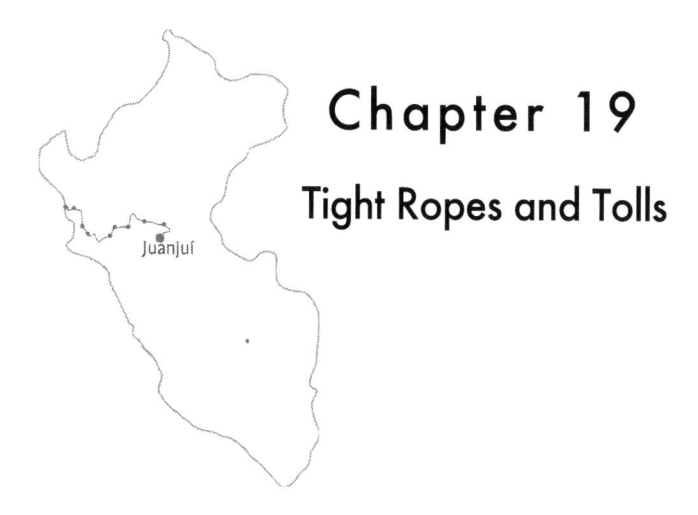

Tight Ropes and Tolls

BENEATH THE AC UNIT was the room's worst spot. Instead of resting, I spent the long night curled into a fetal ball underneath the bed's single flimsy blanket and woke several times shivering, wishing to wrap myself in the thick jungle atmosphere.

In the morning, I took a similar position in the back of the taxi as we searched for a gas station, the ideal setting for our daily oil change. We pulled into one flanked by buildings on three sides; it was like the gas station was placed in a courtyard. The pumps and outbuildings didn't leave much room for a full-size vehicle to maneuver, so I was dismayed with our parking job: not quite next to a pump, yet not far enough away that anyone could use it. My attitude still chilly from the overnight AC, I didn't hesitate to point this out.

"Uhh…this an awful place to change the oil. No one can pull next to this pump…or get around us."

The irritable response: "Well, where would *you* have parked?"

"Over there," I pointed. "Against that wall. You know," I stressed the words, "out of the way."

"Then hop out. Let's push it over there."

I didn't budge. I lathered on the condescension, "Why don't we just drive?"

"Well..." The length of the pause reflected the remark's legitimacy. "...we are about to change the oil. We don't want it too hot."

Un...believable.

The ten seconds the engine would run to relocate the mototaxi didn't compare to the fifteen minutes we had spent driving it to the gas station. I gathered what condescension I had left for this retort...but then I was struck by vertigo, staring into the downward spiral this conversation would become if I were to reply. I held my tongue and took position at the back left side of the frame, my head shaking and eyes rolling.

The station attendants stared at us with cocked heads and tall eyebrows as we rolled the mototaxi out of the pump's vicinity. Was that just curiosity on their faces? Or was there a hint of bewilderment too?

We propped an empty oil container beneath the drain and unplugged it. After fifteen minutes, it was only three-quarters full, and the slow drip wasn't raising the level any—the IV drip of cancer patients is faster. If only our engine had been warmer.

A slew of condescending comments about the concern for the oil temperature flashed through my head. Did I say any out loud? Or did I manage to keep those to myself? That I wasn't left behind in Juanjuí was a strong indication the comments remained within the ether of assholes. My teammates still would've been justified taking such action though—even without me solidifying those comments—when I insisted on pouring the new oil.

"I don't need a fucking funnel."

The first glug of my rushed pour ran down the side of the motor and dripped to the cement. I shook my head, eyes fixed on the amber stream, avoiding the gaze of my teammates. "Didn't need it anyway," I mumbled to myself. "Still a whole cup in there from the *last* quart."

I strode away, spent oil in hand. I flung the container into the trash and asked for *el baño*. I washed my hands of the first glug of oil, and then a second time after the day's third bout of diarrhea. "Is this shit ever going to end?"

I caught my eye in the dull, scratched mirror above the sink. A deep breath. "Don't be an asshole." I held my gaze for a long moment, waiting for the sink's trickle of water to rinse the soiled suds. That comment had been an attempt to deepen the fissure in my personality, to separate asshole from nice guy; and I was trying to place myself on the morally superior side. I was not as easily fractured as that mirror though. My bad attitude wouldn't disappear. It could only go dormant.

I returned to the taxi and my teammates, ready to press on…ready to finish. We returned to the streets and headed south, leaving Juanjuí behind.

* * *

The Overseas Security Advisory Council (OSAC) works with the U.S. Department of State and the American private sector. Its 2014 report on Peru (released four months before our arrival) stated that overland travel was dangerous due to infrastructure alone. This was hard to argue. Peru did have one of the highest road-fatality rates in Latin America.

Apart from infrastructure though, a lot of road danger originated from local criminals and domestic terrorists. Because of this, the U.S. Embassy of Lima designated areas of Peru as restricted to U.S. government employees.

Little did we know, as we left Juanjuí we were crossing into our fourth restricted province in the San Martín Region alone. It was for the best that we hadn't read the report. We crossed a lot of those dangerous, restricted areas. But if we *had* read the report, we would've known that "clandestine, impromptu roadblocks can appear…"

We coasted to a stop.

A thick rope stretched above the road's surface, sagging in the middle, frayed and dirty. On the shoulder, a group of men stood in the shade of a makeshift hut, rifles perched in the crook of their arms. The road cut into a bank, exposing the pink soil. The wound still bled—or so it appeared—as groundwater seeped out, pulling the clay with it and puddling red on the far shoulder.

One of the camo-clad men sauntered over and placed his hand atop the mototaxi. His head dipped below our roof, and he peered over the top of his sunglasses. He spoke, his voice with a serrated edge.

A flash of bewilderment crossed Scott's face before he assumed the stare of a blank wall. When the man finished, Scott shook his head and replied: "No fumar español."

Holy shit.

The man's brow furrowed, accentuated by his dark bushy eyebrows. He repeated himself, the words paced, the syllables emphasized.

My fists clenched.

Scott also repeated himself. "No fumar español." His words were also slower this time, as if Scott thought the man would better understand *him*. It made Scott's ignorance much more believable, even though he understood most of what was said.

The man gazed at Andrew and I. We tried to look pleasant.

The man stood to full height, the top of his head hidden above our taxi's roof. But his chin pointed behind us. Another car had pulled up, and a truck was coasting to a stop behind it. The line was building.

His face reappeared. Fewer words came this time, but with them an obvious gesture: an empty, outstretched hand.

My heart squirted extra blood.

Behind us, the truck's brakes squealed with the arrest of the trailer's remaining momentum. The noise caught the man's attention—he turned his head.

Scott capitalized. He made one of the boldest moves of the trip: he reached out and seized the empty hand with his own, engaging the man in a handshake.

His eyes shot back to Scott. His face was blank. Emotionless. Instead of showing surprise or anger, he just stared. What was going through his head? This was either going very well for us, or very badly. But he gave no hint as to which.

A subtle shake of his head was all we got. His face remained blank, but the shake betrayed him and gave some indication of his reaction. I read it as a dim disgust. He stepped back, yanking his hand from Scott's. He disappeared above our mototaxi's roof for the final time. His shoulders turned to the roadside and he yelled back to the men at the shack. The rope fell to the road, and the man's arm commanded us forward with the energy missing from the handshake.

Scott put it in first and eased off the clutch. Andrew and I caught eyes and gave a mental high five to each other as we accelerated. The rope tightened behind us, the man now leaning against the car. As we lost sight of the roadblock below the crest of the hill, Andrew and I both leaned forward.

"Scott! Holy crap, man!" We patted his shoulders. "What were they asking for?"

Scott leaned back. "Money." He turned his head to yell over his shoulder. "Something about the development and protection of this road." He shifted into fourth gear and the engines rpms dropped, making it easier to hear. "I'm *totally* convinced that's where the money would go," he said with a chuckle. He continued to accelerate, and jumped into fifth gear.

Less than 15 miles later, we coasted…to another stop.

We sat idle, in front of another rope hovering above the road. Instead of rifles, these guys toted shotguns. And our "no fumar español" luck had run out.

Scott made an attempt to use the tactic again. This honcho knew we weren't blind though, so he was more illustrative in his demands. Instead of a second attempt in Spanish, the man marched to the side of the road and returned with a large jar of money. He shook it in front of Scott's face, the coins rattling against themselves and the glass. He pointed to Scott, and then into the jar.

Scott reached into his pocket, feeling for what he thought was the size of the smallest denomination coin. He produced a single coin and dropped it in the jar. The man walked away and the rope hit the ground.

We sped off before they could charge more.

Chapter 20

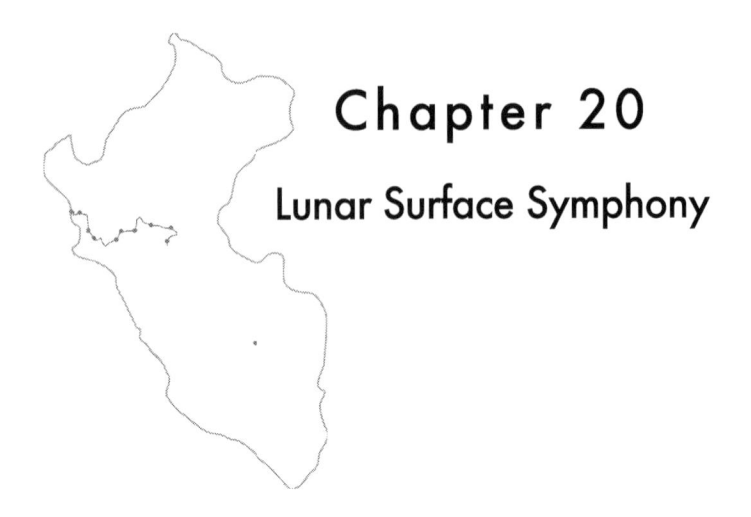

Lunar Surface Symphony

THOSE "TOLLS" that had been collected had developed nothing. After we passed the second roadblock, the road fell apart beneath our tires. Potholes dominated the surface, the remaining asphalt an archipelago of dark mesas vulnerable to the forces applied by motor vehicles. Of course, being lighter than the road's typical traffic, our mototaxi's suspension was put to the test.

The compression–rebound cycles of the coil springs were so constant and percussive that our wheels emanated a grotesque drumroll. Vibrations pulsed through the metal frame, creating a kazoo hum in the tubing. The largest bumps crashed us backseat passengers into the mototaxi's roof head first, like a pair of skull cymbals. And the engine carried the melody, the rpms led by the topography: they whined up on the climbs, and dipped on the descents. As conductor, Scott heard the melody fall behind and the engine go flat as it overheated. We rested on the margin of the road where the jungle was reclaiming the ground.

"Guys," Scott said mid-stagger, "this road is terrible!"

"You should try the back," I said, clambering out.

Andrew began a walk around. "Hopefully this doesn't last much longer." He paused at a rear wheel, bent over and squinted. He stood again. "It'll shake Clifford to pieces."

"It's already shaking me to pieces," Scott said, working an arm back and forth. "Steering is so much worse. The front wheel jerks back and forth the whole time." He massaged his shoulder now. "One of you guys ready to take over?"

"Yeah," Andrew threw back. A quick response. He must've wanted to escape the back as much as I did.

"Good." Scott's face relaxed. "It's getting warm up front, too."

The temperature was trying to match the level of the humidity. We took our time letting the taxi cool and relived the roadblocks with a lot of high fives for Scott's quick thinking and nimble fingers.

"I was feeling around in my pocket for the smallest denomination." He held his hands in front of him, palms up, shoulders in a half shrug. "I didn't want to contribute too much, you know? And look," he pointed back to the road, "I'm glad we didn't!" We all laughed at the gang's cover story. "If only we had gotten a picture with them," Scott sighed. Our "Picture with AK47" square was still in play on our *Peru Bingo* board.

How were our *Peru Bingo* competitors doing? Barry and Gerald were ahead of us. A social media update showed they were a day ahead of us, maybe two by now. Aaron and Josh on the other hand…nobody had heard from them. Were they lagging that far behind? Or had they gone south from Pedro Ruiz? What if they were in the mountains, trying to catch us? That would be awful with their low-performance engine. Or any mototaxi. Ours still struggled over the more uniform terrain of this route. Especially on this decomposing mountain road.

We started again, the monstrous music resuming. I shook to the bones. If I didn't flex my jaw, my teeth chattered. I alternated which arm I braced against the frame above to keep myself wedged in the seat. The conditions persisted, but because of our waning patience, it seemed to get worse. All thoughts were replaced with madness.

The rattling rewired my brain, broke and reforged neuronal circuits, reawakening the asshole that had been quelled in Juanjuí. Not only was he revived, but he drew strength from the heat.

The jungle breathed hard now. My own exhalation was trapped by the buff stretched from my nose bridge to neck back, the elastic fabric hugging my nostrils, lips, chin, and cheeks, restricting airflow above jawline. It was damp with sweat and breath and posed a suffocation hazard; but it was better than the choking hazard offered by tailgating.

We trailed a truck in its dust wake. Why were we so close? Trying to pass? That was impossible. Not only was the road too windy, but we wouldn't be able to accelerate past it on this lunar-surfaced road anyhow. Was I the only one to realize this? Maybe, but I kept my mouth shut.

My tolerance of these driving decisions didn't mute my rewired brain's inner monologue of critiques and criticisms though. Most focused on potholes, the obvious canyons we still managed to strike square. The resultant compression waves traveled up my spine, increasing the tempo at which my thoughts reeled.

Holy crap. You see that coming right? Right? No?! Turn, man!

Bam! Spinal shockwave...

How did you not see that?! It was massive! Couldn't even see the bottom! Just like this one coming up. Swerve!

A slight veer in the handlebars. The front tire missed...the rear tire did not.

Wham! A more intense shockwave...

Oouucchh! Three tires! You have three tires to worry about, three points of contact to consider. Please don't ignore the two you can't see...

Ka-blam! Cymbal crash...

Come on! Left and right man! You're allowed to move in those directions...you should be veering...doesn't even have to be that far. A lot of these potholes are small enough that you can straddle...

Bam! Shockwave...

Jeez! Even the bigger ones would fit if you approached at the proper angle. Look at this oval one coming up! Come at it from the right and swerve...the rear left tire will arc around its perimeter and...

Wham!

No way! That was too easy to read!

Ka-blam!

Are you kiddi...

Wham!

Hopeless! Fucking hopeless! Let me drive. I'll show you guys how it's...

Wha-bam!

Thoughts cannoned through my head. I tried to hush them, but couldn't. We passed the bottom of a small hill and started back up. The front of the mototaxi rose and bars of light penetrated to us, the shafts unveiled by the dust.

The truck pulled away, its rpms constant as ours diminished. Andrew's wrist cycled the throttle, but the engine could not be sustained. It welcomed death.

The mototaxi sat on the road, pointed straight up the hill. Uphill starts...not ideal. It's a challenge easing off the clutch and beginning to climb from a standstill. It would've been better to angle the taxi across the road before it had died.

Andrew folded out the starter and kicked—nothing.

Scott sat forward. "Maybe we should let it cool down here."

I ran my thoughts through some extra filters before I said, "In the middle of the road?"

Andrew said to Scott, "I want to get it to the top of this little hill."

I pulled down my buff. With fewer filters this time, and louder: "We should've stopped at the bottom, where it was shady." Filters began to fail. Andrew continued to kick. "You couldn't hear it struggling on the downhill? It was obviously trying to die." The kicking stopped. "It's not getting to the top of this hill. It died here for a reason."

One more defiant kick, and the engine sputtered to life. Andrew flipped the starter lever in and rolled back on the throttle. The clutch eased out and…

Thunk!

The engine refused to abandon death…those uphill starts, man.

"So…" Asshole-me validated, I took the lead. "…push it off the road?"

There was no response. My teammates just took their positions. We walked it a few feet, uphill, tripping on asphalt ridges and slipping on gravel and cobbles caught in the potholes. We pushed to the road's edge where runoff had carved a deep ditch.

Frustration fueled me. I dug into our cargo bay, searching for the bundle of tools.

Cindy was still there, wrapped in plastic, as lifeless as ever. I chuckled. Most prepared team? Preparations are futile if you don't know what to prepare for. Yes, we had the GPS navigation, throttle-lock, seat padding; the tools and spare parts; the laptop, digital cameras, electricity converter and charging cables to go with; we even had our water filter and MREs. But we weren't prepared.

In Colan, the Scots didn't even have a roadmap. But they had something we did not: history. They had the bonds of friendship and brotherhood. So did the Australian teams. Of the three South Africans, two were blood relatives. And a pair of British teams was one big bachelor party.

Andrew and I had met only three times before the trip. Scott and I had only been coworkers…more than two years ago. We lacked that history the other teams were drenched in. Other teams had grown up together, worked together, traveled together, even done other Adventurist events together. Most? We may have been the *least* prepared team.

I fought the urge to hurl Cindy into the jungle—I still had too much pride to finish without her. I pushed her aside and pulled the heavy tool bundle from beneath her.

Along with our relationships, the road was shaking the mototaxi apart. The two mirrors that hung off either side of the frame had danced with the bumps, throwing light beams like wanna-be disco balls. I found the right driver bit and tightened the mirrors. I also did the walk around.

I bundled the tools and tossed them on top of Cindy. "Most prepared my ass," I mumbled to her. I closed things up and when the engine had cooled enough, Andrew got us to the top of that hill.

Past the hill was more of the same. Potholes, spine-jarring bumps, heavy air, searing sun. My patience deteriorated further, and what had been disdain spiraled to blame.

When you have a crappy, tiny engine, weight is a big concern. Just the previous day we had seen how a team of two moved much faster than us. I had assumed it was because they were lighter. Now I took this assumption as truth.

In a pre-travel team meeting, I had cringed at the amount of stuff that would come with us, but had remained silent. I glanced at the road, its surface, its grade. I should have made my opinions heard.

Our suspension bottomed out. My body was fatigued from the full-body flex that kept me from flailing. And now, in the heat, the engine strained under the load, its tone guttural.

Andrew pulled over when the strain became apparent, into the short vegetation between the road and a small wooden hut. We sat in the shade of its porch.

Before long, I was back at the mototaxi. I tightened the mirrors again…and a wheel hub. I shook my head. What if Clifford's front wheel had fallen off? What a testament to the road's condition that would have been. Lucky I noticed.

Tools packed, I strode back to the porch. Things were quiet.

"So what do you guys think?" Scott prompted.

With a flat tone, I said, "This road sucks."

Andrew only nodded.

"Yeah," Scott came back. "It's pretty terrible."

They both sat on the porch's floor, feet dangling, their toes tickling the tips of shoots. I remained standing, facing them.

"Doesn't help that we have so much weight." The vacuum of silence had sucked the comment out of me.

Andrew and Scott both looked up. "What do you mean?"

"'What do I mean?'" Did they not see the problem? "Guys, look at all the shit we have." My pulse quickened. "Sure, nothing is that heavy, but add it all up—we're fat. And we don't even need most of it."

Andrew's brow furrowed. "What don't we need?"

"Are you kidding?" I lost all filtering capacities. "Tire levers; tubes; the air pump; half the tools we have. That stuff's heavy."

Andrew had assembled our toolkit; there was no doubt who I was attacking. He eyed me. "And what if we broke down—" His voice rose "—and needed them?"

"Sure. They're nice to have—just in case—but really not necessary. There's a mechanic every five feet."

"Haven't seen any today." Andrew's palms pushed onto the porch, lifting his shoulder.

"Fine. Forget the tools. What about the other crap?"

"Other crap?" Andrew leaned forward, as if he misheard. Scott's head followed the exchange.

"The electronics. A computer? Use that a lot, don't we?" We didn't. "Not to mention that heavy converter and all the cables and junk. And how about the GPS; and its mount; and its converter hooked to the battery?" I raised my open palms. "What's wrong with a map?"

"Well, you've been using this stuff so far, just like us."

"Sure. If it's there, I'm going to use it." Another annoyance popped to the surface. "Except that throttle lock. I *don't* use that. Maybe that's why I'm able to slow down for speed bumps instead of hitting them at Mach 1…" My eyes narrowed. "…like you guys."

Silence. Both shook their heads, wounded.

"And that first aid kit, it's the size of a lunchbox." It was packed in my bag. "Why? I've done riskier stuff with a fraction of the supplies. Tell me why Band-Aids and gauze need to be packed inside a hard case."

More damage. Andrew leaned back now.

I threw my arms around like the conductor from the orchestra that had been playing through our mototaxi earlier. I may as well have mimed my questions in concert with half-yelling them.

"And why do we need *three weeks* of MREs?!"

More silence on the porch. The first silence from me.

I concluded: "We have too much stuff. The taxi is struggling and we aren't even back in the Andes yet. How's it going to perform when we spend all day climbing? Think of how slow it's been, how often we've had to stop. We're already six days in, and we're not even close to being halfway." A fear behind my rant came to the surface. "I don't think we're going to finish in time."

It was a strong argument. The lack of response was proof of that.

Andrew rocked forward off the porch, his feet falling the few inches to the ground as he straightened to a standing position. "Three."

"Huh?"

"I didn't pack three *weeks* of MREs," he said calmly. "I packed one." He pointed at each vertex... "Two." ...of the triangle... "Three." ...we stood in. "One for each of us."

He walked away, words reverberating.

My body went limp. I knew he didn't have three weeks' worth. But I had thought he had enough for three days. Scott followed Andrew. I took their spot on the porch.

I shook my head. Day two I had crapped my pants roadside. Andrew had been my hero then, the way he had diffused my awkwardness and shame. And the only mention he had made after was to ask if I was ok. That was a model for our whole relationship. More than once, I had benefitted from Andrew's preparedness and kindness.

And I had just berated him for it.

My hands shifted to my lap, folded into each other. Duncan gave me the one guideline that mattered—and I had failed him. The words came out under my breath: "Such an asshole."

I stared at my hands, my palms. At the taxi, Scott and Andrew were next to the engine, hands outstretched to probe the heat field. They nodded to each other and began to put their things away.

Scott called out. "Nathan? You ready to take over?" There was no malice in voice.

Nodding, I made my voice upbeat. "Yeah." He turned back around.

I rotated my palms down. Meant to protect my hands from the cruelties of the road, I slipped into my gloves now to protect the world from me.

Chapter 21

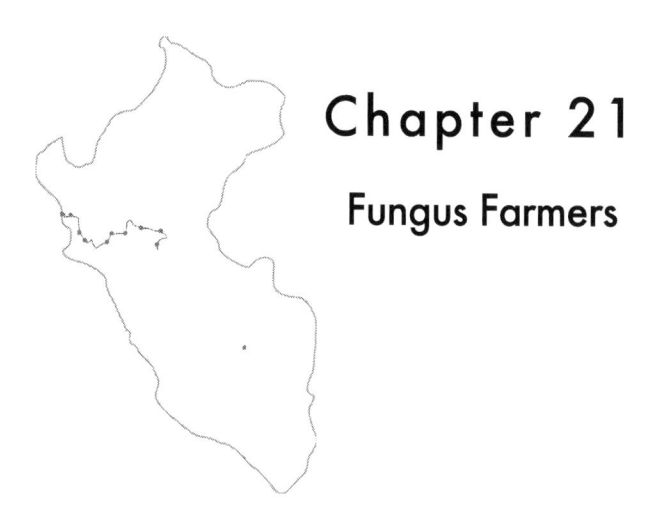

Fungus Farmers

Damn this newfound humility.

I was determined to operate the mototaxi to my own standards. Not to prove anything, but to make the ride for my teammates more pleasant. I owed them that. Of course, this also meant discovering if my standards were even realistic.

It was exhausting. I threw my body back and forth, wrestling the handlebars. They couldn't be forced where I wanted. Instead, I had to plead with them, because the road beneath was trying to steer too. And given that surface, when the road *was* more persuasive, it was a surprise which direction we went.

Yes, steering was very physical. But the route-finding was pure mental.

Potential routes through the pock-marked surface were plentiful, and it was fun trying to select one. My imagination projected three yellow lines onto the road's surface ahead of us—the middle line's origin further forward than the other two—the set weaving back and forth, around potholes, and across the small patches of asphalt and hard-packed gravel. Uniting the simulation with the real world was difficult though. Often, I couldn't muscle the mototaxi down the imagined path.

Having missed the opportunity (and more often than not, striking a pothole), my imagination would have to reset the simulated lines. At the next miss, another reset. Resets were unlimited, making this the most stubborn arcade game ever. And so it went: my body worked hard to meet the navigation demands of my brain while my brain had to contend with the failed execution of my body.

After 25 miles, my brain had overheated...the engine too. I pulled into a spot shaded from the afternoon sun, near a roadside concrete structure.

"Nice job, Nathan."

"Damn, guys. This road *really* sucks." They chuckled and shuffled from the back.

I was pleased with my performance and was confident my driving had been better than my teammates. But I still had to admit that my standards had not been met—my standards had not been realistic.

I dismounted, grabbed my water bottle, and followed my team deeper into the shade. It was difficult to tell if the structures we were stopping at were occupied or not. Were these homes? Outbuildings? No one was around, but things were in too good of shape to be abandoned. And there were chickens at this one, a dozen or so, unbothered by our presence.

I sat on the edge of a concrete slab, a few feet from where Andrew was seated. Scott wandered further, his camera at the ready. The air was thick. Not with humidity alone, but with tensions from my earlier behavior.

"Andrew." He looked up, met my eyes. I pushed through the pride. "I'm sorry about...back there. I'm just tired of this. I knew it would be difficult, but—" My head shook and my eyes fell with shame. "I just didn't anticipate...all of this."

He nodded as I spoke. "I know, man. I'm tired too."

We sat there, the moment's tension replaced by a more supple awkwardness. Before we could cut through that too, Scott called out.

"Guys! Come check this out!"

Andrew and I raised an eyebrow at each other. Scott's enthusiasm was out of place given our day—even for Scott. But his positivity was a needed change. We wandered over. He was squatted, angling his camera at the ground. Andrew and I exchanged another eyebrow.

"What are you doing, Scott?"

"Check this out. How cool is this?"

There wasn't much to check out. Just a lot of dirt. Bare dirt? In the jungle?

"It's an ant colony!"

Scott had discovered the largest ant colony I had ever seen. The hill had been cleared of all vegetation and Scott was squatted next to a train of ants coming and going from the colony, one line leaving empty handed, the other line returning with green fragments.

"Leafcutter ants?"

Scott looked up. "Awesome, right?"

Leafcutter ants are some of the original farmers. These ants don't actually consume leaves. They use the foliage to cultivate an edible fungus in growing chambers deep within their colony. Awesome indeed.

I left Scott and Andrew to track the train back to the leaf source. The ants marched from the colony entrance to the trunk of a tree some fifty feet away. Then the train disappeared into the height of the branches. I leaned close to inspect the ants coming down. Those were small fragments. Didn't ants have one of the best strength-to-weight ratios of any living thing on the planet? As if to answer my question, something caught my eye: a single ant, carrying a single leaf fragment—well, not *just* a single leaf fragment.

"Guys!" I called out, not taking my eye off the ant. "Check out this lazy motherfucker!"

"What?!"

Andrew and Scott both rushed over.

"Look at this guy," I singled out the ant with my pinky. "Right there."

"Uhhh," Scott started, "it looks like an ant carrying a leaf."

"No," I started laughing, "not *that* ant. Look on the leaf itself."

Riding down on the fragment was another ant, sitting absently, like another commuter on the train home. Andrew and Scott leaned closer and started to chuckle. They looked at each other and shook their heads.

"He's not doing anything. Just letting his buddy tote him around like he was royalty."

Andrew grinned, "That is pretty funny."

"Not as funny as your narration, Nathan," Scott said as he turned to me. He raised one eyebrow. "'Lazy motherfucker'? You're a regular David Attenborough." We burst with laughter.

David Attenborough, the British naturalist and narrator of several nature documentaries—*Planet Earth* included—using the term "lazy motherfucker"? I was hunched over. My body convulsed with silent laughter—most of the air had been expelled from my lungs by the hysterics. I had to fight for breath. Our laughter continued and started tears down my cheeks, a muddy trail behind each.

After the spell of laughter, we pieced our composure back together and filled our lungs to capacity. I wiped at the tears, still chuckling at the comment, at its brashness. But it was priceless. We had been so stressed—with the road, the race, each other—we had been on eggshells. But Scott's joke cut the remaining tension, lightened the mood, and brought us back together.

Andrew called from the mototaxi, "Engine's cool. You guys ready?"

We tiptoed back through the line of ants. At the mototaxi, Scott was storing his camera when he asked, "You guys mind if I drive?"

I glanced down the road: potholes as far as the eye could see. I turned back with a smile. "Go for it. You haven't had a turn since this morning."

Andrew and I nestled into the back while Scott triggered the electric starter. The sun was filtered by the afternoon clouds raised from the jungle canopy and was less punishing as it snuck beneath our mototaxi's cover. We pulled onto the road, Clifford's frame swaying, the vibrational kazoo returned to our ears and bones. I looked back a last time. The concrete structure faded into the shadows as we pulled away, the chickens still guarding its patch of jungle. I relived the comment under my breath, "Lazy motherfucker." David Attenborough's voice filled my head, and I cracked a wide grin.

Scott's navigating of the pothole minefield had improved. Or maybe we were just lighter after we offloaded my crappy attitude. In any case, the ride was less punishing. And not long after, it became enjoyable again due to the smooth pavement that took us into the town of Tocache, in the province (also restricted by OSAC) of the same name.

We fueled up in town, under stares from the locals. Some pointed. One group of women even laughed at the *gringo*-filled mototaxi.

I looked at my teammates with some of the same sentiment. In Colan, we had *not* been the most prepared. We lacked the history from which the bonds of friendship are forged, the experiences that forever tie people together. I laughed at the absurdity of it all. For our trio, having a short personal history and a lack of shared experience would not be a problem after this race.

Chapter 22

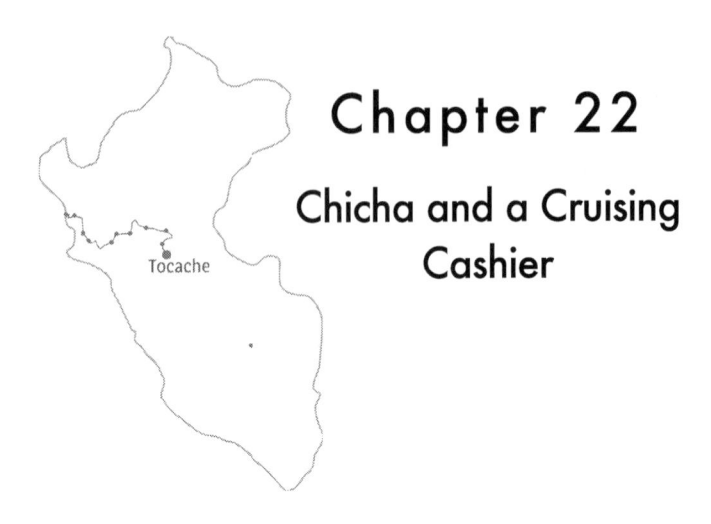

Chicha and a Cruising Cashier

ANDREW FLEW US to Nuevo Progresso. Even in Tocache, with 29 miles to go, I didn't think we would get there—the light was failing and rain clouds were moving in. On top of that, our lights weren't working—markers and headlight both. Maybe our electrical system had suffered from the shaking? Whatever, it didn't matter. The road we followed may as well have been polished for how smooth it was. Andrew capitalized. He rolled the throttle wide open and made up for the time we had spent clambering over the lunar-surfaced road.

In Nuevo Progresso, Scott and I negotiated for a hostel room—meaning I watched Scott jabber with the owner. With no garage for the mototaxi, we would have to leave it parked on the town's thoroughfare for the night. We hauled everything into our room…everything. Then we set out to find dinner.

We wandered into the *Plaza de Armas* and a restaurant sign called to my hunger and beckoned me.

"Scott." I pointed to the sign, trying to reserve judgment lest I be disappointed. "Is it safe to assume this restaurant serves Chinese food?"

Scott shrugged. "I'm willing to try it." He turned his head. "Andrew?"

"Let's do it," he replied.

We walked into the restaurant and sat; we were the only patrons. An older man delivered glasses of purple liquid and spoke with a matter-of-fact tone as he set them down. Scott nodded and the man walked toward the large brick oven at the back of the restaurant, where large metal skewers meant for rotisserie hung still and empty.

"What was that about, Scott?"

"Uhhh." At the back, the man spoke to a young boy, eight or nine-years-old. The boy nodded and darted out the back door. "I think he was saying we have to wait for the chef to show up." I turned to face Scott. Over his shoulder, through the front windows of the establishment, the young boy whizzed by. I smirked at the relaxed nature of things.

We sipped at our purple beverage. Then gulped. What was this potion? It was delicious. Back in the kitchen, a grill ignited and the man set a large wok to the heat. As he poured in some oil, the boy appeared at his elbow. The man gave a single nod. After the boy had caught his breath, the chef arrived.

He strolled through the back door, unconcerned by the presence of seated customers. His hands snatched two rags from a neat stack as he passed a shelf and entered the kitchen bathed in the light of the dining area. He was well built, young, in his twenties—close to our age, maybe younger. His brown skin stood in contrast to his white shirt, but it didn't hide the lighter-hued burns on his forearms. He tipped his head to the man, who responded with our orders. There was a casualness between them, but still an air of respect. Father and son? The chef's hands set to work before the man finished, his chin dipping after each order was recited.

Dinner was prepared with flair and in the time counted by a few flickers of the flame and a few tosses of the wok.

This was *Chifa*, Chinese with strong Peruvian influences. The preparation and appearance looked Chinese, but instead of rice and noodles, the main carbohydrates were rice and fried potatoes. With the South American spices, we could taste the intertwined traditions. I didn't motivate myself to eat—my dish did that for me. It was my first full meal in days. And the purple drink, called *chicha morada*, washed it all down.

Stomachs satisfied, we ambled to the one register situated on the counter separating the dining area from the kitchen. Since our supply of small bills was dwindling, Scott asked if we could pay with a large-denomination bill. The owner snapped the paper, held it up to the light, flicked a corner. He shouted over his shoulder and then spoke to Scott.

"Sí, claro," Scott replied. "Muchas gracias, señor." The owner nodded and walked to the back of the restaurant.

Our large-denomination bill disappeared. Andrew and I raised an eyebrow each in Scott's direction. His eyes shifted between us. "Sorry, guys," he blurted. "I'm not great at translating." Over Scott's shoulder, the young boy disappeared out the back door again. "The owner said he can break the bill, but he didn't have the right denominations in the register. He's just going to the back office to grab our change."

A silhouetted shoulder poked out near the back door, the outline backlit by the twilight outside. I cocked an eyebrow. Back office, huh? I turned to look out the front windows of the restaurant. Outside on the sidewalk, the boy whizzed by again.

"I don't think they had enough change." I got the raised eyebrows this time.

"How do you know?" Andrew asked.

I nodded to the sidewalk. "Keep an eye out for the little boy." We leaned against the counter, our attention bouncing between the young chef in the kitchen and the sidewalk. Three minutes passed before the boy sprinted by in the opposite direction. We turned to the back of the restaurant and waited. He shot through the door and his thin silhouette made a handoff. The owner reappeared, apologizing for the delay. We all tried to wave off his apologies, Scott expressing our appreciation of him accepting such a large bill. He handed Scott the correct change and bid us farewell.

We emerged onto the street. "He really didn't have enough change," Andrew said.

"That's why he took the bill," Scott said. "He sent the little boy to break it."

"That was very nice of him." We all nodded.

We started off before Andrew said, "I wonder how many places the little boy had to try before he found someone willing to give him change." We all nodded again, our appreciation of Peru's people swelling.

We strolled down the sidewalk with a certain contentedness. I glanced through shop windows we passed, until something caught my eye.

"Guys!" Andrew and Scott stopped a few paces ahead of me. "How about some ice cream?"

My body had been improving. My appetite had returned first. Then hunger. Now I had a craving, the first in many days. This had to be an indication my bowels were headed for a recovery, that my plight of diarrhea was nearing its end.

We found small plastic cups of ice cream—those instantly recognized by my inner child—and made our way into the square where we settled on a bench beneath a lamp. In the growing dark the light popped on. We pried the cardboard lids, damp with condensation, from the orange and white mixture. Scooping ice cream with the flat wooden spoon had not gotten any easier since childhood, but it forced us to take our time, to savor each bite.

We sat in silence as we scraped and scooped, facing west. A large cloud bank sat on the horizon, its gray facade intercepting any sunset light bound for Nuevo Progresso. But above it, clouds were ablaze, a blinding white that faded to a pastel and then a vibrant orange straight above us. The town bathed in the soft light. A drop of condensation fell into my hand. I glanced down. Along the tilted cup's edges, the few remaining bites of vanilla were melting, dripping to the pastel puddle in the middle of the cup before running across the sherbet orange at the bottom. I rotated the cup a quarter turn to align the color gradient below with that above.

Chapter 23

Wind-Whipped Drips

Nuevo Progresso

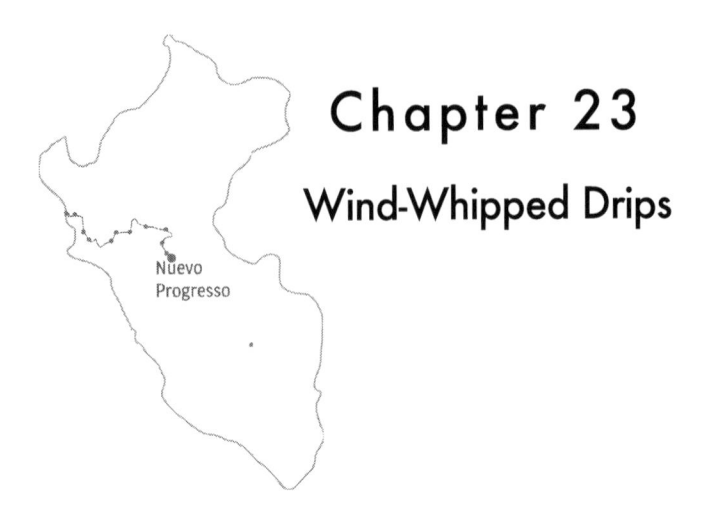

I BOLTED UPRIGHT, ALERT. We had gone to bed early, well fed and worn down, looking forward to a long sleep. Still adjusted to the darkness of unconsciousness, my eyes scanned the room.

Andrew and Scott were asleep; our stuff was still piled against one wall; all seemed in place. The hostel was quiet and the room a lovely 78 degrees Fahrenheit. So why my sudden start?

A memory floated to the surface, one I had recounted for Bren and Emma—the Australian cyclists—less than a week ago. I had woken up like this during my mountain bike tour. In *that* situation, I had been sleeping inside a sealed bivy sack, the lack of air circulation slowly suffocating me.

My fingers shot to my jugular. Was my heart racing? My breathing rapid? The pulse I found was calm, and my lungs were steady. So...not suffocating. Then what the heck?

Had my dreams woke me? They *had* been crazy. What were...? The dream narratives had slipped past remembrance, but not the feelings. My dreamscape this night had been bizarre. But not enough so to wake me.

I drew a breath meant for a sigh of exasperation. My lungs refused to be filled, then forced a cough. What!? Why the protest? I drew another breath, slower this time.

Holy shit!

I jumped out of bed. I dismantled the pyramid of our things, block by baggage block. The mototaxi was outside. We had brought in everything. Everything! The bottom row of the structure included the large green duffel that held our miscellaneous items. It was half full, its loose fabric draped over the adjacent item: a plastic container of a similar shade of green. I yanked our jerrycan from under the fabric and walked it to the hall.

One set of fingers locked on the door frame, the other curled around the handle, I swung the door open, close, open, close. How contaminated was our air? And what effect would the gasoline fumes have? Was it worth waking up Scott and Andrew? I slowed the door fan. They were both still breathing; the fume source had been located; the air quality was improving. What action could they take? No, I'd let them sleep.

After five minutes of cycling the door, I propped it open and sat in the frame. I tried to purge my lungs. My chest and abdomen inflated my lungs as much as possible, then tried to squeeze all the air back out. It's impossible to completely empty your lungs, but a few large breaths would dilute any residual fumes. The solution to pollution, right?

Now for the cause of the problem: what to do with the gasoline?

Hallway? Too much liability. Mototaxi? Too far. I glanced over my shoulder, into our room. I settled for locking it in the bathroom like an adopted pet set on wreaking all sorts of domestic havoc. I repositioned the duffle's loose fabric to guard against any fumes escaping under the door.

The bed welcomed me back. In the fresh air, my alertness ebbed while fatigue reclaimed me. The bathroom was tiny compared to our room. How bad would its air be in the morning? I was sure I'd find out…diarrhea and all.

I lost consciousness.

* * *

Even in the gasoline fumes, my morning bowel movement was a success. There was even a chunk present in the liquidy discharge. And I farted. Milestones! Along those same lines, even though the jerrycan had long since been removed from the bathroom, the fumes persisted, so the door remained open while I used it, facilitating more team bonding. We talked about our gasoline dreams.

We packed and, our room empty and smelling more like a garage now than when we checked in, we returned the key and hit the road.

The polished road continued past Nuevo Progresso. The mototaxi still without lights, our speed kept us from being run over in the din. It also helped the rain penetrate our vinyl defenses. Drips of rainwater caught on the front of the roof were whipped back by the wind and smacked us. Water streamed off the front tire, a constant spray. We wore our waterproof layers. This wasn't the soft, warm rain you imagine in the Amazon, falling from the finite wisps of a cumulus cloud born from the forest, its margins a silver lining. No. This rain was cold, violent, and persistent, originating from the nondescript mass of gray that stretched out above—no silver lining included.

We had been making good time again when the engine sputtered. My eyes snapped to the indicators. No useful information there. Another sputter, more persistent this time. Andrew's wrist rocked the throttle. The rpms rebounded and the smooth cycling of the piston was restored.

Sputtering wasn't strange. We heard it all the time...but when the engine was too hot. A drop caught my forehead. We were in a rainstorm. The easiest way to convert an air-cooled engine into a water-cooled engine is to drive in the rain.

Another sputter. The rpms fell lower this time. Andrew's throttle rocking wasn't enough. His left hand went for the clutch and eased the stress on the engine. The clutch-squeeze/throttle-rocking combination kept the engine sputtering, but no recovery came. Another drop in the rpms. It was all over. The engine ceased. Andrew shifted to neutral and steered us off the road with the momentum we had left.

Clifford came to a stop, rain pattering on our vinyl top. Andrew gave me a look over his shoulder. We were thinking the same thing: no way was it too hot to die. I shrugged my shoulders.

He gave a single nod before leaning and folding out the kick-starter. One… Two… Three attempts and nothing.

"Andrew." I pinched my eyelids closed. I couldn't handle the strain of mechanical thinking when I had so little knowledge to build on. My parted eyelids revealed Andrew turned toward me, pulling his goggles up onto his head. "Water in the gas tank?" He sighed as he considered it. "It's just…" I fished for logic. "This is the first rain we've had. I mean…it's rained before, but this is the first heavy, consistent rain." He nodded.

Scott leaned forward. "What's the deal with the water?"

Andrew's head rolled to the opposite shoulder to address Scott. "If water gets into the carb, that could stall the engine." Andrew turned back to me. "The problem with that theory is we've been driving in the rain for a while. If we were going to have an issue with water, I think it would've happened already."

He was right. We'd been driving in the rain for an hour and a half. Why the delay?

I cocked my head to see past Andrew's shoulder. "Look," I nodded. "Water on top of the gas tank, right at the lid." His eyes tracked my gaze. "It could've taken a while to collect."

He let loose another sigh while he shook his head. "I don't think so." He turned back. "I inspected the lid's seal back in Colan—it looked pretty good."

I nodded. I didn't doubt him. But it was too much of a coincidence that we were having this problem in our first heavy rain.

Scott chimed back in. "Try starting it again."

Andrew nodded. "Why not?"

He did the awkward half squat required by the short distance between the kick-starter and mototaxi's roof frame. One kick… Two kicks… Slipped boot. Andrew repositioned his foot on the rubberless kick-starter, the metallic lever slick with moisture. One... Two attempts and the engine fired up.

He sat and gave a don't-have-a-clue shoulder shrug before folding the kick-starter back in. Clutch, first gear, and we were off.

I wasn't buying it though. We had had a problem, then recovered without a solution? I went back to my water theory. What could be done after the next engine failure?

Ten more miles and another sputter. Andrew kept the engine purring. Ten seconds later—another sputter, another recovery. Eight seconds—sputter and recovery. Seven—sputter, recovery.

We rounded a bend. Ahead was a dilapidated gas station. It still had the large roof structure that had once sheltered the pumps. Beneath it: dry ground.

Andrew made a beeline, the engine's sputter and recovery no longer distinct. The engine died as we hit the edge of the dry ground and we coasted the last fifteen feet to the middle of a gravel patch.

"Nice park job," I remarked, sliding out of the back seat.

"No kidding," Scott said. "Way better than out there." He nodded to a patch of grass between the building and road where a series of discarded cans and buckets lay, ones in the upright position full and hosting the slow and random oscillations of the overflowing water that streamed down their sides.

"Yeah, lucky this was here," Andrew agreed.

"Lucky we made it here."

Andrew dismounted and headed to the back. It looked like he had a plan.

"What are you thinking?"

He worked the cargo ropes free and dug into the green duffel.

"I'm thinking it's the carb again. It's been a while since it was cleaned. And it's not as obvious that it's dirty when we aren't climbing." The duffel's zipper whined as it slid along the temporary seam. "We have to pull the fuel line off the carb anyway, so if there's water, we'll see it." Andrew's hands reappeared, holding the black bundle of tools.

A green square came around the corner, Scott's fingers clamping each side, his legs below it. His head appeared as the top half of the map folded down. "Looks like we're close to Tingo María. It's only another 15 miles...tops. Should we try to drive it there? Find a mechanic?"

Andrew spoke. "I'd rather not attempt it. I don't think we can cover another 15 miles." He glanced around. "If we have to do roadside repairs ourselves, this spot is probably the best we could do."

"I agree," I said. "It's going to be easier to work here than in the rain...and a lot more pleasant."

Scott nodded and refolded the map. "That's settled then." He tossed the map into the back seat. "So what next?"

Andrew unrolled the tools. He slipped a wrench from its fabric sheath and passed it to Scott. "You pull the seat off, Nathan," he turned. "You kill the fuel, disconnect the line from the carb, and—once Scott gets the seat off—remove the gas tank"

"You got it." *Look at this guy.* We may have been broken down in a rainstorm, but we were dry, had a plan, and had someone who had taken charge. Things weren't all that bad.

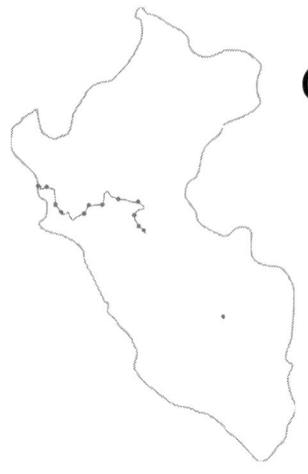

Chapter 24
Wound Up

ANDREW SAT ON HIS KNEES, legs folded underneath him. Next to him sat a tray I had retrieved from the grassy patch of water-filled containers. It had held all the loose bits during disassembly, cleaning, and reassembly. It was nearing empty…for the second time.

"Scott, can you hold this?" Andrew didn't look up. He was focused, determined to get the mototaxi running.

"You bet!" By this point, Scott's perpetual positivity had replaced Andrew's plan as my source of hope.

Andrew had been right though—the carb had been filthy. Nearly as bad as the first time the halves had been cracked apart. So Andrew had cleaned it, his attention focused, his moves deliberate, his process thought out. It had gone smoothly—he had obviously paid attention during all of our service stops.

Andrew had also been correct about the water. With the gas tank free from the frame, we had dumped the lid's moat and opened it for inspection. The seal had looked great. And with no water flowing through the lines, we had assumed our fuel was water-free.

"Feed that cable right through this hole, Scott."

"Here it comes."

Seeing our carb, we had assumed it was the problem. But after the first reassembly, the mototaxi still didn't start. It had taken twenty minutes of kicking before it fired up. The engine had gasped and taken a drink of fuel, slowly winding up. But this initial climb of the rpms had surpassed our set idol. The rpms kept climbing, faster and faster. In the four seconds the engine had run, the rpms rose to a dangerously high pitch.

"Ok." Andrew sat back on his heels, taking one last look before moving on. "Nathan, we're ready for the gas tank."

Our hearts had jumped at the sounds of combustive life, but had been left frozen by that new sound. Fortunately, it had been Andrew on the bike when it had started. He had used the kill switch before the engine could blow up. None of us knew what the sound meant, so we started over and tore everything apart a second time.

I waddled the gas tank over to the frame. "Here it comes." I slipped the front end into the frame.

Now, we were almost back together for the second time.

"Scott, can you guide the fuel line through the frame as Nathan sets the tank down?"

"You betcha."

"Here we go," I warned, lowering the back end of the tank. I lined up the tank's single bolt flange with the bolt hole in the frame. The tank nestled with a thunk, gasoline sloshing inside. "Down," I said while I spun the bolt finger-tight.

Scott knelt on the left side of the engine. "Got the fuel line connected."

Andrew was still on the right side, doing one last visual inspection. He nodded, rolling back onto his feet and standing up. "Go ahead and turn the fuel on."

Scott turned the valve while I secured the seat. Andrew gave us a tight-lipped look as he folded out the kick-starter. It took several attempts, but the engine did fire up, and quicker this time.

The engine purred back to life, raising itself to a steady idle, forcing the moisture out of the cylinder. But the upward trend didn't stop. Just as it had the first time, the engine revved up higher and higher. Andrew hit the kill switch.

We exchanged glances.

"Well, now what?"

Andrew shrugged. "I don't know what's causing that," his head nodding to the motor. "I think it's safe to say a third attempt would be a waste of time."

Scott and I nodded. Less than two hours earlier, we had been filled with hope. We had had a problem. We had formed a plan. It had been empowering to act independently. Now that independence was squashed beneath our lack of troubleshooting experience.

"I can drive it," Scott said.

Andrew and I gave a simultaneous, "Huh?"

"It sounds like it's at full throttle, right? I can drive it. Use the clutch like crazy." Scott looked back and forth between Andrew and I, then shrugged at our skepticism. "What?"

"I don't know, Scott," I said. "Seems...dangerous. Plausible, sure, but what if something goes wrong?"

Andrew nodded. "I agree. Besides, it could be bad for the engine. We don't want to fry our motor."

Scott conceded. "So if driving isn't an option, are we talking about a tow?"

"How far did you say the next town was?"

"About 15 miles."

We turned to the road. There had not been a ton of traffic, but several cars had passed since we had stopped.

"Scott...feel like flagging someone down?"

"I can try." He paused, eyes on the ground. "Actually," he looked up at Andrew and me, "it would probably be better if you guys tried."

Andrew grimaced while I suppressed a chuckle. "Uh...Scott, we don't speak Spanish."

He nodded. "Exactly. It's harder to turn down someone who's hopeless. People will probably just say 'no' to me, because they *can* say 'no.'"

"Good point."

"Let's all go," Scott said. "And try to look miserable."

"Shouldn't be too hard."

With a new plan to restore some hope, we put Clifford's red engine paneling back in place, packed our stuff, and abandoned our shelter to stand on the rainy roadside, waving down cars.

Forty-five minutes later, a piece of dirty plastic separated Andrew and me from Scott. It was the rear window of a tuk-tuk, sworn enemy of the mototaxi.

The tuk-tuk was another compact, three-wheeled vehicle used for taxiing, and in many cities directly competed with the mototaxi. On top of that, instead of being a mishmash of metal and rubber around a motorcycle engine, the tuk-tuk had actually been engineered. You could tell by the maneuverability of its small wheels, the added comfort of its enclosed passenger bay, and the customizable combustion system which could utilize either natural gas or gasoline.

On the roadside, most people had blown right past us. Of the few that had stopped, none were willing to tow a mototaxi. A few had even laughed at the request. With the tuk-tuk driver though, we tried a different approach. It wasn't until after Andrew had reeled him with a discussion of money that Scott took over the negotiation, mentioning our mototaxi for the first time. After some smooth talking—and paying the fare up front—Scott had convinced him to tow us.

Andrew and I crammed into the back of the tuk-tuk. It was a tad smaller than the mototaxi's bench seat, but since it was enclosed, there was no tire spray to worry about. Instead, we worried about Scott—on the mototaxi—and craned our necks to keep an eye on him through the dirty plastic. Lacking a proper tow strap, we used a length of rock climbing webbing. For the task, it was an uncomfortably short piece of webbing.

We took off, a gradual acceleration under the weight of an atypical passenger. The flat went well. Then we started up the one ridge between us and Tingo María. The uphill was slow, but easy. We crested, then started back down.

It was tense.

Scott rode a razor's edge, trying to balance the coasting with the braking, the potential ramming of the tuk-tuk's bumper with the potential yanking on its undercarriage with the strap. This wasn't Scott's only feat of balance though. The webbing was fixed to Clifford's front fork in such a way that crossing over the strap would cause the front tire to jackknife. We couldn't say what would happen if it did, but it couldn't be good.

Every time Scott gained on the tuk-tuk, the tow strap slackened and dragged on the road. My heartbeat was sporadic at these moments. "Tight man! Keep it tight! Don't cross over the strap!" He couldn't hear me. But I still yelled and mimed against the opaque window that Scott couldn't see through. The webbing now tattered, the road leveled off.

Our tuk-tuk driver must have savored towing a mototaxi—he delivered us to the best mototaxi mechanic in town, to the front of the shop, to the large bay doors, honking as we came to a stop. The mechanic could help, but not before finishing a few other projects. Most of the day had already been wasted—what was a little more? We agreed to wait, cut the webbing, and turned the tuk-tuk loose.

Chapter 25
Bright Lights

TINGO MARÍA—not a tourist hot spot. Flanking the city was a maze of stunted, pointed peaks which bore no resemblance to the Andes. These peaks were not solemn, not regal. They were noisy with critters hidden in the flora fed by the tangle of clouds captured by the valley.

Built at the confluence of the Huallaga and Monzón rivers, Tingo sits in the Upper Huallaga River Valley and only became reachable in the late 1930s, a reason Tingo has been slow to attract tourism. Another reason: trafficking of that famous Peruvian crop. The Upper Huallaga and Monzón river valleys host some of the densest growth of illicit coca in the world. That put us in the middle of cocaine alley.

The few tourists that do make it to Tingo seek out a nearby national park, which is home to one of Peru's most popular caves. But a lesser-known attraction (and only a single kilometer from town), is the garbage dump known as *Moyuna*. It has been in operation for more than thirty years, and in 2014 it was estimated the dump received between thirty and thirty-four tons of garbage…daily.

How much garbage is thirty-four tons? No idea. But that is *all* of the area's garbage, including the hospital's biohazard waste. And every last bit goes straight into the Huallaga River.

Was that worse than leaving used oil on the side of the road? Irrelevant—we had our oil changed in Tingo as well. We can all guess where it went. May as well have tossed it into the waters ourselves. But I'm getting ahead of myself. The last thing the mechanic did to our mototaxi was change the oil.

* * *

Street and sidewalk puddles had stilled, their surfaces reflecting the gray threat of more rain. The mechanic used the dry spell to accomplish all he could. When it was our turn, we skipped the verbal explanation. After several kicks, the spark caught. The engine revved again, as high as the kill switch allowed. The mechanic nodded and set to work.

After twenty minutes, he waved us out of the shop. With a single kick, he fired up the engine, and revved it a few times. Then the rpms fell back to an idle. A fat smile spread across the mechanic's face, as if to say, "stupid *gringos*." Before we could get excited though, the engine sputtered and died. With a scowl, he looked back to us. We shrugged. He nodded, then sat back down on his stool and picked up a wrench.

Our afternoon was dominated by boredom. Once the mechanic threw our motor's generator coils into the basket of his moped and disappeared down the street, we also set off into town. We had lunch at a restaurant with a full menu, at a large table, flanked by padded chairs, atop a clean tile floor, with views of the outside world available through plate glass windows.

After, we got pictures with some police officers standing guard outside a bank. All wore camouflage, while some held riot gear and others held weapons. No doubt the Aussies and Texans would allow a grenade launcher to substitute for the "Picture with AK47" square on our *Peru Bingo* board.

We reviewed the pictures as we walked away. A grenade launcher? What was the purpose of the guards? We had assumed they were protecting the bank *from* criminal activity.

But given the valley's cocaine production, was it possible that criminal activity was protecting the bank? Who better to protect drug money than off-duty cops? It seemed plausible, but who can be sure?

We wandered some more before we doubled back to the taxi. It was in more and smaller pieces now, with several specialized tools strewn across the ground, thrown down by a mechanic showing signs of frustration. I smirked. Who looked stupid now?

He and Scott chatted. Our taxi wouldn't be ready before tomorrow.

"Clifford's finally living up to his name, huh?"

"Yeah. 'The Big Red Piece of Shit.'"

"So when will he be ready tomorrow?"

Scott shook his head. "He doesn't know. He said maybe in the morning..." Scott glanced at the mess of our machine. "...maybe later in the day."

We nodded and watched. After half a day, his movements were still quick, his effort persistent. It reminded me of Andrew tearing apart the carb.

"At least he seems competent."

"Oh yeah," Scott said. "He's determined to get this thing fixed. Said he hasn't had this tough of a repair in a while."

Spectating brought back the boredom. We grabbed our things and crossed the street to a hotel. We checked in, deposited our belongings in a room that overlooked the mechanic's street, and headed back out for dinner.

The disappearance of the sun caused a role reversal. In the day, it had been the surrounding jungles abuzz with life; in the night, it was Tingo María itself that bustled.

Sidewalks were shoulder to shoulder. We walked even with each other when we could, but were forced into a single file most of the time. Street-facing shops were open for business, the white light falling onto the faces of passersby through large windows and open doors. More bulbs and neon signs hung outside the shops, and the markers and headlights of tuk-tuks and mototaxis crept through throngs of pedestrians, who diverted like water around a rock. Music spilled out from *discotecas*, mixing with the shouts of peddlers selling sweets. The scent of freshly baked bread wafted up the street, the ovens' escaped air still dry in the jungle humidity.

One sign caught our eyes: "Hamburguesas." No translation required; our stomachs identified the core meaning. We went inside. Like the sign, what we were served only resembled hamburgers.

The buns were flat. Inside, the beef patty was thin, but supplemented with a slab of bologna and a fried egg, all sandwiched with the classic lettuce, tomato, and onion. Also crammed inside were fries. Their thin slicing gave them a crisp surface—like the *papitas* in Juanjuí. Their saltiness brought variety to the flavor, while their texture added a crunch to each bite. Munching was the only sound at our table.

Bellies full, our beds called to us.

Navigating to the hotel, we detoured past the mechanic's. The city life had not spilled onto his street. His shop was the only one with lights still on and we were the only pedestrians. That made it easy for him to spot us. He yelled and ran to the mototaxi, which was back together. He used the electric starter and it purred. Then he revved it, winding up the engine. Back at an idle, he tapped on our marker lights—all aglow—and flipped our headlight on and off. His grin had grown into his eyes.

He had stayed late to fix it. He had called on other mechanics for diagnostic advice and other shop owners for recommendations. He had even bought parts through a competing supplier. He had replaced the entire electrical system, including the generator coils. Paired with the other routine maintenance he had performed, it was a new machine. He joked about its new ability to do 60 mph.

And the bill was too low. Parts aside, he only charged 30 soles for labor. An entire afternoon of work, of failures and mental anguish, of phone calls and errands, and he was only asking for US$10. We tried to pay more, but he refused. Then he offered to store our taxi for the night.

Our day had not been great. The rain, the failed attempt at repairing Clifford, a crazy tow, and the fact that we had covered almost no ground—putting us even further behind schedule—had all been frustrating. Our mechanic friend though, he had managed to turn it all around. A tuned mototaxi that would be ready for our rested bodies and minds the next morning? The day could not have ended better.

Chapter 26

Cinematic Slumber

THE GRAY LIGHT pried my eyelids open. Through our floor-to-ceiling windows was Tingo María, in the shadow of its eastern mountain. Dawn had been delayed by yesterday's trapped clouds, which had rallied and risen against their earthen captors and out of the confining ridges. Now—with the extra altitude—they caught the sunlight and scattered it down like a vaporous chandelier casting brilliant, golden light into the fog below.

"Hey, Nathan." My sheets crackled as I rolled to my back. My head turned. Scott and Andrew were laying on their sides, heads propped on pillows, staring through the window as I had been. Scott had a smirk on his face. "Ready for us to sing?"

I cringed, but the expression was hijacked by a yawn—a jaw-stretching, back-bending, straight-armed-sized yawn. My lungs expelled the fatigue gathered during the maneuver, and my arms fell back to the bed. "That's not necessary."

"Andrew?" Scott said.

"Start us off," he smiled.

In the traditional melody: "Happy birthday to you... happy birthday to you..."

We lay in our twin beds, the song filling the room. I smiled at the finish, mood shifting from miffed to grateful.

"Don't worry," Scott said, sitting up. "We'll spare you the twenty-six spankings."

"Good!" My neck straightened, eyes looking into the space above my head. "I'm sure the road today will give me *more* than twenty-six." Scott and Andrew laughed and clambered from bed.

I rolled back to the window. The fog was burning away, enough to reveal the silhouette of the backlit ridge. The extra light stirred the red and yellow paints, bringing a blush to the city. The singing had brought a similar color to my own face.

I sat up and tossed my legs over the side of the bed. The white sheet fell from my body as I stood and stretched for a second time. Our chandelier's golden glow was intensifying, and below it, our mechanic friend was pushing Clifford onto the street. I smiled.

We packed and hustled down to the mechanic's, loaded up the taxi, and departed.

Five miles from the city, the road degraded. The handlebars became epileptic on the road, jerking back and forth through the potholes with no control whatsoever. It wasn't as bad as the infamous stretch, but I still superimposed the three imaginary yellow lines onto the road's surface to navigate. Hopefully it wouldn't get worse.

Another 5 miles, traffic from the roadway was diverted to a parallel track. Past the junction, large piles of coarse gravel spanned the road at ten-foot intervals. Two, three, four piles I counted before the temporary road fell away from the original. At the bottom of a hill, we crossed a temporary bridge and saw the reason for the closure. Up the gully, the permanent bridge's steel underside was cracked through. Heavy equipment sat on solid ground at either side while a group of hard hats stood on the bridge, looking down at a few men dangling from the ropes thrown over the side.

We exchanged a look. That would have definitely qualified as a "Rickety Bridge Crossing" in *Peru Bingo*. If only we had crossed before it had been blocked off. Instead, our tires were slipping in the wet clay of the temporary track downhill from the bridge. I downshifted and gained the traction that would pull us back up to the official road. Its cracked and potted condition continued as we began to climb.

The road didn't improve. Good thing the mototaxi had been at the mercy of the mechanic the day before. Would it have been able to perform on this road otherwise? I was skeptical. After several hours, several switchbacks, and several cool downs, we crossed a ridge. Wisps of moisture streaked the sky ahead, the adjacent clouds darker and threatening to paint their own rain. We pulled on waterproof layers and an edge of apprehension.

We were descending toward Huánuco. We had been in cocaine alley for a few days, but were now approaching cocaine central. Huánuco is a major hub for drug trafficking and was the only city our Peruvian liaisons had warned us about. They didn't tell us much beyond suggesting we pass straight through and, if that wasn't possible, pleaded we not be out in the city at night.

It was a long descent.

Our approach through the outskirts and into Huánuco proper left me underwhelmed. The ramshackle appearance of most of the buildings paired with their short stature was unthreatening. Where were the mansions? The villas? The private helicopter pads? Where was anything typical of a Hollywood screenplay?

We pulled into a gas station where a motorcycle and mototaxi were parked next to the pumps. The taxi driver was lying across his back seat, legs sticking out the side. The motorcyclist sat on a curb, knees pulled up to support the crossed arms on which his forehead rested. We stretched and walked circles to restore some circulation, waiting for an attendant to appear.

"Is there no one around?" I said, giving a wary eye to the motorcyclist. Was he sleeping? Or was he waiting for a target assigned by his employer? Would we be witness to a drug war assassination?

"Looks like someone's inside," Scott said squinting. "I'll check."

Motorcyclist in my peripherals, I walked away from the pumps, toward an empty concrete slab. The city stretched up the hillside in front me and down the valley to my right. Maybe the city's vibrancy had been washed out by the gray sky. Or maybe the city was just pale compared to my imagination.

"Blackout," Scott yelled to me from the mototaxi, his shoulders shrugging.

I glanced up and down the street. Maybe the blandness was just due to a lack of light.

Andrew was untying our jerrycan as I returned. Scott looked up as he pulled the key from the ignition. "There's an electricity shortage–" He slipped the key into our gas tank's lid. "–so the city has a daily blackout."

"Daily?" I glanced at the motorcyclist again. How do you not plan your fuel needs around a blackout? Maybe there *was* going to be a hit.

"Yeah, but it sounded unpredictable," Scott said, nodding to the mototaxi in front of us, to the feet sticking out, still motionless. "The attendant guessed the power would be off for another three hours."

Andrew uncapped our spare fuel. "Figured we didn't want to wait around here any longer than we had to," he said as he moved into a pouring position.

My heart fluttered at the thought of waiting around in cocaine central.

"Yeah, let's fill up and get moving." Was that fear in my voice? "You know," I covered, "got to make up the distance we lost yesterday."

Andrew's pour was steady, but gasoline clung to the plastic and a sequence of drops ran to the bottom corner and dripped to the concrete. The puddle on the ground grew rectangular as Andrew tipped the jerrycan further and further, spreading the drips in a line.

"That's—" Scott started as he stared into the tank, stretching the word before ending with a punctuated, "–good." Andrew and Scott capped their respective containers.

"Almost empty," Andrew said, shaking the jerrycan. "Hopefully the next town doesn't have a blackout too."

Scott locked the gas tank. "We should have enough for the rest of the day, right?"

Andrew nodded. "Assuming we don't drive into the night."

Betrayed again by my emotions: "Not that we want to be driving around here at night, anyway."

Andrew and Scott both nodded.

We secured the jerrycan, rotated drivers, and fired up the mototaxi. I kept an eye on the motorcyclist as we pulled out of the gas station, half hoping he would still play a part in my Hollywood screenplay, half hoping he was still asleep.

The whole city was in a state similar to the motorcyclist's slumber. People were present, but there wasn't much activity. Did everyone head into the hills for work? Was Huánuco's pulse like Tingo María's, a slow thump during the day, a rest period that allowed it to flutter at night? We didn't find out.

We left the city and returned to the country's dirt and gravel, this time *sin* potholes. Late in the afternoon, the mototaxi was passed back to me.

After the long morning of mountain roads, a sluggishness had returned to Clifford. Even then, we caught a slow line of traffic. I pulled my buff over my mouth and nose as we joined the end and—with what was left of our tire tread—contributed to the trailing dust cloud. The road's curves kept the length of the line a secret. Spurts of downhill traffic prevented passing. And vehicles accumulated behind us.

After several long miles in the dust accompanied by a chorus of climbing engines, their abundant exhaust giving extra power to the day's penetrating heat, our procession of cars, pickups, and trucks halted. A construction zone. A few enterprising individuals ran up and down the single-file parking lot with homemade sugary drinks and snacks for sale.

After twenty minutes, traffic started again. The line of trucks ahead was slow to accelerate under the load of their cargo. I swerved out of our place in line, wrist rolling the throttle, and zipped past the larger vehicles. I tapped the horn: "See ya, suckers!" With the other cars and pickups, we traversed a short construction zone, then past a long line of downhill-oriented vehicles.

Traffic petered out again, us falling between the fast and slow-to-start vehicles, many of which passed us on one of our cool down sessions, anyway. That was fine. Traffic was not something I wanted to deal with. But as our stops became more frequent, I had to wonder if that traffic might end up being beneficial.

Chapter 27

Birthday Brew

CLIFFORD got us to the village of San Rafael. It was small and beautiful. Traffic was channeled through town on smooth pavement with enough space to park next to robust curbs that guarded sturdy sidewalks full of pedestrians. Buildings were brick and stone stacked multiple stories tall, with front doors situated at the top of concrete stoops. People congregated on the steps, leaning, sitting, chatting. The structures' crisp colors, height, and bustling occupants had an urban air. This wasn't a city, right?

We found the one gas station, and its electricity was flowing. We examined the map as the fuel pumped.

"There aren't any other towns for a while," Andrew said. "Maybe we should stay here tonight."

The valley was still bright, but night would come fast.

"We *have* covered a lot of ground today," I added.

Scott killed the flow of fuel and shifted the nozzle from the gas tank to the jerrycan. "We could get Nathan his birthday dinner."

Andrew gave a single nod. "Sounds good to me."

"Me too."

Fuel thirst quenched, we headed to a hostel. Scott and Andrew went in while I sat with the mototaxi. It was a strange ten minutes.

On the road, oncoming cars slowed. On the sidewalks, people came to a standstill. Stoop conversations paused. Everyone stared. I waved to a few people, but when they didn't wave back, I gave up. A good thing, too, because my arm didn't have the required endurance. People started to appear in doorways, hands shielding their eyes against the sun. After a moment, they disappeared only to return with their friend, their brother, their mother, pointing.

This was weird. I busied myself with the ropes of our cargo rack. While fumbling with a knot, three young girls walked by. All did a double take. A comment made them all laugh. The word I caught: *leche*. They had to be talking about my skin, and I suppressed my own chuckle.

"Nathan," Scott said coming down the steps of the hostel. "We got a great deal on a three-bed room."

Another night with my own bed? This *was* a birthday treat.

"Awesome."

"Yeah. And do you mind unpacking that letter?" I was in charge of race documents. Included was a letter that explained our ordeal in Spanish, compliments of Duncan. "The owner didn't completely understand what we're doing, but was really interested."

"Of course. It'll be nice to get some more use out of that thing." I handed off Scott's and Andrew's bags. "Hey, Scott." I passed the green duffel. "*Leche* means milk, right?"

"Yup."

I slung the strap of my own backpack over a shoulder and smiled as we climbed the hostel stairs. "That's what I thought."

* * *

"What?" Scott drew out the word.

"You don't?" Andrew tried to confirm.

"I'm guessing," I raised an eyebrow, "you both do?"

"Are you kidding?" Scott scoffed. "We're programmers. We would get IVs if we could."

A fresh cup of coffee sat before each of us. Steam rolled off the dark surface.

"How is that possible?" Andrew said.

I laughed an, "I don't know," then gave it a moment's thought. "I mean, I've sipped before."

"And didn't like it?"

"It was ok. But in college I had some friends that were going to Starbucks every day...sometimes more than once." Scott and Andrew nodded. "I thought that was a waste of money. Maybe I became a little prejudiced against it."

Andrew picked up his mug and tested the temperature of the brew against his lip. He set it back down without taking a drink.

"Still, you're twenty-six. How is this your first cup of coffee?"

"Who knows," I shrugged. "Maybe it will be the first of many."

The coffee had been served inside a restaurant, one of those small operations that served whatever dish had been prepared that day. It was close enough to the hostel that we had found it with our noses. We sat at one of the five tables—only one other was occupied. First came the coffee and my offhand comment about my first cup.

The disbelief dissipating, Scott picked up his mug and sipped. The skin beneath his chin wiggled as he swished the drink across his tongue. His throat bulged with a swallow. Then a slow exhale. "So good," he whispered, eyes fixed on the mug.

Andrew's turn; a similar reaction.

Then both looked at me. It was an expectant stare. This had better be good—they'd probably kill me if I didn't like it. I wrapped my fingers around the mug and raised it to my face. Heat ran up my fingers, collected in my palm, and ebbed at my wrist. My lips brushed the mug's rim, and I inhaled the steam, the aroma familiar. With a slight tip of the wrist and aid from my lungs, I pulled a small volume of the liquid in through pursed lips. My tongue rolled like a straw and held the liquid, letting my taste buds revel until I swallowed, the warmth spreading through my stomach.

Andrew and Scott waited.

"Pretty good." I set the mug down. "A little bitter at the end."

"It is pretty strong," Scott conceded. "Especially since you're not a coffee drinker."

"Add a little bit of sugar," Andrew said.

A small scoop and quick stir later, I took another sip.

"Damn. This is really good." I kept the mug in hand. "I might have to start drinking coffee."

Scott and Andrew laughed. My eyebrows raised.

"This *is* Peru, Nathan," Scott said. "Don't get much closer to the source than this. They probably grew and roasted these beans out back." He took another small drink. "Coffee's not like this back home."

Andrew nodded. "This might be the best cup I've ever had."

Scott looked up, pondering. "It might be for me, too."

"Well," I extended my mug into the air in front of me, above the center of the table. "This is definitely the best cup *I've* ever had. Let's cheers to that."

Scott raised his mug saying, "Because it's the only cup you've ever had."

Andrew raised his mug and smirked, "Details, Scott. Details."

We laughed as our mugs clinked.

Dinner was served: a beef stew ladled over rice. We couldn't have found a better birthday meal in all of Peru. We ate and sipped in silence.

After we cleared our plates, Scott struck up a conversation with the neighboring table, the occupants of which had been giving us the occasional glance. Scott explained to the older gentleman that it was my birthday, and after many soft *feliz cumpleaños* were offered, Scott explained the race.

As was the pattern, the men didn't believe him at first. Piura to Urubamba...by mototaxi? Scott laughed with the men, holding his ground. Then one man spoke. The others at the table went quiet, as did Scott.

Andrew and I plucked up. "Scott, what did he say?"

Scott continued in Spanish. A few exchanges passed before Scott translated.

"He knows about the race...says he saw a team."

"Really?" I sat up, the coffee in my system enabling the speed with which I did so.

"Two white people...a man and woman."

Scott asked for more details.

Andrew caught my eye. "Could be Sue and Dorian."

"We haven't seen them since day one," I said. It was they who had passed us outside Piura...being towed by a pickup. "Think we could catch them?" It was the first time in days we had seen or heard of another team.

Andrew shrugged and turned to Scott. "When did he see them? How long ago?"

Scott's Spanish was a little twisted with the excitement. He asked several more questions.

Then Scott's brow furrowed. "Tres años?" he repeated.

The man confirmed. "Sí, tres años."

"Sí," Scott smiled and his tone relaxed. "Claro."

Scott looked at us, "Uhhh." He chuckled. "The team he saw came through three *years* ago."

We smirked, the excitement of the moment replaced with humor.

"Sorry, Nathan," Andrew said. "I don't think we'll catch them."

We had a good laugh, then bid farewell to our company and returned to the street.

"That's pretty cool," Scott said.

"What's that?"

"That guy. He knew about the race." We started down the sidewalk. "He said he keeps an eye out for teams every year. That he remembers seeing a team three years ago really puts into perspective how excited he was about it. There's probably people that feel the same way about *us* being here." I glanced around. Stares still came our way. "To think they might remember us years from now...." He sighed. "It's cool we can bring that kind of excitement."

We walked on, nodding silent agreement.

Ahead was a small grocery store.

"Dessert, anyone?" I asked.

"Think they have a birthday cake?"

We walked into the store. The owner helped us pick out treats, guiding us toward favorites of his and his children. With a bag of Peruvian sweets, we made our way back to the hostel.

Inside, I learned a valuable lesson: never trust a fart—at least not after a bout of food poisoning.

I had been digging in my bag when the urge came. I had farted a few times in the past few days, so didn't think much of it—not until the supposed fart started to trickle down my crack. I clenched the whole walk to the communal bathroom.

I inspected the damage while seated on the toilet. Still mostly water. Sheepish at the fact that I was officially twenty-six years old and still crapping myself, I returned to our room to retrieve my toiletries and excused myself for a shower/laundry session.

My bed thanked me for my liberal use of soap as I crawled into it, clean and refreshed. It was not ignorant of such bodily functions. At least that's what the plastic-wrapped mattress suggested—the very talkative plastic-wrap. Every time I repositioned, it crinkled and squeaked. About the time I dozed off, I woke back up to snoring. Then diarrhea struck again. Then once more. I sat on the toilet, cursing the fact I was a light sleeper and cursing my diarrhea. I stumbled back to the room, situated at the end of a long, hallway, lit by a single, bare, incandescent bulb.

The door squeaked. The noise was not a problem though—our room was already noisy. The tune had changed though; the snoring had been replaced with unconscious moaning. My stomach wasn't the only one with issues.

Sleep did not come until the morning's early hours.

Chapter 28
Negotiation Navigation

"...WAKE?" THE SOUND WAS DISTANT.

I lay on my side. The mattress crinkled as my knees curled toward my chest. I grunted through the blanket draped over my head. The inflection made it a question.

"You awake?" Scott said again.

My eyes were fat with fatigue. No way could they be convinced to open. Instead, I slipped the blanket off my head and rolled to my back, letting the room's light fall on my face. Some photons made it through the skin of my eyelids, past my pupils, and illuminated the jelly inside my eyeballs. My optic nerves fired—a lovely tannish red. Maybe this was enough stimulation to stir me.

"Never mind," Scott chuckled. "Are you even alive?"

"Doesn't feel like it," I groaned. After a few deep breaths, I pleaded with my eyelids. They surprised me and parted. "Nope." The light was intense. "Definitely not among the living."

"Well you better get there," Scott said. He turned back to his things arranged on the bed in front of him. "We need to get going."

I sat up. Andrew was gone, likely to the bathroom. No hope for a rebellion against Scott, then. Maybe I could sleep in the mototaxi. "Here we go," I said to myself. I rocked out of bed and set to packing.

By the time Andrew got back, Scott was ready to go. He sat on his bed, the map spread in the air before him. Talk turned to the route while we finished packing, but the timeline wasn't making sense. Andrew and I crowded around Scott, fingers tracing our proposed path.

"We still have a lot of ground to cover."

"Then let's get going," Scott urged.

Andrew stood. "Scott, that's not…" Scott turned to Andrew, his expression a mix of confusion and expectancy. His thoughts hadn't aligned with ours; he didn't see what was coming. Andrew took a Band-Aid approach. "We might need to truck."

"No way!" Scott jumped to his feet. "We're doing good." He looked at me. "The mototaxi just got fixed." Back at Andrew. "We're cruising again!"

"Yeah, but we were never cruising fast enough to begin with. Our pace has been too slow from the start."

Scott collapsed the map's accordion folds. "Come on guys. No trucks. We've got this." He slung his bag onto his shoulder. "I'm going to do the walk around. Let's be out of here in fifteen minutes." Andrew and I exchanged a glance as Scott stalked out. We didn't talk, but finished packing and headed downstairs.

Loading took longer than anticipated, as we all decided to unpack an extra layer. The sky was drab, the atmosphere chilled. We pulled on sleeves. I unpacked my rain jacket too, and at full height again, I glanced around. The streets were quiet and the sidewalks unpopulated. A tingle sat behind my abs; waves of uncertainty crept through my limbs. Shop doors were closed and stoops empty. I bent over to secure our things.

Cindy's face disappeared as I snuck closed the green duffel's zipper, the song several octaves below its usual tune. Then I bent the blue tarp around our bags and tucked its edges in, as though folding a favorite blanket. As I stretched the ropes, the tarp's crackles were obnoxious. The morning shouldn't have been disrupted. Not because it was so calm, like a pristine pool of bright water you leave alone because of its beauty. Rather, the morning was stagnant, like the murky pool of dark water you don't disturb due to a primal fear of what's below the surface.

Packed, we crawled into the taxi. The engine's ignition was the most noise we had made before we pulled onto the main street of San Rafael, heading for the edge of town. All the buildings and doors were dark and still, oblivious to us. Without the stares and the sincere curiosity about our foreignness, the tingle in my core flickered faster, as if the white noise captured by an old television. I shifted in my seat. Were we sneaking out of town?

I sighed. Sneaking out? That made no sense. The town had been lovely; we had had a great time; and all of our interactions with the locals had been amazing. The taxi gave a lurch under a new gear, the throttle pushing the rpms higher. Maybe it wasn't the village we were sneaking away from. Maybe there was something else from which we wanted to conceal ourselves.

My forward-leaning posture was pulled back into the passenger bay by exhaustion. My back against the seat, the view was limited to the road ahead. We passed the edge of town, leaving only our engine's echoes, a goodbye deteriorated by the somber stillness.

The road was just as it had been the day before: dirt and gravel and uphill. Today though, the grade increased and the dreaded potholes made a resurgence. There would be no sleep in the back seat; I needed to be conscious to keep myself from being bucked out. Conscious, but not attentive.

My mind wandered. That is, until I stumbled upon a problem: why were we still climbing? Our map had no elevation marks along this route, no symbols to denote a mountain pass. All our major climbs to this point had been obvious on the map. So what was this? I shrugged it off. The road would probably level off around the next bend...or the next...maybe the next?

It didn't. The ravine funneled us higher and higher, the pale browns and tans seen around San Rafael transforming to the darker, richer browns that could host a whole slew of greens, mostly grasses and small shrubs. There were some trees, but fewer the higher we got. Despite the cool air, the climb pushed our engine to its heat capacity. We pulled over.

Even though we tried to sneak away from it, the tense atmosphere created in the hostel had followed us all morning. We left Clifford, each of us in a different direction to stretch our legs and recover some vitality. Andrew and I returned and we couldn't help but pull out the map.

We bent over it, scrutinized it. We counted the miles behind us and those ahead. My journal confirmed our tally of days and route conditions we had seen. Rough sections had taken much longer; so had stretches of climbing. And of course, our map didn't indicate rough or steep sections.

We consulted the GPS unit. We had spent the entire morning climbing. That was no secret. But the elevation we had gained thus far was impressive. We were already higher than the top of our first pass, back near Olmos. Andrew and I were encouraged by Clifford's performance, but not by our progress. The day's accumulated mileage was only half of what we had planned to cover by this point in the day. Andrew and I talked over the realism of our goals.

Scott hadn't come back to the mototaxi. He was just far enough away for our low mumblings to be lost among the whispers of the breeze. I made the short walk to where he stood: a small precipice that looked down the valley.

"Hey, Scott."

"What's up, Nate?" He didn't look at me.

I stepped next to him, mirroring his position. The view was narrow, constrained by high ridges on either side of us, the tops concealed by the clouds draped over them, like bed sheets on a clothesline whose white hems brushed green grass blades.

"We need to talk about our pace," I said with a low voice, afraid to disturb the valley. No response. "It's just too slow."

"Yeah?" Both hands were in his pants pockets, jacket was zipped.

"This is already day nine, and we're just over half way. So Andrew and I tried to extrapolate." He stayed quiet. "It's not just about making the Finish Party, or even the finish cutoff date." I kept staring down the valley, but concentrated on my peripheral vision. His head angled toward me. "At our pace, there's a chance we won't make it to Cusco to catch our flight."

Scott's head angled forward again. I stayed silent, waiting for that to sink in. This had surprised Andrew and I too, but there was no argument to be made against it.

"Hmmm." My peripheral vision detected a small movement: a bob of Scott's head. His audible thinking having already broken the silence, he continued. "I just didn't want to resort to that, you know? I really wanted to finish this thing."

"Me too." I kept my eyes forward. "And I still do." The sympathetic tone dropped out of my voice and I turned my head to look at him. "But it's not like we're giving up…or cheating. It's just not what we expected." The breeze carried away what was left of the morning's bad air. "We *are* going to finish this thing—maybe just not the way we'd imagined."

He nodded this time before turning to me. "Yeah, I guess so."

"Besides, we all want to be at the Finish Party, to see everyone again, to hear about the shit *they* went through," I said with a chuckle.

"Yeah," he said. "And we did all agree to finish with enough time to see Machu Picchu."

"That's true."

The dialogue stalled. Our eyes returned to their down-the-valley stare.

"Hey guys!" We both turned at Andrew's call. "Engine's cool. We can go whenever you're ready."

Our gazes returned to the valley for another long moment.

"You know…" I started back in, seeking a resolution. "…we don't have to truck the whole distance. We don't even need to worry about it today. But in the next two or three days, we do need to make some decisions."

His body turned to me. "Sounds good." I met his eyes. He must have seen some skepticism there. "Really," he assured, a strong gust of wind whipping our jackets. His eyes were softer, his shoulders held upright instead of folded forward. His enthusiasm had returned. Actually, I'm not sure Scott can operate without it. Rather, his enthusiasm had realigned. I was relieved to have the *Three Tired Travelers* united again.

He set his hand on my shoulder. "Ready to get going?"

I cracked a smile. "If you are."

He squeezed an additional affirmation. "Let's do it."

We walked back and prepared to leave. The boys crawled into the sofa half of the mototaxi while I pulled on gloves and took my position straddling the motorcycle half. I fired up the engine and eyed the road ahead of us. It drunkenly stumbled and crawled beneath stone outcrops, around cut banks, and past floodplains, the inefficient use of rock and gravel ever climbing until it vanished from sight.

I gave it some throttle and eased off the clutch. I called out, "Here we go!"

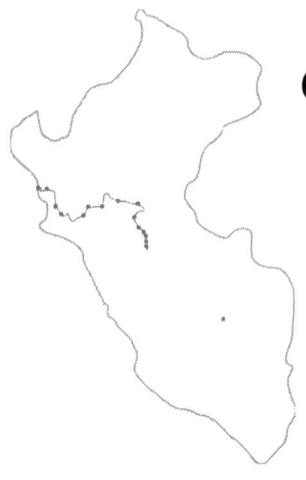

Chapter 29

Concert Hall

THE INEFFICIENT USE OF ROCK AND GRAVEL had become an inefficient use of pavement. The road smoother, our ride was a lot more enjoyable. Faster though? The grade had remained consistent. Dumbfounded, we all watched the altitude on the GPS unit tick away meter after meter.

3400m…

3500m…

3600m…

I glanced to the back seat. Andrew's shoulders shrugged. His hands secured one side of the map Scott was leaned over. Passes were marked. So what was this?

3700m…

3800m…

Would we break 4000 meters? Could the engine handle the elevation?

The road curved around a jutting outcrop, and the view opened. Our road, which had slithered all morning, now began to coil. It stretched up the valley in a straight line, made a wide, 180-degree arc across a hill, and climbed the other side of the valley. Opposite us was the mouth of a narrow ravine. Where ravine met valley, high above us, a rounded face of concrete stood out from the hillside, crowned by a guardrail.

A single eyebrow lifted.

I looked back at the road to correct my lane position before checking the GPS.

3900m...

There was no doubt—we would cross that altitude threshold we all had been so curious about. Why 4000 meters? When hearing about our intended route, one of our mechanics had laughed. He explained that mototaxis don't run well at high elevations because of the low oxygen availability. Because we didn't have a high-performance engine (or a decent-performance engine for that matter), it was more problematic than usual. There was little hope that adjusting the idle speed—the typical solution—would do much.

So, what had this mechanic considered to be high, to be the threshold above which we would have serious problems? You guessed it.

The LCD display showed the counter click right up to the threshold. I held my breath until...

4000m...

That's more than 13,000 feet above sea level...almost 2.5 miles.

I sighed, and the display clicked right past and continued the upward count in ten-meter increments. We rounded the large turn. While wrenching the handlebars by leaning backward off the left side of the seat, I chanced a glance at my teammates. Andrew gave a thumbs up. Scott shook his fists above his head—well, more like ear level, since there wasn't much room below the mototaxi's vinyl canopy.

The pavement straightened. Below—on the valley wall opposite us—was our road, smaller, the few cars and trucks along its length matchbox size. At the pinnacle of the view was a leftward curve, guided by a familiar guard rail. We rounded the bend and started up the ravine.

4050m...

My hands over gripped the handlebars—with excitement, not apprehension. Above 4000 meters and still running? The struggle was apparent, but was it any worse than any climb had been, at any elevation?

4100m...

Another small celebration. Every meter we gained was an act of rebellion, and I was leading the charge. But how long would this uprising last? We had no idea what this road was going to do. What if we started descending? It was time to give someone else a chance to drive at elevation too. I peeled my eyes for a shoulder.

The ravine walls were steep and the road narrow by necessity. Ahead of us, was...a pedestrian? I swerved to the center line, leaving room for the man on foot. My head snapped back for a closer inspection; but the road's curves brought my eyes forward again, just in time to pull onto a small patch of gravel.

Kill switch engaged. Usually when we stopped to cool the engine, it keeled over like a spoiled child at the end of his ignored dramatics. That the taxi didn't die on its own did not go unnoticed.

"Cooling the engine?" Andrew asked. He leaned forward, still seated. Scott had clambered out and was headed to the edge of the gravel for a look. Andrew's focus was on the mototaxi though, and there was a fearful suspicion in his eyes. There had been no sputtering, no strange noises. So why had I pulled over?

"Nope," I smiled. "Just wanted to pass the reigns while we're above 4000 meters."

Andrew leaned back. "Oh," he said with a disbelieving relief. "But does it feel like it's running ok?"

"I'm actually surprised by how good it's running."

He nodded, still seated in the back. "No loss of power?"

"Mmmm." Each word came out slower than the last: "Not that I can tell." The shadow of an inflection cast doubt on my assessment.

Andrew gave a skeptical look. My excitement faded, and I was more critical in my second analysis.

"Well, no," I said, my voice stronger and more certain. "I haven't noticed a loss of power. More than usual that is—so it is struggling, but it feels like it always does. However..." Andrew cocked an eyebrow. "...I have been driving for a while and we've been climbing the whole time. And the atmosphere has been thinning the whole time." Andrew's other eyebrow raised, considering my point. "If there was a change, I'm not sure I *could* have noticed."

He nodded. "So it's possible none of us would have noticed a change." His eyes flicked past me. I turned. Scott was walking back toward us, wondering aloud why we weren't taking in the view.

I turned back. "You should drive next. You're the only one who hasn't driven today. If anyone's going to notice a difference, it's you."

"Guys," Scott half yelled, only able to half suppress the delight in his voice. "You've got to see this view!" Andrew got out of the mototaxi and we started back to where Scott had been standing. "And did you see that guy?!"

"Yeah," I half yelled myself. "What was he doing?"

"I don't know," Scott shook his head. "He wasn't dressed like any Peruvian we've seen so..."

The thought went unfinished as we stepped to the edge of the gravel. We looked out at the landscape, our toes brushing the bent blades of bunch grasses that marked the boundary between safety and a long tumble.

Our atmosphere is mostly nitrogen and oxygen gasses, both of which scatter blue light. While other colors pass straight through, blue bounces every which direction, giving the sky its color. At elevation though, less atmosphere means fewer gaseous molecules to bounce the blue. So while the morning's slate gray had been replaced with a torn white sheet, the whole backdrop had become dark, strong, pronounced. Blue patches bled through the cloud edges to produce a whole palette of blues—it was more watercolor than reality.

Below, the crisp gold of dead grasses intermingled with the soft and too-fresh green of new shoots. Spiny shrubs were on their way to dark green, but with so few leaves, black branches darkened whole swatches of hillside. On a peak in the distance, a light beam illuminated the umber of decaying mosses. Among all this, sturdy gray outcrops and spines striped the hillsides, threatened only by the slow digestion of lichens.

The wind animated it. Air that shook the grasses and shrubs also stretched and reshaped the condensation above, shifting layers and sheets, casting to the ground wandering beams of light. Gusts of maniacal laughter rang in my ears while my hair was tousled and jacket whipped. In its warped hug, I realized I had a down jacket in the mototaxi. Before I could turn to go grab it, Scott spoke.

"What do you think those are?" He pointed.

In the bottom of the ravine, about twenty-five feet across, stood a series of stone circular structures.

"Animal pens?" Andrew guessed.

"Maybe old building foundations?" Further up the hill was another structure. Stone, but capped with a metallic sheeting; corrugated tin? "Maybe they were built by the people that live there," I said pointing.

At that moment, someone stepped out of the structure.

"Should we ask?" Scott joked.

We never got to laugh. When the woman had stepped out of the structure, she had called out.

Her voice rebounded off the opposing side of the ravine before she had finished. Anticipating the echo, she raised the pitch of her voice. It rang clear, several notes above the echo, and with such musical quality that she had to be intentionally harmonizing with herself. She stopped. But the tones continued to bounce, wall to wall, until the first faded to nothing, then the second.

Our heads snapped right, toward the sound of a return call. The man we had seen walking on the road. He was much higher in the ravine. His voice echoed only once. His reply was too short to need any tone adjustment.

Our eyes snapped back to the woman. Her response was longer, necessitating her voice climb higher through the octaves with each successive echo, timing the syllables into the gaps, the slight syncopation creating random rhythmic phrases as her voice climbed. The layering and overlapping created something between a chant and music.

Her tone dropped back to the first she had used, where the echoes had already faded. Her voice climbed again, so that mid tones were loudest, supported by low tones, and accented by lingering high tones. She stopped, but her choir continued, echoes dissipating in the sequence they appeared.

The greens, tan, and grays all flickered through the various shades of an applauding audience.

The man replied once more, then silence.

The air was calm, and though the ravine was quiet, the sounds still echoed within us.

Someone spoke. "Wow."

Then the wind returned, biting. My down jacket...the mototaxi. Before turning around, I stared, the extra moisture in my eyes wicked away.

We walked back to the mototaxi. It was understood that we were leaving. What else could be gained from this place? How could anything top that moment?

After we pulled on another layer, Andrew fired up the taxi, and we left. I turned around, and watched the shoulder disappear. Within minutes, we began to traverse the hill at the top of the ravine. We got one last look at the mysterious stone circles, at the stone hut, at the woman's concert hall before the road coiled back on itself and the ravine vanished.

Chapter 30

Altitude Antidotes

I WAS WEARING my base layer, both my shirts, my down sweater, and my jacket. My buff I wore as a beanie and I had zipped my down sweater to the collar. I had pulled on my jacket hood and, fully-zipped, the jacket came to my nostrils, which I now yelled through.

"Whadayahink?!"

No response from Andrew. I tapped his shoulder. When his head turned, I yelled again. His head shook. He *could* feel a difference in the taxi's performance. Not far past the singing ravine, we had crested. Well, technically we hadn't...the road had just stopped climbing. There was no top, no descent, just a flat plain. And even here, Andrew could feel a difference.

I leaned back, hugging my body. If Clifford's performance was getting worse, then we had made the right choice to go to Cerro de Pasco. It wasn't on our route, but it was the only notable city we could hope to reach that day.

As we approached the city though, I called that decision into question. It had been another short climb to the outskirts. We were pushing 4,300 meters now, 14,100 feet—2.7 miles above sea level.

The landscape was barren, tans and greens absent. The ground was one rocky outcrop where only the most persistent of soils collected in strange angular fractures and windblown hollows. The quality of the soil was reflected in the minimal plant life present, their greens an aching hue of desperation.

Closer to town were the occasional structures. Industrial maybe? They were made of concrete, rebar ends poking past wall surfaces and through the tops of columns. Most were abandoned, bolstering the despair that came from the environs. More inspiring was the city's arch. Every Peruvian city had an archway that straddled the main road. The arches we had seen so far had all flowed gracefully over the roadway as a single arc, painted a warm red. This one: angular shafts of concrete, propped against each other to make a triangle. I cringed. Hopefully no fragments would flake off and fall onto us as we passed below.

We made it through unscathed, but where was the city? The arch was usually in the thick of it. But there was nothing here. A few small buildings on the ridge ahead, but apart from that…

"Holy shit!"

The words made it through my jacket, no problem. The mound on our right had fallen away, the slope running down from us to reveal the city. It was as if the city had been built inside a funnel and we were driving along the rim. The slope below was covered in roofs of a hundred shades and sheens of gray. Beyond this slope, the city extended and wrapped around the hill, circling back onto itself.

Scott laughed and turned to me. "Welcome to Cerro de Pasco!"

Cerro de Pasco is one of the highest cities in the world at 14,210 feet (4,330 meters) above sea level. Like many high elevation cities, this one was sustained by mining. Also sustained by the mining have been a slew of health problems caused by lead poisoning, where piles of tailings sit adjacent to urban neighborhoods and not far from schools and health clinics. In 2008, Peru's congress passed Law No. 29293. It's objective: relocate the entirety of Cerro de Pasco, a city of

70,000 people. Six years after the passing of the law, no progress had been made.

Though its funnel-like geography gave us quite a view of the city, it did not help us navigate into its depths. On top of that, the mototaxi was struggling. Conserving our momentum on the open road had helped performance; the stop and go of a city did not.

After an hour of aimless driving with the occasional engine failure, we paid a mototaxi driver to guide us through the city. After a block, our taxi died. He circled back around and parked ahead of us. We vacated the taxi and propped the front tire of our taxi into the cargo bay of his. Then we all three squeezed into his back seat.

Our second tow.

This was the sight delivered to the mechanic: three *gringos* with borderline altitude sickness stumbling out of a mototaxi towing a similarly altitude plagued taxi with a number of other underlying issues that prevented it from running. Scott talked to the mechanic, and, as often happened around Scott, a group convened. It wasn't long before men were laughing, the mototaxis in need of fixing falling by the wayside.

Scott brought them back around and talked more seriously with the mechanic. He agreed to help, but after he finished with a few other taxis. We took a seat on the sidewalk, Clifford parked in line with a few other taxis on the side of the low-traffic street. There was a break in the clouds and sunlight fell across our sidewalk. The rays were intense, the thin atmosphere not able to filter the sting from their warmth. I spread my legs out to absorb the rays. I reveled as the warmth spread through me, and still sitting up, I drifted into sleep.

* * *

Another hot mug was set in front of me at another restaurant, vapor dancing in the thermal currents above the surface of the liquid. I leaned forward to peer into the mug. Not coffee. The liquid was a light hue, letting light penetrate to the bottom and then escape again, revealing the leaves. I grinned and looked at Scott and Andrew.

"Do you guys know what kind of tea this is?"

They both leaned forward.

Scott looked up first. "Is this..."

Andrew, still staring into his mug, finished *and* answered Scott's question. "Coca tea."

Resting idly beneath the wisps of steam coming from my mug, the leaves looked innocent enough. Especially since we knew they would help our altitude sickness. They certainly didn't seem as though they could create a whole drug trade.

Ceramic plates clacked as they were set onto the thick table and slid in front of us, piled high with food.

My upward-sitting sleep at the mechanic's had been interrupted by the choking protests of our mototaxi. According to Andrew—who had been watching the mechanic work on Clifford—no real improvements had been made. Scott joined us and we had discussed the trucking option. The engine was struggling at elevation. If there was a leg we had to truck, this stretch would be a good candidate. Scott had asked the mechanic about a truck and before long, a meeting with a driver had been arranged. With some time to kill, we went for food.

Our plates were half-cleared and mugs full, leaves still steeping, when two men stepped into the restaurant. They did not sit, but stayed at the door, their Spanish capturing Scott's attention. He turned in his seat, spoke a few words of his own. They gave an explanation.

"Sí. Claro." He turned in his chair and began to stand saying, "This is the truck owner and his driver. They want to talk outside."

We stepped outside. We confirmed the destination of Huancayo, a suggestion from the mechanic because it was a major city. Apart from covering a good chunk of ground to get there, its size guaranteed plenty of mechanics and, if worst came to worst, another trucking option. But their price was more than double what had been quoted over the phone.

We had expected a price jump, but not double. Scott haggled, but they wouldn't budge. We took a different approach. Scott said we needed to discuss it as a team. We arranged to meet them at the mechanic's shop in half an hour—plenty of time to reach a decision and to finish our interrupted meal. Plenty of time to let them sweat.

Back at our meal, we talked it over. The cost seemed expensive, especially since the price had doubled. But trucking meant less stress over the mototaxi and gaining ground on the other teams. Once we converted to $US, it seemed a fair price for peace of mind and we agreed we would pay it.

Our plates clear and mugs empty, we returned to the street. If we were going to truck, we needed a picture of the taxi loaded up—that would fulfill one of our *Peru Bingo* squares. If the truck ever came…

After an hour, the truck still hadn't shown. Sure, it was possible there had been a miscommunication. But Scott had proven his Spanish abilities numerous times. Probably the men hadn't anticipated us accepting their terms, and so bailed on the arrangement altogether.

Their loss, sure…but ours as well.

The decision already made, we began to search for another truck. We wandered the area, unable to find the trucking garage the mechanic had told us about. When we returned, a group of men had reconvened, most of them brought by rumors of mototaxi-driving *gringos*. Hearing our troubles, several men made suggestions. One even pulled out his cell phone and started making calls.

The man arranged the whole thing for us, and for the same price we had already agreed to. Within thirty minutes, the truck arrived. It was a large box truck, with no ramp. So the group of men crowded around our mototaxi and ten of us lifted it the four feet into the back. Shouting and smiling our thanks, the three of us crammed into the two passenger seats in the cab, and we began the spiraling climb out of the pit of Cerro de Pasco.

Chapter 31
Pearl of the Andes

Cerro de Pasco

I SMILED at the central highlands of Peru through the passenger side window of our truck, but not in wonder at the view, for the scene carried only a desolate kind of beauty. Rather, I was smiling at the fact that I wasn't crossing the central highlands by mototaxi. The cold was still biting, which didn't pair well with the landscape's monotony. But inside our fast-moving truck, my cheeks were flushed.

For the first hour, we followed one long, flat stretch of pavement. It was a decent road, one Clifford would have liked. But then we made an abrupt left turn, abandoning the pavement for a gravel road, one defined by a dreaded feature: washboards.

We had our map handy and Scott, squished between Andrew and me, flattened the folds in front of us.

The paved road we had just abandoned stretched all the way to Huancayo. It was the obvious route, the one *we* would have taken. So where were we going? Scott asked our driver.

"He says this route is better." We bobbed up and down in the seat, jarred by the larger bumps.

"Better?" Andrew's eyebrows shot up. "Is he on the same road as us? This is not better."

"I don't know." Scott's shoulder shrug stalled under the bodily resistance of Andrew and me. "He does make this drive a lot."

"I guess," I said in a washboard vibrato. "But my brain is rattling inside my skull. I'd take the extra half hour if it meant smooth pavement."

There were large trucks on the road, but not much other traffic. That made sense. Who would want to be on this road? Vehicles resonated with the washboards, humming, threatening to fall apart.

After half an hour, a symbol of modernity appeared. The structure grew as we crested a hill and approached, making our way around its base. It loomed over us, a pale tan building flanked by steel towers and all manner of confused and tangled piping, some only a few inches in diameter, others a few feet.

The driver spoke to Scott, forcing a chuckle. The insides of Scott's eyebrows raised while the outsides curled downwards just slightly. "Sí?" The driver nodded. Scott mimicked the driver's laughter, muttering, "Claro."

"Apparently," Scott began, giving up the gossip, "this building is a concrete plant."

"But," Andrew leaned forward, forcing his shoulder from its cramped position behind Scott's so he could look out the windshield, "it's in the middle of nowhere."

"Yeah," Scott continued. "Trucks drive a long way to deliver it. And there are loooooots of trucks."

I nodded. "That explains the washboards."

"Why wouldn't they pave the road?" Andrew said.

The front driver-side wheel hit a large bump, letting the cab dip before rebounding and sending Andrew into Scott into me, who bounced off the door back into Scott, who bounced back into Andrew.

"And miss out on potholes like that one?"

The conversation was cut short by another deafening section of washboards. Shockwaves moved through the jelly of my eyeballs and blurred my vision.

We had followed the road three-fourths of the way around the cement factory. The only explanation for this roundabout route was the immensity of the concrete plant; it was so massive that its gravity had curved the road into an ellipsis, like the orbit of our planet around the sun. If only our ride was as smooth. The occasional meteoric hiccup wouldn't be so bad, but the endless earthquake that was our gravel road was driving us...

Another bump—not a meteor impact or earthquake aftershock, but the transition from gravel to a hard, consistent road surface.

The silence was... Well, it wasn't. The engine still purred, the rpms rising and falling at the commands of the throttle and transmission; our seats still squeaked; there was a heartbeat pounding in my ears. So much noise, but in the absence of the washboards, it was all discernible.

The new road surface came up against a low rock wall and then dropped. The valley floor was naturally terraced, each floodplain making an abrupt descent to the next. The concrete plant disappeared behind us, but villages and farms stretched down the valley.

We passed through the first small village, the road of cobblestones flanked by pink and reddish walls on either side, only wide enough for a single vehicle. Other streets were infrequent, and the village roads meant for motorized traffic were few. At the angular collisions of streets, I craned my neck to look up the incoming road only to find more walls.

Below the village, the valley showed off its cultivars. Hillsides sucked up the red light in their molecular traps while casting out greens and blues. The clouds broke and threw an intense light over the valley, and the sun was soaked up to staggering effect. The bleached browns of wooden fences, the eroded tans of rock walls, and the enriched reds of the soil made the black leaves and their blue shadows deeper. It was like watching a painting get darker under a brighter light.

Where the hill crested above us, small backlit shadows moved against the sky. My head snapped to the opposite side of the valley. The hill was dotted with people, strolling between rows of crops, bobbing in and out of sight, with large baskets propped on a hip. Most were working their way down to the road, another day behind them, ready to return home.

The road continued to drop stepwise, the valley walls growing larger. The crops which had dominated in the upper reaches of the valley became interspersed with unmaintained natural vegetation; lower in the valley, the landscape transformed to natural vegetation interspersed with crops. The drive had been silent, our eyes too busy to allow our mouths any freedom.

Tarma, the Pearl of the Andes, jumped in front of us then. Really. This city is so well concealed within the deep valleys and gorges of the Andean foothills that it was impossible to see it coming. Now we were driving down narrow streets, edging through crowds of foot traffic, our route crossing back and forth over what appeared to be the main thoroughfares, though they were quite underwhelming, as if the growing mountains were squeezing everything in the town closer together.

The streets emptied as people made their way to restaurants, to markets, to home. The driver picked up some speed and we were able to get out of town faster than we had made it in. Our street fell out from the confines of the tall buildings and began to wind up the hillside, escaping the shade of the valley.

We swung through switchback after switchback, all hidden among the various homes covering the hillside. Our last switchback had a guardrail and a view though, and below us was Tarma, spread out like a spilled drink, the appendages of buildings extending up each of the several valleys that all intersected at the town center. The nose of the truck angled through this last turn and we popped up onto another flat plain. Behind us, Tarma was gone, every trace of it concealed from sight in the valleys below.

* * *

It was late.

The sun had set hours ago.

Tarma was a distant memory.

The four of us lowered Clifford from the cargo bay of the truck. Well, really, the four of us slowed his fall to the street. Handling the weight had been much easier with ten men.

The driver spoke to Scott, pointing up and down the street we were on. It was a branch off the main artery that led into the city's center. Scott nodded at the driver and gave our thanks.

Huancayo is Peru's fifth most populous city with 380,000 people, and is considered the cultural and commercial hub of the central Peruvian Andes region. It lies in the Mantaro Valley, an unusual geographic feature of the Andes given its broad valley floor that is filled with cultivatable soils, making the area an important agricultural center for the Andes as well. The city derives its name from the Huanca, a Quechuan people who were conquered and subsequently incorporated into the Incan empire, but who later—during the Spanish conquest—provided men and supplies to the Spanish army.

"Well," Scott said, turning back to Andrew and me, "he says this street has a lot of hostels on it. They get a lot of people from the road, so most should still be open. We might even find a restaurant that hasn't closed yet."

The truck fired up and pulled away from the curb. It made a U-turn, and the driver waved as he passed by.

We watched it go, standing in a silence that felt out of place in the city.

"Shall we?" Andrew said.

He and Scott took off to the nearest hostel, leaving me with Clifford. If we couldn't find a good price here, we would drive down the street to the next group of hostels. Just in case, I decide to warm up the engine. Ten minutes later, I straddled the taxi's motorcycle seat, my elbows propped on the handlebars, my forehead resting on my crossed arms. I couldn't get it running. I had tried every trick I had learned in the past couple of weeks, but the engine didn't even sputter.

The drive from Cerro de Pasco had been relaxing on a mental level. It was not at all physically comfortable, but it was a welcome change to not have to worry about the taxi, to not fear having to troubleshoot a mechanical problem, to not be disappointed with or even concerned about our pacing. In Cerro de Pasco, we had estimated it would have taken a day and a half to cover what we would cover in the truck. But on the outskirts of Huancayo, after crossing the landscape, we decided it would have actually taken three days on the mototaxi. Not only was that a huge disparity, but it carried uncomfortable implications about the rest of our projected progress.

"Nathan!" I lifted my head. Scott and Andrew walked toward me from across the street. "This is the one." Relief surged through me. "It's a really nice room. And a fair price." Scott said, Andrew nodding beside him. "And there's a garage just up the street where we can store the taxi. So fire this thing up!"

They got to the mototaxi, eyebrows raised when I didn't move to start the engine.

"Umm…" I started. "…about that."

Together, we pushed Clifford back up the street and into a gated courtyard with some flimsy tarp coverings for shade. In the hostel, we discussed our options for the following day. Push on with Clifford? Find another truck? Would the train be an option? The taxi not starting wasn't something that had happened before. We had tried again in the garage, each of us making several attempts. Had the truck ride caused something that prevented it from starting? Our consensus was to not worry about it. At least, not until morning.

Each of us in our own beds, we laid down.

Sleep came easily.

Chapter 32

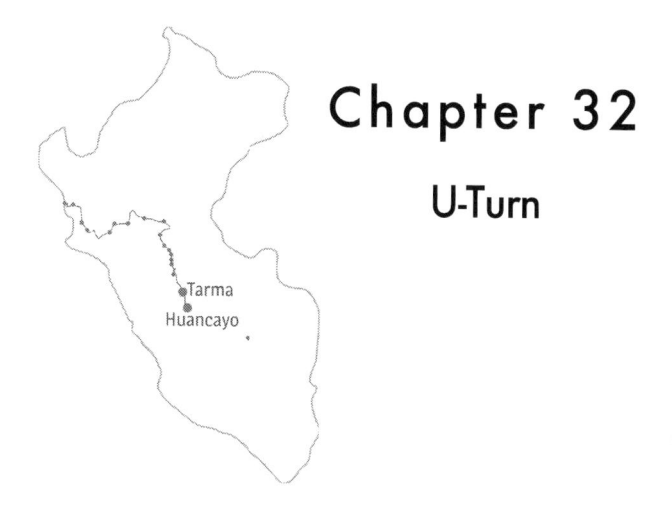

U-Turn

Tarma
Huancayo

INHALATION. EXHALATION.

My forehead's thin film of sweat started to bead. My heart thrummed. The mototaxi had been so resistant to starting that we had been taking turns at the kick-starter. After fifteen minutes of near-continual kicking, the engine had sputtered for the first time since Cerro de Pasco. It sounded like mechanical death, but at the same time, like hope.

Now, I crouched above the seat, chest bent over the handlebars so I wouldn't hit my head on the canopy. I focused, pushing all my mental capacities into the toes of my right foot, concentrating the energy there as though the electricity of my central nervous system would spark the cylinder. My left foot took my weight as my right foot settled into position on the starter lever.

One kick.
Nothing…
Two kicks.
Nothing…
Three kicks.
A sputter…

The sound startled me. The engine was actually grasping for life. Shock was cut short by instincts. I eased the throttle back and forth, milking it, giving the engine small bursts of fuel to build its appetite before serving it a feast. My wrist broke backward, further and further with each roll until...

The engine caught its rhythm. Andrew and Scott shouted. I revved the engine higher. It sounded horrible. Andrew and Scott froze at the sound, celebratory fists stalled above their heads. I continued to work the throttle. The sound, it was still rhythmic...but not good. Our engine may as well have been gargling.

I sat now, feeling Clifford's vibrations in my legs. He may have sounded awful, but he felt normal. I cut back on the throttle and started to bring the engine down to an idle. Scott and Andrew, arms crossed now, watched with clenched jaws as the decibels bouncing around the garage dropped. My wrist action reached subtlety and then stillness. I eased my grip and straightened my fingers. My eyes wouldn't blink, wouldn't twitch away from the throttle grip. They remained poised on the target so I could make a quick save if necessary. The seconds passed though, and the rhythm was unbroken.

I looked to Andrew and Scott, both leaning forward. I lifted my right hand from its hovering position above the grip and brought it to shoulder level, leaving Clifford to idle independently. Andrew's body relaxed, straightened, and he gave a nod of his head. Scott threw his arms up and ran his hands through his hair.

"Shall we?" I said, shoulders shrugging. "I know we have no idea where we're going, but right now we at least have the *option* of going."

Scott and Andrew glanced at each other.

"It doesn't sound good," Andrew said, eyeing the engine.

Scott laughed. "Yeah, but..." Both hands opened toward the engine. "...it's running."

Andrew looked back at me, at my eyebrows raised to just above optimism. His pursed lips parted as he turned to Scott and said, "Let's grab the door."

I pulled onto the empty street, pausing long enough to let the guys jump in the back. We headed back to the thoroughfare.

After experiencing the ease of trucking and then losing even more confidence in our mototaxi, we decided to truck another leg. That decision was made even easier by the complete lack of Junket teams we had seen the previous day, even moving at the faster pace of the truck. Was it just because of our route? Bad timing? Or were we actually that far behind?

Our plan was to find a bus or train station. We figured transportation hubs overlap, so maybe we could find a lead at one of these terminals. The plan was simple enough…on paper.

On the streets of Huancayo though, our plan was less than ideal. Driving around in search of road signs with a bus or train symbol was hopeless. Getting directions was difficult. And the city was too big for us to accidentally stumble upon something.

We spotted a traffic cop. I made a hard turn onto a side street to stop and let Scott work his magic. With vague directions to a train terminal, we plunged down a single-lane road, the high buildings funneling us into a mess of crooked streets and no-left-turn intersections decorated with an array of road signs that I swear all displayed the same name.

Miraculously, we found the road we were supposed to be on—the traffic was insane. I dusted off those horn-honking skills and let Clifford shout, "Excuse me," "Sorry! *Gringo* at the wheel," and "Can you please let me in? I'm dying."

This didn't help as we approached a crucial intersection. I was trapped in the flow of left-turning traffic when we had the last-second realization that we needed to go straight. A braver man would've gone for it.

"We'll just make a U-turn," I shouted.

"Yeah," Scott shouted back. "I got the street name. I know where we're going."

The turn complete, I began to make my way from the right side of traffic to the left, hoping for an intersection where we could turn around. But a pair of railroad tracks ran down the middle of the road, flanked by guard rails, separating the two directions of motorized traffic. We took the tracks to be a good sign, but they were a nuisance nonetheless. We had to travel several blocks before I spotted a crossing. That was when it happened: the engine gave a death-cough.

My heart skipped. The engine had always died on country roads and in small villages where there was no such thing as an inopportune moment. The possibility of stalling on the busiest road in one of Peru's biggest cities hadn't occurred to me...until that cough.

The single cough became a second, which morphed into a sputter. I milked the throttle and established the smooth rhythm again as we coasted to the intersection. We made it halfway through the U-turn when we stopped on the tracks, traffic whipping past in front of and behind us. I squeezed the clutch and revved the engine, trying to keep Clifford alive. His sputtering only worsened.

Andrew tapped my shoulder and pointed through the traffic. "There! A parking spot."

An oasis in this desert of hope.

"But the train station." I worked the throttle. "We're so close."

"We won't make it. The engine's ready to die."

"Nathan!" Scott slapped my other shoulder. "Here comes a break."

Down the road, a gap in the cars was approaching. I nosed out as far as I dared, reducing the distance left of the three lanes we needed to cross. I revved the throttle higher, willing the engine to stay alive for a few more seconds. If it died mid-road, we were screwed. The gap came. I wrenched back on the throttle and let out the clutch. We crossed the three lanes before the engine choked and lurched. Another desperate surge on the throttle got us to the curbside parking spot. The engine died before we stopped.

"Well done, Nathan," Scott said from behind.

"No," I shook my head. "I missed the turn. If I hadn't, we might have made it before the engine died."

Andrew spoke above the roar of traffic. "Is it just hot?"

I ran my hand through the space around the engine.

"It's hot for sure. *Just* hot though, who knows?"

"Hey," Scott said hopping out of the taxi and onto the sidewalk. "There's another traffic cop down there. I'm going to go make sure we have the right directions." He took off.

Andrew and I did a walk around, traffic threatening to tag our shoulders on the street side. It did seem like the engine was just hot. Hopefully after it cooled, we could start it again. We moved into the shade of a building.

Scott returned and repeated the directions, working them into his memory while the engine cooled. According to the cop, we were close. This small glimmer of hope was beginning to brighten our little patch of sidewalk when a passerby broke our circle.

"Mmmm...is that..." he said, struggling with the words. "Is that your...taxi?"

English? From a Peruvian's mouth? It had been a long time since that had last happened. He took our silence as affirmation. "It's..." He went with body language and pointed "...look."

We turned. Gasoline dripped from the carb into a small puddle. Then it erupted into a waterfall that cascaded down the engine, sending clouds of gas vapors into the air with a violent hiss. We gave a collective yell and rushed for the mototaxi's fuel valve.

Back on the sidewalk, we watched the spilled gasoline boil off while talking to our new hero, Cesar. His English was quite good now that he was calm. He had learned a lot of English while living in Idaho (the state adjacent to our native Washington) and was using it to figure out what three *gringos* were doing with a gasoline-spouting mototaxi.

"Piura to Urubamba? That's quite a drive," he said before turning to the taxi. "Mototaxi or not."

Further questioning brought our mechanical issues to light, as did the cloud of gas vapor, and our desire to find a truck. Cesar knew of a place, a shipping company. It was only a few blocks away.

"Can you give us directions?"

"Yes." He thought for a second. "But I will take you there."

"Really?"

Cesar nodded enthusiastically while we exchanged glances.

"Well," Andrew started, "it might be a while before the taxi cools down. Not to mention it might not start. And if it does, we might spray fuel everywhere again."

"Yes," Cesar chuckled. "That's why we are going to push it."

"Push?" I glanced at the bustling traffic. "Down *this* road?"

"Of course." He smiled. "We are not far from the trucks."

Pushing a mototaxi down the road was not what we had wanted to do. But Cesar's confidence inspired us to do just that. So for fifteen minutes, the four of us walked the mototaxi down the right side of the road, the outside lane of traffic aggressively merging left while their horns blasted "What gives?" and "Out of the way!"

I was hunched under the canopy, pushing and steering. I glanced at the three pushing at the back, and had to smile. Who had ever pushed a mototaxi down one of the busiest roads in Huancayo in peak morning traffic, Peruvian or not? I thought back to Emma and laughed.

Cesar led us all the way to the shipping company as promised. Then translated. This company was no help. They would ship the mototaxi, but without us, and not until the day after we needed to arrive. After Cesar explained our situation, an employee suggested a smaller trucking company down the street.

While they went in search, I stayed with Clifford. It was the same story: lots of stares. But I was used to it by this point and tried to engage some people with my limited Spanish. Two women were interested enough for me to provide our letter of explanation. They had some difficulty reading it, but I pointed out all the important bits. They smiled and said something I didn't understand while making the sign of the cross. At least we had some prayers coming our way.

Down the street, Andrew and Scott—with the help of Cesar—had worked out a deal. A truck would pick us up that afternoon and take us and the mototaxi to Ayacucho, the last major city before Urubamba.

"So we have some time to kill?" I asked.

"Yeah, a few hours," Andrew said.

"What do we do until then?"

"Explore," Scott said.

After we said our goodbyes and offered many thanks to Cesar, we pushed our mototaxi down the street to the shipping company, which agreed to store it until our truck arrived. With the taxi safely stowed, we set out into the city, on foot.

Chapter 33

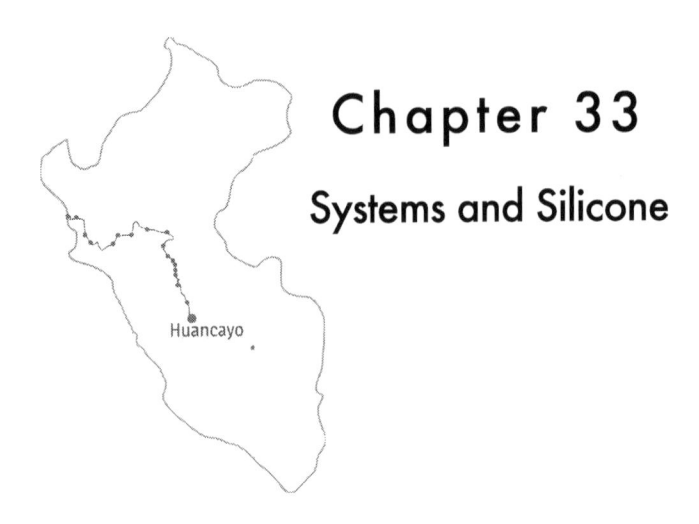

Systems and Silicone

WE WANDERED through a large, indoor market spread across multiple stories in multiple buildings. We strolled past stalls filled with purses, shoes, hats, sweaters and emerged at the top of a flight of stairs. The steps fell to a wide, open floor, the entirety of which we could see below.

The room was lit by skylights mounted in a series of A-frame roof segments held up by large green columns. Several partitioned, three-walled stalls stood in rows running across the floor. The first row of booths was tiled and plumbed and decorated with cookware—kitchenettes. Each had a small counter mounted on the open side, under which sat a few stools. Some were occupied, plates of food steaming in front of their patrons. This must have been the food court.

In the next row, meat hung on the walls and dangled from thin wires stretched across the stalls. At the top of the stairs, the aromas of the kitchenettes were suppressed by the fragrance of rawness. There was something missing from this row though.

Nitrosyl hemochromogen: if raised in Western society, this color might be one of your favorites. Or, at least, one of your favorite pigments. Let me explain.

Sodium nitrite is as ubiquitous as any chemical, with a long history that stretches back through the Middle Ages of Europe, past the 10th century AD in the Byzantine Empire, and into the 2nd century AD in China. Some scholars even claim that Bible passages reference this salt specifically. This rich history is due in large part to its antimicrobial and antioxidant properties, both of which are necessary to prevent food spoilage. As such, sodium nitrite has long been used as a curing agent. It also adds to the flavor and aroma of meat. But from a marketing standpoint, maybe the most important function of sodium nitrite is to provide color, one missing from this market.

We descended the stairs and crossed the room, the smell of meat pungent. Vendors displayed several cuts, which included whole pork legs, headless chickens, fleshy cow skulls, and small mammals still recognizable. And the meat? No reds. No pinks. Just the flat gray of aging and oxidation.

Hemoglobin was the primary oxygen-carrying protein in the circulatory system of all the vertebrates hanging in these stalls. This is the same protein that gives blood its red *and* blue color by virtue of the bonds formed by the iron atom at its center. One such bond is with nitrite. When hemoglobin picks up nitrite—in the same way it does oxygen—it creates the pigment known as nitrosyl hemochromogen, and a familiar red color is produced.

When strolling past the meat wall at your supermarket, the reason the meat is not gray is because of this salt. Yes, the sodium nitrite pushes the expiration date, but it also produces that familiar pigment, turning the meat a lovely shade of appetizing.

That shade wasn't a marketing device here. There was no sodium nitrite to be found, and no nitrosyl hemochromogen either.

My eyes scanned the grayish cuts before flicking between the first and second row of stalls. Such a large cultural difference, the raw meat being so close to where people routinely prepared and ate food. What does that say about Western cleanliness? Is it a means which promotes sanitary practices with better health outcomes? Or has this cleanliness become its own end, its own cultural obsession?

We left the market and continued through the streets past more shops and smaller markets and a church capped with a blue dome. After a few hours, we started back. If our truck showed up early, we didn't want it leaving without us.

We were too early getting back to the garage though...way too early. And since our bodies weren't using the time to explore, it was our minds that did the wandering.

"You don't think a system which contains information has cognitive abilities?"

Scott threw his arms wide. "Of course not!" He fell against the mototaxi's canopy, looking at me. I was in the back seat, knees bent, feet resting on the driver's seat back.

To kill time, Andrew was tearing apart the carb. Meanwhile, Scott and I were discussing books that were fresh in our minds. The book I had brought along for the ride was Lewis Thomas' *Lives of a Cell*, a collection of essays written by a biologist. One of the major themes he presented was that life is scalable. A cell, organ, animal, ecosystem: the lines which separate these—the lines we draw between *inside* and *outside*—are fairly arbitrary.

Scott sighed. "Look, I can have a spreadsheet of data. But just because it contains information, that doesn't make it intelligent."

"Right," I nodded. "But that's a database, not a system. The spreadsheet isn't doing anything with the information."

Another biology concept fresh in my mind was presented in Maturana and Varela's book *Autopoiesis and Cognition*. They argued that a self-regulating process is a form of cognition, and therefore, all living systems are cognitive systems.

"Ok," Scott conceded. "So if the spreadsheet has a basic algorithm that crunches the data, you're saying that's cognition?"

Andrew was seated on an overturned bucket next to the mototaxi's engine. He looked up.

"Well..." I considered my initial thesis. "...if the data somehow affects the function of the spreadsheet, then yeah."

Scott pushed off the taxi and looked to the sky. "But it doesn't even know it's processing information!"

Scott was going crazy over an idea I had proposed. Just like when I combined a rock climbing technique with a bowel movement, I couldn't resist hybridizing the concepts presented in these books for the sake of invigorated ideas.

"But it doesn't need to know!" I yelled back. I'm saying cognition is scalable across those arbitrary lines of life. I didn't say anything about awareness."

Scott gave me a cynical squint. "Are you kidding me?"

"Why not? Think of beehives, anthills, termite colonies. The individuals in these superorganisms don't realize their behavior is actually a self-regulating process. They literally don't have enough brain cells to know what they're doing. But they are still a part of a self-regulating process, a cognitive process."

Scott gave me a placating shrug. "Sure...but how does that scale?"

"Think about it. Remember the ants we saw, my David Attenborough narration? Individually, those ants were unaware of how their behavior affected the colony as a whole. And there's the famous example of wolves in Yellowstone. Reintroducing the wolves completely altered the park's ecology. But it's not as if the wolves did it on purpose. So what if *we* are the ants? Or the wolves? What if our behavior is somehow part of a self-regulating process that we are just completely blind to?

After a moment, Scott just shook his head, unconvinced. Andrew stated his skepticism with silence.

I wagged my finger. "I don't think you get what I'm saying." Scott scoffed as I straightened up, restructuring my argument. Andrew's eyes wandered back to the carburetor.

The conversation continued on in circles, until...

"Holy crap," Andrew said from the overturned bucket, half the carburetor in each of his hands. He held them out to Scott and me. "No O-ring." The two channeled grooves which would have held the O-ring were both empty.

"That explains why gas was spraying everywhere this morning," Scott said.

"Yeah," Andrew said as he stood. "Doesn't explain why the taxi is running like crap though."

"Every little bit helps. Should I see if I can pick up a new one?" Scott asked.

We had covered a fair amount of ground that morning, both by taxi and by foot. "I don't remember seeing any mototaxi parts stores or mechanics around here."

Scott glanced at his watch. "And the driver should be here soon."

Andrew cocked his head to the side. "Well, I do have a silicone gel I can put in the groove temporarily."

I put my finger back up. "Haven't we tried that before? I don't remember that turning out well."

Andrew nodded. "Yeah, but in Chamaya we didn't give the silicone a chance to set. We immediately turned the fuel on and fired up the engine. If we let it dry, it might work."

"How long does it take to dry?"

"A few hours. It could be good to go by the time we get to Ayacucho."

"What if the gas dissolves it like last time?" Scott said.

Andrew, still sitting on the upturned bucket, opened his hands to the dismantled components in front of him. "I am getting pretty comfortable cleaning the carb."

Scott and I gave each other a half-shrug followed by an approving nod. "Go for it," Scott said. "I'm going to go check on our ride." He headed for the office.

Over the next two hours, Scott made several trips between the mototaxi and the office, searching for information. Everyone he talked to said our ride was coming, it's still coming, it's still on the way, it's en route. But no one could say when it would arrive.

Then, in the following hour, everyone seemed to forget who we were. They didn't know what we were talking about, didn't know what arrangement had been made that morning, didn't know what truck we were asking about. How could you forget the *gringos* with the mototaxi? Was our driver actually three hours late? Or had we been left behind?

"Wait!" Scott said, eyes squinting toward the front of the garage. "That's the guy from this morning." Scott took off.

Our time in the garage had been stressful given the uncertainty of our future, but Andrew had still made good use of it. He had cleaned the carb, reassembled it with the gel, and remounted it. After he cleaned and organized his tools, we sat in the back seat together munching on some cereal that had been packed away next to Cindy, who, despite the heat and her plastic cocoon, was still doing quite well, proven by her continued singing of *Yankee Doodle*.

"You want any more of this?" I angled the open end of the bag toward Andrew.

"Nah."

I made my way to the cargo rack to pack away the cereal. I glanced toward the front of the garage.

"Looks like Scott found someone who remembers us." I leaned against the mototaxi, trying to get a sense of how the rest of our day was going to turn out. The local was nodding his head and talking to another employee. Then he pulled out a cell phone. Scott turned and gave a thumbs up.

"It's looking good," I said to Andrew.

The phone went back into the man's pocket with a lot of head-nodding. Scott repeatedly pointed to the watch on his wrist. There was more nodding and then the trio disbanded.

Scott came back, walking a little taller and with a little more bounce in his step.

"That guy remembered us from this morning and knew exactly what I was talking about," Scott said. "He couldn't believe we were still here, so he called the driver to make sure he hadn't left us. Apparently there was some bad traffic. He's only 10 minutes away."

Twenty minutes later, he arrived.

We had relocated to the street. Not only was our driver's arrival time underwhelming, so was his vehicle: a Toyota Hilux, the equivalent of a Tundra. This was going to cart our mototaxi? Would the taxi even fit? A slow groan leaked from my chest. Had we just wasted the whole day waiting for a ride that wouldn't be able to take us? The box truck had hardly been wide enough for the taxi; the Hilux was smaller, right? Scott ran off to find our contact.

Andrew and I stood, staring at the pickup. Scott returned, standing shoulder to shoulder with Andrew and me. "Yup, this is our ride. And they are *fully* aware that we are bringing the taxi." Andrew and I turned to each other, our faces skeptical.

This *was* an adventure.

My mouth warped into a grin. Andrew shrugged and returned my smirk. "Why not?"

Eight of us lifted Clifford and walked him into the bed. His rear wheels were barely wider than the wheel wells of the Hilux. Mototaxis are pretty flimsy though, so as we set the taxi down, his wheels bowed in far enough for the tires to reach the bed. This let his engine rest on the open tailgate while the front tire hung out the back.

The shipping guys did a lot of rope work in the bed, trying to ensure Clifford wouldn't go anywhere. Then our driver went for a bite while the rest of the guys had a good laugh, each getting a picture at the handlebars of our mototaxi.

Thirty minutes later, our driver came striding down the street, his pace fast.

We stood. "Here we go."

Chapter 34

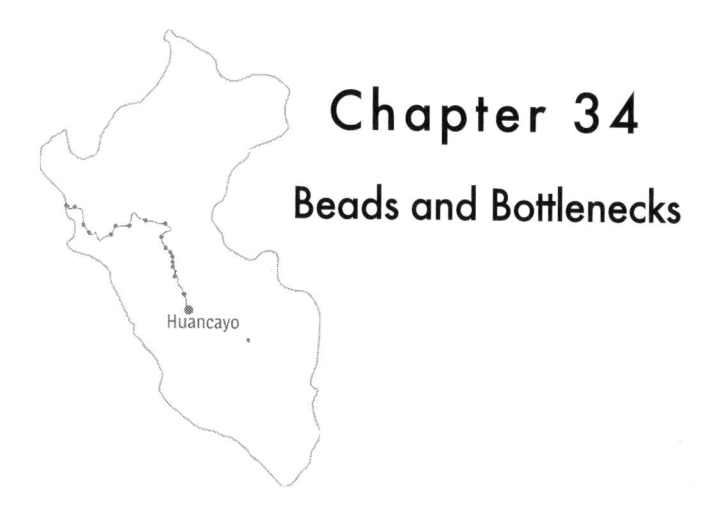

Beads and Bottlenecks

SPECTACLES, TESTICLES, WALLET, AND WATCH.

This punch line from a joke about a Catholic and a Jew actually guides one through the sign of the cross. But I grew up Catholic—that motion will not soon be liberated from my muscles. Nor would it be liberated from the muscles of our fellow passenger.

We were finally on the road, but only after an awkward moment in Ayacucho prior to leaving, in which our driver asked us to pay the full amount we owed up front. We were hesitant, but we were already in the pickup—Clifford included. No way could he leave us behind. But to make the most of the trip, our driver was still looking for another passenger.

An hour into the drive, we picked up a fourth passenger from the roadside. This woman fit the stereotypical traditional Peruvian. Her wrinkled skin had been tanned to leather despite a wide brim hat. Tucked away in her long skirt was an assortment of goodies, including snacks and—of all things—a cell phone. That didn't fit the traditional stereotype, but her cargo did. Packed into the back seat of our mototaxi were a few sacks of potatoes.

She sat between Scott and me on the rear bench. Andrew—prone to carsickness—sat copilot. I was behind the driver, staring at the growing cliffs outside of my window. The road had wound into a canyon, and its surface was narrowing.

"Whoa," Scott and Andrew said together. Only the back of their heads were visible.

"What's up?"

Scott turned to me. "I can't see the road through my window." He turned back and searched for another long moment. "It's just a drop-off."

A seatbelt clasp clicked in front of me, and the hidden coil spring retracted the belt into the wall. Why would the driver *undo* his seatbelt? To my right, our fourth passenger made the sign of the cross. My seatbelt hugged tighter as I eased forward to look at Scott. We grimaced at each over the silent prayers of this woman. Hands unguided by sight, she produced a rosary from the folds of her skirt and started to cycle the beads through her hand.

Now it was apparent where we were: a stretch of the 3S between Huancayo and Ayacucho known as Peru's "Death Road."

The road was constricted on either side. On our left, we were at the bottom of a cliff; on the right, we were at the top. I wasn't able to see the drop next to us, but meanders gave ample opportunity to see the road in front of us as it twisted and wound through the canyon.

The painted lines disappeared. We rounded a sharp leftward bend, the cliff on the inside of the turn concealing what was just beyond. The road funneled us into its single lane, where there were no defined boundaries—the reason the road was unpainted. The road opened back up to two lanes after the next bend. Another turn and another segment of road only a single car-width across. There was another expansion to two lanes for a turn, then another bottleneck.

After a mile, the narrow segments ruled. To fight the blind corners, our driver turned to his horn. On the approach to every turn, the horn blasted as he tapped out an incomprehensible rhythm. It was not the blasts of our mototaxi that often said "in your blind spot" or "squeezing into your lane." This blare was of desperation, yelling, "I'm coming around this corner! If you can hear me, please stop so we don't have a head-on collision and careen off this cliff into the raging river below and either get crushed in the wreckage or perish in the frigid water!"

I know…my translation is a little rough. But it is fairly accurate.

More than once, the horn was the only thing that kept us from just such an accident. Our driver's hearing was razor-sharp, able to detect the horn of an approaching car even under the noise of our own. In those instances, both drivers jumped on the brakes and hoped for enough room to crawl past each other. More than once, we had to reverse to a wider spot. Our driver wasn't above folding in his side mirror, even. Being four inches closer to the cliff face made all the difference.

Of course, we had heard of this stretch. Now we understood that its reputation was deserved. This was no place for tourists. This road's drivers were all experienced, all familiar with its curves and bends and twists. All knew the risks and did their best to minimize them. They had to. How else could such a stretch of road function?

Sweat accumulated on our driver's forehead, even though the cab was still cool.

"Guys," Andrew said. Happy for a reason to stop counting the number of laps my neighbor had made on her rosary, my eyes traced the direction his finger indicated. A mototaxi was parked on one of the road's rarities: a wide spot.

Scott spoke to our driver while rolling down his window. The pickup slowed as we pulled alongside the taxi. The South Africans.

"Hey, guys!" Scott's enthusiasm managed to percolate into even the tensest of situations.

"Hey," they chorused, hard-pressed to echo anything upbeat. Their faces were covered in dust, and no smile could be managed. Only a smirk.

"Quite the chariot you've got there."

"Yeah," Scott said. "Our taxi has kind of crapped out."

"Ours is having problems too. There's something wrong with the electrics. Our lights flicker on occasion." His eyes looked down the canyon, where long shadows were growing and merging.

Another jumped in. "Can you ask your driver how much further this stretch goes?"

Scott exchanged words with the driver. Our driver's fingers were still wrapped around the steering wheel, foot on the brake, the gear selector having never left "Drive".

"It's another 40 kilometers," Scott said through the window.

"We better get going." He spoke to his teammates more than us. "Things are only going to get worse in the dark."

"How's it been so far?"

"Been nearly run off the road three times." He shook his head. "I'm pretty sure one driver did it intentionally."

My chest became aware of my seatbelt again. I had taken the restraint for granted, had taken the experience and skill of my driver for granted.

The pickup's brakes eased off the discs. We inched forward.

"Listen," Scott rushed, "do you guys need flashlights? Or headlamps? Something…in case your lights go?"

They glanced at each other. "I think we'll be alright."

"Yeah," another chimed in. "We'll see you fellas at the finish line."

We wished them luck as we pulled away.

Death Road? In the dark? With no lights?

The seatbelt couldn't be blamed for the tightness across my chest. This wasn't just a dangerous road. This was the stretch where, a few years previous, a Junketeer had died. Duncan had made us all aware of this prior to our departure from Colan, but details had been hard to come by. We had heard the taxi had gone off a cliff, taking the team with it, but we hadn't heard much else.

The rumor I found most tragic was that it had been a passenger that died. I couldn't imagine knowing I had been the driver leading up to an accident in which a friend perished. I glanced through the back window toward the South Africans, only to have my view blocked by our mototaxi. I turned back around, glancing at Scott and then Andrew. I *couldn't* imagine? Maybe I just didn't want to.

Darkness settled, which worked in our favor. Instead of the horn, the flicker of our headlights alerted oncoming traffic of our position. Even us novice Death-Road-navigators could discern when an oncoming vehicle was concealed by a blind turn, because the dust suspended in the air glowed. And where the dust was too thin, the canyon was still narrow enough that light was visible on the opposite wall.

More and more two-laned stretches appeared, and oncoming traffic became less threatening. Soon, the road widened further, following the canyon's morphology. After crossing a bridge, the road crawled onto a gentler landscape, one illuminated with large floodlights.

This construction zone was large, well-lit, and well-staffed. Flaggers stopped us at a roadblock while a hillside was blasted away. These crews worked around the clock, and with so much blasting, it was fortunate our wait was as short as it was.

Some teams were not so lucky here and had to wait for hours. But one team had topped us all. The Kiwis reached the construction site in the middle of a several-hour road closure. Trying to gain position on the large trucks waiting to be piloted across, they had made their way to the front of the traffic column. There, they had been waved through by the flagger. Of course, the Kiwis had been wearing their team uniform this day: the orange coveralls they had won in Colan.

The flagger must have assumed they were part of the construction crew. And who can blame him? Three guys in orange coveralls? Who—other than construction workers—would be dressed like that? So with an all-access pass, the Kiwis had made their way through the construction zone, unscathed by any roadside explosions.

Chapter 35

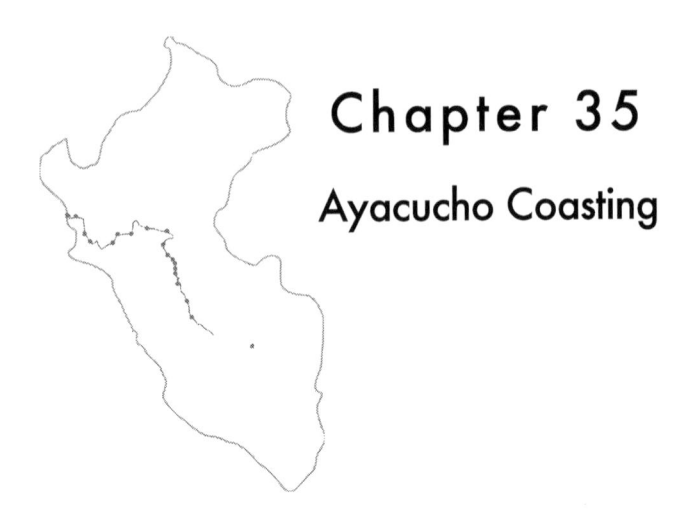

Ayacucho Coasting

"CAN'T BLAME THEM," Andrew said.

"Not at all."

"Probably the most suspicious thing they've seen all night."

"Probably all week."

Our night drive was dragging. We had made it past Death Road, through the endless construction, and back onto pavement. In one village, Andrew had spotted the parked mototaxi of a British team. In the next village, we had dropped off our praying passenger. Not long after, we had passed another team, still driving through the night: the Australian team *Macho Picchu*, Barry and Gerald. It was the first time we had seen them since day two, all the way back in Olmos. We had whooped and hollered at them through open windows. Given the cargo, we had figured they could guess who was inside the Hilux.

"Hey Nathan," Scott said, poking his head into the cab. "Can you get the paperwork out?"

"Yeah, of course."

I reached for my bag. We were stopped on the outskirts of Ayacucho at a police checkpoint. Apparently, a mototaxi being carted around in the back of a pickup wasn't a common sight here. That it happened to be the dead of night didn't help law enforcement suspicions. Scott had tried to talk our way out of it, but the police remained skeptical. They wanted to see some papers.

I emerged from the pickup and passed the documentation to the officers, the letter of explanation on top. They both leaned over the paper, one of them directing a flashlight beam onto it. They traded several cocked eyebrows and, before they even read the whole first page, the letter was shuffled below the registration and insurance. Scott and I exchanged our own weary glance.

Then, out of the dark, came the high whine of an engine struggling to keep up with gravity's pull. We turned toward the few marker lights that dotted the blackness. A single headlight arced down the hill toward the checkpoint. The taxi's brakes squealed as they approached the checkpoint's exaggerated speed bump. Once illuminated by the checkpoint's floodlights, the Aussie's returned the cheering and hollering we had given them, waving like madmen, as unapologetic as ever. Scott and I returned the encouragement, yelling and pumping our fists as they rolled over the *rompemuelles*. Their transmission dropped a gear, the throttle wound up, and they disappeared back into the dark, the slow climb of rpms and the continued Australian yells the only evidence of their brief appearance.

Scott and I faced the officers again, with wide smiles. They exchanged one more expressionless glance, then handed back our documents before wishing us well.

We jumped into the Hilux. "Andrew, did you see Barry and Gerald?"

He laughed. "How could I not?"

Scott laughed with him. "Their timing was perfect. I don't think those cops would have let us through if the Aussies hadn't shown up." We pulled onto the road and started the climb to Ayacucho's center. "I hope we catch them again." We did. Then passed them too, with more cheering.

We didn't get as near to the city center as we wanted, but our driver knew of a very steep road where we could unload the taxi without straining ourselves. As soon as we were out, he hopped back into the driver's seat and disappeared into the streets.

We spent the next ten minutes taking turns at the kickstarter. It finally caught under Andrew's efforts and sputtered to life.

"Andrew, think your impromptu seal will hold?"

"Guess we'll find out."

Andrew rocked the throttle, smoothing some of the crackles and trembles out of the piston's voice. I grasped at Clifford's frame, excited to be sitting in the back once more, in the company of the jerrycan and bags stuffed under the sofa, the cool breeze running across my cheek. My hand bumped against the frame's marker light—it wasn't on. Neither was the other side's marker.

"Andrew!" His head turned, lining me up in his peripheral vision. "Are the lights on?"

His thumb cycled the switch. The markers didn't so much as flicker. Scott and I hopped off, circling the taxi. We leaned under the canopy to talk with Andrew, raising our voices over the motor's.

"They're all dead. Headlight too."

"We must have lost our electrical system again."

"What now?"

Whatever we came up with, it had to be quick. It was only a matter of time before the engine died.

"Let's just use flashlights and headlamps," Andrew said.

"They aren't that bright. Will you be able to see?"

"We're in the city. Streetlights should be a lot of help." We glanced down the road. It was lit well enough. "We just need to be seen by everyone else."

Scott and I reconvened at the back of the taxi and unpacked all of our lights. Andrew was fitted with the brightest headlamp; Scott and I both held lights to our front; and the red blinking

LED was secured to our back. We edged onto the road and made for the center of Ayacucho.

It was mildly sketchy at worst. As traffic increased, so did the street lights. The consistent illumination made it easy to spot not only us, but those on the roadside too. Before we covered a mile, Scott was tapping Andrew's shoulder and pointing.

"The Aussies!"

We pulled to the curb behind them. Scott and I jumped off while Andrew milked the throttle, sustaining the engine's life support. They had stopped to get directions, and we agreed to follow them in search of a place to stay.

On the first uphill they pulled away, far enough that it became the back seat's job to keep tabs on them. It felt like we were tailing them, staying back far enough that we could still see them, but not getting so close that we would be obvious. Our lack of lights made it that much more authentic.

Of course, any proper tail would have a decent vehicle. On one cobbled street, our engine died. Scott and I jumped out and started to push, hoping to avoid an ankle sprain on the cobbles. Once up to speed, Andrew popped the clutch. Clifford's momentum turned the engine over, and the spark caught again. We piled in and continued down the street, our mark lost in the night.

"Just keep going straight. They'd notice we weren't behind them."

We coasted through intersection after intersection after intersection, eyes peeled, uncommitted to any direction. Maybe this was hopeless. Maybe we should have been searching for a place to park the mototaxi for the night instead of Barry and Gerald. For all we knew, they were still moving.

"There!"

Scott pointed to our right. Down the street perpendicular to ours stood Barry, next to their parked mototaxi. Andrew wrenched us around the corner and pulled behind them, Clifford's engine dying again as we came to a standstill.

"I thought we lost you guys."

"You did."

Gerald appeared from a doorway. "No good." He rested hands on hips. "Not enough room for all of us. But they said something about a traveler's hotel just down the road there." He pointed down the hill.

"We'll just keep following."

"Sounds good."

Gerald and Barry loaded up and started down the hill. Andrew tried the electric starter...nothing. Then the kick-starter...nothing.

"Andrew!" Scott pointed at the ground. "Kill the fuel!"

The carb again. We all looked down as a slow drip transformed into a pressurized spray. The gas was squeezing past Andrew's makeshift seal. He reached for the fuel valve. The hot gasoline spilled onto the road, washing dirt and oil from the ancient cobbles before being funneled down the hill by the mortar channels holding the surface together.

"Well..." Andrew leaned back. "...now what?"

We stared down the hill, to where the Aussies had vanished from sight.

"Screw it. Let's coast."

"Huh?"

"They said this place was just down the road. What if it's literally down this street? We can coast it."

After a quick discussion to hash out the details, Scott and I abandoned the sofa to stand on the rear cargo rack so we could dismount in a hurry and push the taxi if necessary. It was also nice knowing I could bail at any second. Ready, Andrew slipped the transmission into neutral, eased off the brakes, and let gravity take us.

Before the end of the block, we had picked up enough speed for the lane's cobbled rhythm to be dampened by our suspension. The warm night air dropped a few degrees as it accelerated past us, tousling our hair. The rush of air, the squeaked compressions of old suspension springs, and the clatter of chain links spinning their sprockets were the only sounds in the dormancy of our engine.

"Woooooo!" To my right, Scott was leaning back, arms straight, chin pointed to the sky. My face relaxed into a cheek-bulging smile and I yelled with him. Clifford achieved an impressive speed for being accelerated by gravity alone. Then again, our yelling drove him faster, past his known limits.

The city's culture was instilled into the air, like incense. It energized us. We leaned off the taxi, ignoring the potential traffic at each intersection. Our bent knees took every bump the taxi could not, our calves absorbing and recoiling with the energy. We glided near the ground, with no lights, like a predator in the dark. No flight could have been better.

Our bird of prey cried out, the brakes squealing. Scott and I stood straight again. On the sidewalk, Barry and Gerald both pointed to a large garage door. We lost momentum in the corner and on the incline of the garage entrance. Scott and I hopped down and helped the mototaxi to where the Aussies had left their own.

"We lose you fellas again?"

"Fuel problems."

We made our way into the building and found a room for the night. It was an expensive, high-end hotel, one that required the front desk to keep a copy of our passports. This was the first place we had stayed with the ability to *make* a copy of a passport, much less even have the desire to *see* one. But after such a long day, I practically threw my passport across the counter.

Rooms secured, bags stored, and taxis stabled, we made our way into the streets in search of a restaurant still open for dinner. We introduced Barry and Gerald to *Chifa*, the Peruvian–Chinese food. We sat around a large table and placed our orders.

"So gents," Gerald said, elbows on the table, rubbing his hands together. "Any favorite moments so far?" We pondered for a second. "Nathan?"

A firm "Yeah" came from my mouth, almost involuntary. I recounted for the table the moment outside Cerro de Pasco, standing above the narrow ravine where the woman was calling out, her voice echoing and re-echoing across the landscape.

"It was..." I sighed through a smirk. "...incredible." Andrew and Scott both nodded agreement.

"Sounds like it," Gerald said. "But..." his eyebrows dropped and eyes narrowed. "...you do realize she was probably yelling at him to pick up some eggs from the market, right?"

We laughed and imagined what other everyday, mundane remarks might have left us all captivated. We continued to swap tales of the road over our food, and thanked the Aussies for getting us out of the situation with the checkpoint police.

"Wait," Barry jumped in. "That was the first time you had to talk to the cops?"

We chorused, "Yeah."

Barry and Gerald laughed. "We've been stopped by the cops every day since we started."

We also recounted our experience on Death Road.

I half yelled through a mouthful of food. "The woman with us was praying."

"So was the driver," Andrew added.

We laughed, unconcerned about tempting fate since that particular danger was already behind us.

"And did you notice the driver took off his seatbelt?"

"I did see that," Andrew said.

Gerald jumped in. "We heard about that. They do that so they can jump out of the vehicle in case it goes over the edge."

The air stilled with seriousness.

After a pause, laughter shook us all again—it was the boyish laughter used to celebrate the slaying of imaginary monsters. Our monsters may have been just as intangible, but their threat was much more real. And the safety of hindsight made them that much more laughable.

It was well after midnight by the time we made it back to the hotel. Our room had a narrow balcony, the wrought-iron railing framing the city lights on the hill above us and the cobbled road below. We showered with hot water and fell into separate twin beds, looking forward to joining Barry and Gerald again the next morning for breakfast.

Chapter 36

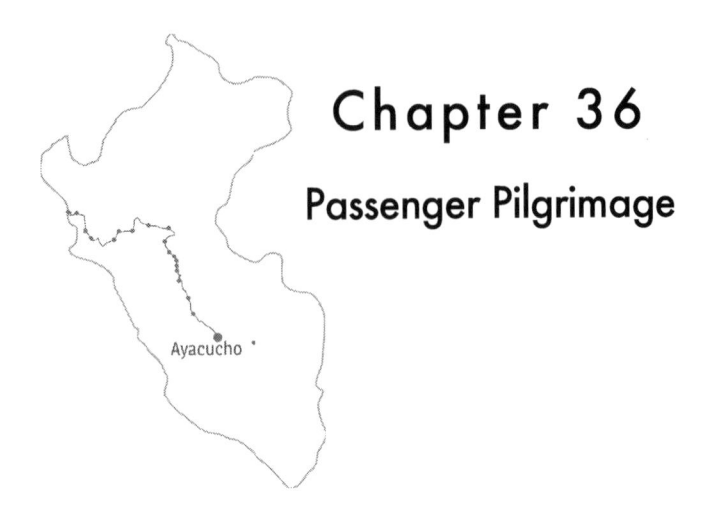

Passenger Pilgrimage

Ayacucho

"YOU REALIZE what's going to happen, right?"

Andrew was arranging bags in the cargo rack. Scott was searching for something in his daypack. The hotel parking lot was empty, but it felt strange to speak above a mumble.

We had eaten breakfast with the Aussies. The spread lined one wall of the hotel's dining room. Tables were covered in white linens, polished silverware, and glasses of water with ice. Cushions covered chairs. I had made three trips to the buffet, admiring my reflection in the stainless-steel-hooded food trays each time. I was pretty ragged.

That was one reason our table had stood out. None of us wore shorts, or fanny packs, or money pouches. Instead, we sported unkempt facial hair, sweat-stained buffs, and long pants splattered with oil and caked in salt, dried mud clinging at the hems. Another reason was our bantering and shit talking. Our table alone filled the dining room with jeers and cackles that drowned out the smattering of polite conversations at other tables.

When we had left the dining room, a breeze rushed past our ankles—I suspect it was the room's collective sigh at our departure. No matter though. We had important things to tend to. After collecting our bags and settling the bill, we headed for the garage.

Scott was still elbow-deep in his backpack. Andrew pointed to my bag. I passed it over and he set it in the cargo rack amidst the folds of our blue tarp.

I continued. "They're going to try to convince us to finish this thing out on the mototaxi." It was a hunch, something I picked up on at breakfast.

Andrew paused and his eyes found mine. He understood what I was trying to say: that we needed to be on the same page. Would their efforts change our minds to truck it? Not likely. But would the conversation create tension within our team? I thought back to San Rafael, where we first discussed trucking. Scott had been so adamant that we not truck.

"Scott?"

"Got it!" He yanked his arm free, camera in hand.

The sun had already heated the air to an uncomfortable temperature. "Scott, did you hear me?"

He checked the status of the camera battery before looking at me. "Huh?"

"I was saying the Aussies are..."

"Hello, fellas!"

I turned. Barry and Gerald were crossing the garage, baggage in hand. Had they heard? Had Scott?

Scott fired up his camera and walked up to the Aussies. "So, what do you think of the mototaxi?" he prompted with an interviewer's cadence.

Without pause, Gerald responded to the camera. "All I can say," a single finger pointed at the taxi, "it's a shopping trolley with a motor."

We chuckled. It was hardly an exaggeration.

Barry said, "So boys, still planning to truck?" His eyes fell on each of us.

"That's the plan," Scott answered, his camera falling to his side.

"Are you fellas sure?" Gerald said, arms crossed on his chest. When none of us answered, he began again. "Listen, you guys should just get a brand new carburetor put on your taxi and finish this thing out." Without turning, he pointed over his shoulder at their own taxi. His tone was very matter-of-fact: "We've replaced ours twice already."

"Yeah," Andrew said. "But the carb is only *one* of our problems. The engine is still running like crap. And now that we've lost our lights for a second time, I'm wondering if the entire electrical system doesn't need to be replaced, wiring and all."

"Besides," Scott jumped in, "we're so slow compared to you guys. You think it will take you two days to make Urubamba. That's at least three days for us, without any mechanical issues." What were the odds of that? "I think we're all enjoying the trucking pace anyways." Gerald nodded, arms still crossed. His concern was fatherly, as though he was worried we were missing out. Trucking felt like the right thing to do, though. This task presented its own challenges and let us glimpse more of the urban lifestyle of Peru. "Plus, negotiating transportation for three *gringos* and a mototaxi is a great way to work on my Spanish."

Gerald nodded, the corners of mouth tugging upwards. "Alright. Just wanted to make sure." His arms fell from their folded position and his hands found hips to rest on. "So you're off to find a truck?"

"We hope."

"Any ideas how?

"The front desk gave us a map and marked out a shipping company on it. We'll start there."

"This is it, then," Gerald said, his right hand extended. Our teams shook hands in every combination while we wished each other luck. "See you boys at the Finish Party."

The Aussies' suspension squeaked over each stone paver before reaching the door and accelerating onto the smaller cobbles of the street. The sound of their engine faded behind the high garage wall.

"Well," Scott held up the map, a circle scribbled in black ink. "Shall we?"

* * *

Ayacucho is Quechua for *the corner of death*, a name the city acquired from the decisive battle over Peru's independence from Spain. However, it also translates as *the corner of spirit*. This is fitting, as the region's people have always had a reputation for great spiritual devotion, as illustrated by the city's 33 churches—one for each year of Christ's life.

We saw a few as we wandered the city on our own pilgrimage, searching for salvation. Our first lead of the day—the inky circle—had not panned out. When we had reached the location, large posters of even larger busses covered the windows. Flags from all over the world bordered the door. We still asked, just in case, but as we suspected, they could do nothing for our mototaxi.

It was time for our second lead. On our way to the inky circle, we had walked past a large, roll-up aluminum door, half-open and half-concealing a flatbed truck.

We returned, the door now fully opened. The white cab sparkled. Tire sidewalls gleamed. A sturdy steel rack painted matte black separated the cab from the bed. A row of hooks offered easy attachment for ropes and straps. The cleanliness tipped us off; this was a dealership.

Still, Scott explained our situation. The young woman behind the desk produced a stack of business cards. She pulled out the most promising, scribbled down the address, and made another dot on our map.

That street number had vanished. We did find the two adjacent numbers and their doors, but between them was only blank wall. Even a few police officers on foot patrol were baffled by the address and its lack of a door. But for transportation concerns, they recommended a tourist information center at the *Plaza de Armas*. They were confident we would find information on shipping companies there.

The girl behind the counter there put their notions to rest—she had zero information.

People must have misunderstood our intentions. When a *gringo* explains that he needs to get from Ayacucho to Urubamba with a mototaxi, and is in search of a truck for the job, which is more likely? That he needs a truck for his mototaxi or that he speaks piss-poor Spanish and actually wants to get from Ayacucho to Urubamba in something *like* a mototaxi or truck? That would explain all the bus businesses that people had been suggesting to us all morning.

So, it was back to the dealership. Maybe another business card would hold more promise. Maybe we could raid the whole stack and go door to door until we found what we needed.

The secretary looked surprised when we walked in the second time, a couple of hours later. Scott explained that the business she had sent us to was no longer there. She pulled out the stack again.

"Scott, do you think the letter would help?"

The girl looked up.

"Couldn't hurt." He asked her to read something that explained our task. She agreed, so I dug out the letter. Her eyes moved back and forth, down several lines before glancing at us with a smirk. She swiveled her chair and called toward the back of the building. A young man in coveralls appeared. He bent over and propped an arm on the desk as he read over her shoulder. Their cheeks pulled at the corners of their mouths.

"Scott..." Another idea. "...can you explain our taxi is broken?" I pulled out my camera and cycled through the pictures backward. I stopped on the image captured during the previous day: our mototaxi strapped down in the Hilux.

Scott showed them the picture, reiterating our need for a truck. With the letter and the picture, Scott's question finally made sense to someone other than us.

The young man stepped out to make some phone calls on our behalf. Meanwhile, the young lady posed with us while a third employee took our picture with her phone. Things were friendlier now that we seemed...less crazy? Or maybe it was because we now understood each other.

After several pictures, the young man reappeared. An acquaintance of his was coming to talk with us. We were shown to the back of the building where we would meet this guy. The business cards lay forgotten on the desk.

Everyone got back to work and left us to mill around the dealerships garage. The wait for our meeting was tense. What if this guy wasn't for real? What if arrangements couldn't be made? That would mean more time wasted.

After twenty minutes, the acquaintance showed. We all shook hands with Carlos, then Andrew and I leaned against that back wall of the garage and let Scott do the talking. After another five minutes—and mid-negotiation—the tension was taken up another notch.

Scott's hand was bent to a right angle at the palm, fingers held horizontal as they made incremental jumps upward in unison with the Spanish words. Carlos stood facing him, nodding, nodding, nodding until, "No, no, no."

Andrew and I exchanged a glance. Scott was learning the words for the number corresponding to the price this trip would cost. It wasn't that Scott had a limited vocabulary of numbers; it was just that Carlos' price quote had been stated in a dialect that made a direct translation sound odd. Scott was taking the time to clarify.

Once Scott had the word, surprise jumped into his voice. Carlos confirmed. I produced a pen and paper, just to make sure. Carlos scratched across the surface. We broke our gaze with the paper to look at each other.

"Un momento, por favor," Scott said to Carlos. We stepped away to speak with each other.

Andrew stated each word slowly, his inflections stressed: "Fifteen hundred soles?"

"That's way more than I expected," I said, eyebrows higher than my voice. "And way more than what we've paid so far to truck."

The cost of a one way trip for three *gringos* and their mototaxi from Ayacucho to Urubamba was roughly US$500—three times our most expensive trucking bill thus far.

Scott nodded. "It is expensive, but look how long it took us to find someone willing to do it. What if we say 'no' and can't find an alternative? We won't care about price then."

"That's what…$170 apiece?" Andrew said. "That's not…terrible."

We swapped pensive glances.

"Why not?" I said. "It'll probably be worth it."

We nodded consent. Scott returned to Carlos and conveyed our agreement. We all shook hands on it.

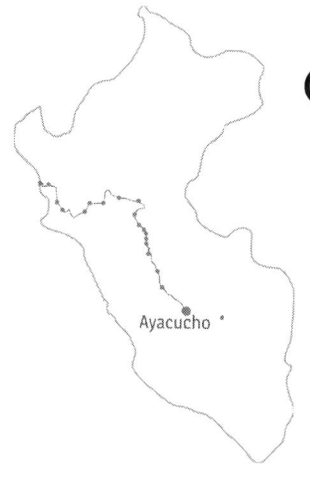

Chapter 37
Slicing Lights

"Fucking…" Eye roll. "…awesome."

We had been standing on the sidewalk outside the hotel garage waiting for our ride. Even through the glare on the windshield, the identity of the driver was unmistakable. We flagged Carlos down, directing him into the garage.

"It worked out last time," Andrew said.

Carlos turned off the road, the transition across the sidewalk throwing an awkward wobble through our second Toyota Hilux.

"I guess so," I chuckled, eyeing the extended passenger cab as we followed on foot. "At least we'll be comfortable."

Carlos stepped out and greeted us all with a handshake. He looked the same as when we had first met: designer jeans hugged his legs, faded and worn in all the right places; light brown leather shoes covered his feet; an intricately patterned button-down shirt spread across his torso, the collar extra angular and reaching for his shoulders since the top few buttons were left undone, showing off the gold chain that hung there. The accents on the frames of his sunglasses matched the occasional glint from the rings on his fingers. Talk about a sharp-dressed man...a sharp-dressed man whose mid-week commitments weren't so pressing that he could take two days to drive a few *gringos* and their mototaxi to Urubamba?

What exactly did Carlos do for work?

Despite his clothes, Carlos didn't hesitate when we loaded Clifford. The four of us and two garage attendants lifted and slid him into the bed. The wheel wells were bigger this time, so we couldn't get the rear wheels to sit flat. We left one wheel resting on the bed while the other sat on a wheel well. We stepped back to assess the awkward angle at which Clifford was perched.

"We'll just...tie him down really well."

This proved difficult. Carlos wasn't really in the business of transportation...not cargo of this nature, anyway. He had no rope, no bungee cords, no tie-downs, nothing that would have been useful. We wrapped our one length of webbing around the engine, each end hooked on opposite sides of the bed. The few feet of excess rope from our cargo rack tethered the mototaxi's rear bumper to the headache rack of the Hilux. And our single bungee cord stretched through the front fork to prevent the wheel from swinging.

We evaluated our handiwork while Carlos made a call on his cell phone.

"Is this way sketchier, or what?" I said. Our previous Hilux ride had had all kinds of rope. Those guys had even rigged a system to support the tailgate, to distribute the weight of the engine and ease the stress on the gate's stock cables. It had felt secure. *This* on the other hand...

"¿Listo?" Carlos slid the phone into his pants while walking toward us.

"Sí," we answered, each of us with a leery eye on our cargo. We crawled into the pickup.

Though Carlos was prompt picking us up, our departure from Ayacucho was anything but. First, we stopped for diesel. The second stop was a whole service: oil was replaced; air and fuel filters were cleaned; brake, transmission, and power steering fluids were topped off. The final stop was to fix a puncture. While the right rear tire's new patch dried, the rest were inflated as well.

What had this guy been doing in the hours before picking us up? Was that not the appropriate time to take care of this? Maybe not... Maybe he needed to be paid before making these investments.

That didn't stop me from rolling my eyes at every stop though, counting the seconds lost as if I had somewhere to be. That was the surprising part of the situation: my dissatisfaction was in regard to details that hadn't even been discussed. Carlos hadn't promised we would depart at a certain time. He had not agreed to deliver us to Urubamba by any specific day. He had not laid out a plan or itinerary at all. It was my own expectations that I held against him.

Really, I should have just trusted him. He said he would get us there—my expectations should have been for nothing other than that. But of course, I was in a different frame of mind, and reduced to pouting in the back seat.

I clung to these feelings even as we left, unable to shake them on the innumerable turns. The series of switchbacks persisted through the outskirts and past the edge of the city, taking us higher and higher up the ridge, our departure from the valley synced with that of the sun's. The city's earthy tones glowed in the golden light, emphasizing how the city spread through the valleys, occupying what land the mountains allowed.

Scott's demeanor was ever-friendly, and he chatted with our driver. Carlos said he worked at a university as a teacher: chemistry and physics. Best-dressed professor ever—chauffeuring us? He wasn't missing class? Didn't need to grade some papers? Whether he was really a teacher or not, I had no doubt Carlos knew *some* chemistry. Unfortunately, before Scott probed deeper, the conversation shifted to Quechua, Carlos' heritage and first language. Scott had been dying to learn some, so he picked our driver's brain.

After night had come, the road topped out on a high plateau. The dark was immense, and the stars beamed, their viewing enhanced by the elevation. My forehead would've been pressed to the window if not for my breath condensing on the glass. Instead, I was content staring toward the horizon until we started to descend.

We worked down another set of switchbacks. I half leaned to the middle of the bench seat, to see past Carlos' chair. The darkness was dense. Our headlights penetrated the blackness only far enough to keep us between the road's painted lines. A flash caught my eye.

Andrew, sitting shotgun, looked back. "Did you guys see that?"

Scott also turned. "Was that a person?"

Several hundred meters past the alleged pedestrian we saw another flashing light. Carlos eased the brakes. The light was strange: not flashing per se, but shaking. Or maybe waved...by hand? Our headlights cut into the dark far enough to illuminate the scene. One person stood on the road's edge, shining a flashlight back and forth to alert drivers of the hazard down the hill from him: a mototaxi. A second person was bent over it, his purpose obscure before we passed at a crawl.

Scott uttered quickly to Carlos and we stopped just downhill from the stopped taxi. We hopped out, our own lights in hand, but didn't get two steps before the South Africans met us.

"It's good to see you lot."

"Your mototaxi broke down?"

"Still runs fine," one said. "We just lost all our lights, though. Even the markers."

"No one can see us," the other jumped in. "Almost got hit a couple times."

"Can you ask your driver how far it is to the next village. We've been looking for a place to stop for over two hours now...and it's getting really cold."

Scott leaned through the open door for a quick exchange with Carlos. He turned back around, lips pursed. "It's still another 25 kilometers to the nearest village."

They looked at each other, desperation on their faces. "What are we going to do?"

Andrew jumped in. "Do you guys need more lights? We have flashlights and headlamps. I have some gloves in the cab too."

"So do I. You guys are more than welcome to have them."

"Gloves would be great. We didn't think it would ever get this cold, but we've just been stuck driving all night."

We retrieved the gloves and handed them over.

"Lights too?" I asked.

"No. They aren't bright enough." He let out a sigh. "And this road is crazy. Going over the edge is a real possibility."

"Let me talk to our driver," Scott said. A few minutes reasoning with Carlos and Scott had hatched a plan.

"Listen, you guys are still running, right? Our driver has agreed to go slow enough so you can keep up. Just stay on our tail. You'll be able to follow us to the bottom of the grade. Our lights should help you see and be seen."

"That would be fantastic. Let us fetch Tully and we'll be ready to go."

They retrieved their third teammate from up the hill and taped whatever spare lights they had to the taxi frame. One of the rear passengers held the brightest flashlight, which would act as their headlight. We returned to the cab of the Hilux, our eyes on the South Africans illuminated by our tail lights and the flash of our hazards.

The driver gave a thumbs up. It was an eerie gesture in the glow of the red brake lights.

The shoulder gravel crunched beneath us as we rolled back onto the road, beginning a slow descent. Scott asked Carlos to slow down again and again and again when he began to pull away from our mototaxi tail. The constant switchbacks and steep road made it difficult to be sure, but given how frequently Scott was asking, it seemed like Carlos wanted to pull away. Good thing he didn't have a delivery deadline to hold over us.

Time crawled. Our speedometer displayed the lowest speed we had seen since leaving Ayacucho. But the pressing darkness paired with the repetitive switchbacks started to dissolve time altogether. Was this curve the same as the last? Or was that three turns ago? Wait, how many switchbacks have we passed through? Eight? Eighteen? Thirty-eight?

Near the bottom, I broke eye contact with the South Africans to survey the stars again. Looking up, half my view of the night sky was obscured by the silhouette of the ridge we had been descending. Replacing the stars was a more impressive display. I was reminded of a lighthouse in the dead of night, as seen from a distance, when the only evidence of its presence is the beam of light arcing through the dark, rotating around an unseen source. Above us, I got the impression of several lighthouses, stacked in rows that crawled from valley floor to ridge top. Against a perfect black backdrop, beams of light arced across the night as their unseen sources rounded the road's switchbacks. There were a half dozen beams at any instant, some close—the section of road above us—and others far above, near the top—a place we had been nearly an hour before.

My breath fogged the window. My chin dropped and found the South Africans again, their lights a feeble twinkle compared to those slicing the night about us. Another switchback and the road was less steep, and where the next switchback should have been, the road only veered slightly. I turned. There were lights ahead—street lights.

Carlos pulled off the road and into a gas station, the South Africans still on our tail. On the other side of the road was the village, with well-lit streets. We all hopped out, exchanging hugs and handshakes.

"Hey, we really owe you guys."

"Yeah, don't know what we would've done if you hadn't come along."

"No kidding," Scott said.

"Good thing we found you guys. Glad we could help."

Carlos had the pump running and our tank filling. He walked over and explained how to get to the main road of the village, where there were a few hostels. The South Africans climbed back into their mototaxi, the prospect of sleep calling them.

"Thanks again so much. After we finish, our first round of beers will be for you guys."

"Sounds good to us," we laughed.

They fired up their mototaxi once again, lights still dark.

"Hey," Scott yelled over the engine. "No more driving at night." He winked. "That's an asshole move," he chuckled. They returned the laughter.

"See you in a few days!" They pulled across the road, and disappeared below the crest of the hill.

Our fuel replenished, we crawled back into the Hilux and continued down the road, leaving behind the lights of the village. How terrifying to be on a mototaxi, in the dark, invisible. The South Africans' situation had altered my perception of the day. Every inconvenience and delay was now just fate adjusting the clocks so we could—with seeming serendipity—find them at their moment of greatest need.

A shadow of their relief also coursed through me. The stress that I had built up all day vanished, just like our headlights in the dark. A sigh escaped my lungs, and I dozed off.

Chapter 38

Balloon Fight

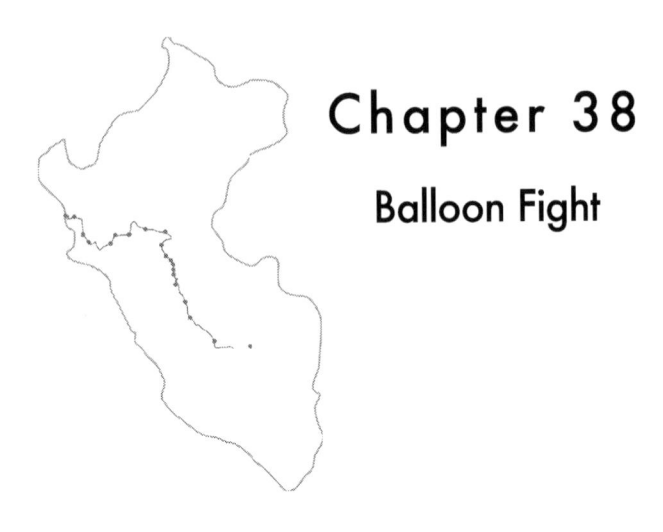

EVER HEARD OF *HOMO ECONOMICUS*?

These economic discussion can get a little abstract, so let's ground ours with an example.

Our hypothetical market will deal in water balloons, because who doesn't love flinging those encapsulated spheroids of icy surprise? And for simplicity, we'll say there's only one store in town that carries these.

First, let's define supply and demand. The supply is the actual number of balloons *available* at the store. The demand is the number of balloons you and your friends *want to buy* from the store.

Got it?

Now let's say there was a last-minute water-balloon fight announced. This means the demand for balloons is high, because more balloons is better. The manager of the store also heard about the fight, and so increased the price knowing your friends would pay. Now let's look at two laws governing the price of those balloons.

The first is the Law of Supply: as price increases, supply increases. Even at the higher price the balloons are still flying off the shelves. So what's the manager do? He runs to the back for another box and restocks the shelves as fast as he can—there's money to be made.

The second is the Law of Demand: as price increases, demand falls. As the cashier rings up your basket of balloons, you start to sweat at the sum cost. Balloons aren't usually this expensive, right? That's when a squirt gun catches your eye. You stop the cashier mid basket, and swap the balloons for the gun.

There you have the two laws. As price increases, supply increases and demand falls.

What if we manipulate the supply though?

Let's say that manager had forgotten to order balloons last week, so our store only has a few packages left. Everyone is demanding water balloons, so he increases the price in proportion to the difference between the number of balloons *available* and the number of balloons *wanted*. That's a big discrepancy, so the price jumps way up.

Being rational people, you and your friends realize you don't want to spend that kind of money. If anything, you can wait until the store has been restocked and then have a reasonably-priced water-balloon fight. Here is the Law of Demand again and because this time the price skyrocketed, the demand plummeted.

What does this have to do with *Homo economicus*? Rationality. To demonstrate, we need to tweak our example though. Those balloons...fill them with cocaine.

Now, let's venture back to Peru. You may recall the underdeveloped infrastructure in *la sierra*. Without it, economic development has been slow and governance is difficult, making the judicial system more akin to the honor system.

In these areas of little governance and little prosperity, coca is a lucrative crop, an economic opportunity. Given its illegality though, concealing its growth is crucial. This is pretty easy in the mountainous region, where farmers only need to venture into dense growth of the lush valleys. Not easy is environmentalism.

Away from prying eyes, these farmers clear forest (typically by slash-and-burn) to create a plot for their coca crop. Then they clear more land for their subsistence crops. If they're lucky, they'll have some livestock which will require even more land. And should the farmer bring his family—or other workers—that's even more forest to cut down.

Also, as with most agricultural process, chemicals are used to ensure the crop's viability and to increase its yield. These chemicals typically have a negative impact on the surrounding environment.

If the farmers sell their coca as dry leaves, this list of environmental problems stops growing. However, should they decide to process the leaves further, we find a whole new array of chemicals.

To get from dry leaves to the end product, cocaine hydrochloride, these rainforest chemists use a number of chemicals: an alkaline material, kerosene, sulfuric or hydrochloric acid, potassium permanganate, ammonia, and acetone or ether. None of these are particularly good for the environment. And of course, the typical disposal method is dumping these chemicals onto the ground while the cocaine is loaded onto a plane. Oh yeah, that plane's runway…probably another product of deforestation.

This is not a comprehensive or exhaustive discussion of the environmental costs, but you get the basic picture. Now back to our balloons.

The general approach to the War on Drugs (especially cocaine) involves manipulating economics. On the ground, this approach isn't exactly conscientious of the environment either.

Task forces seek out coca farms and seize crops, either removing the plants by hand or spraying them with another batch of chemicals—the kind that kill plants indiscriminately. This apprehension or destruction of coca crops causes further damage to the environment. It also creates a commodity vacuum in the marketplace though—just like when the manager forgot to order balloons. And just like it did in the store, this drives the price of cocaine sky high.

You may recall it was this price that dissuaded you and your friends from buying those water balloons. So is it safe to assume that cocaine users will make the same decision?

Therein lies this strategy's logical error. Many economic models portray humans as consistently rational and narrowly self-interested. However, economists acknowledge that most humans don't fit this description (as proven by our desire to throw latex-wrapped liquids at each other). This is the reason researchers have invented their own economically driven man who does fit this description. His name: *Homo economicus*.

I am not rational. You are not rational. *Humans* are not rational. Therefore, cocaine users are also not rational. That sky high price...that doesn't dissuade them. If they have the motivation and the means, they will make that purchase.

Now, governments continually try to reduce the supply of cocaine, thereby increasing prices and lowering demand. However, the economic irrationality of cocaine users (or *Homo sapiens* in general) keeps the demand high. Remember the Law of Supply? Because consumers maintain that high price of cocaine, supplies increase.

This means anonymous and undetected farmers clear more land to plant more coca. They acquire and use more agricultural chemicals. They acquire and dispose of more processing chemicals. They hire more hands and plant more subsistence crops. Meanwhile, the farmer whose crops were seized has to relocate and begins deforesting and polluting anew to recover his losses.

As you can see, it's possible to argue that the War on Drugs perpetuates not only the production of drugs, but the destruction of rainforest as well.

How's that for rational?

* * *

It was still the dead of night. We were traversing the area known as the VRAEM, an acronym for the Apurímac, Ene, and Mantaro River Valleys, Peru's major cocaine-producing hot spot, which turns out more than 200 tons of cocaine annually.

The area has played host to a guerilla force, the Shining Path, that has historically resisted the Peruvian government. Small skirmishes between the guerillas, law enforcement, and improvised self-defense militias have further delayed development in the area. Starved of resources and opportunities for economic growth, many locals have turned to the most consistent source of income: coca. Whether supporting the guerrilla efforts or just supporting their families, the economic circumstances of these farmers and their workers are such that raising coca is the only way to guarantee their well-being and the well-being of their kin.

I leaned to my side, trying to stare through the windshield of the Hilux. Nausea had jolted me awake. I focused on shaking it. We crested a ridge, and spread below was another city.

Carlos said something. Scott gave a short reply.

"What's going on?" I said.

"We're going to stop in the next town," Scott explained. "Carlos says we're picking up a friend of his who knows the route better. They're going to take turns driving, too."

I nodded, keeping my eyes fixed on the road.

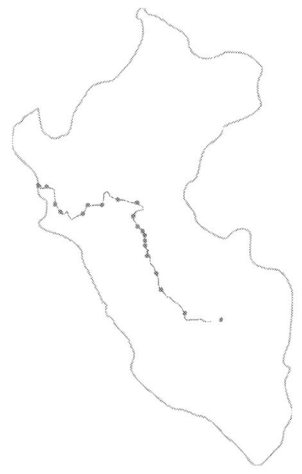

Chapter 39

Hostel-ities

WROUGHT IRON sapped the warmth from my palms and fingers. The town streets were deserted, the sky dark. A parade of empty benches lined the city's thoroughfare, a strip of manicured vegetation flanked on either side by a short fence, sidewalk, then street. I grabbed the fencing and gave a shake. Sturdy. I leaned against it, happy for the contrast to the plush seats of the Hilux.

Scott leaned next to me. "Feeling alright?"

I was losing heat where the fence held me. There was an excess in my stomach. It felt good to have some siphoned off.

"I dozed off for a bit," I said. "Woke up nauseous. I've got it mostly under control now."

"Same for me," he replied, gazing at the empty street.

Past Scott, toward our pickup, was Andrew. He had collapsed onto a park bench after having jumped out of the pickup before it had even come to a full stop. He was hunched forward, face buried in his hands, diaphragm pulling lots of crisp air into his lungs.

"How's Andrew?"

Scott's head took a slow turn in the same direction. "Miserable."

After we had said goodbye to the South Africans, the windiness of the road had persisted. This was problematic. Motion sickness is a product of conflicting sensory input. While we were flying around those corners, our inner ears detected the change in direction. But in the dark, our visual cortex could not infer the same motion. Our eyes disagreed with our ears. The product was nausea.

"What's the word on Carlos' friend?"

Scott shook his head. "He's supposed to be here anytime."

"Maybe it's good he's taking so long. Seems like we could all stretch our legs." Andrew shifted on the bench. "And get some air."

Scott nodded. "You think some food would help? At least some fluids or something? Maybe we could grab something while we wait."

"Let's go ask. Andrew will know better than us what might make him feel better."

We pushed off the fencing and wandered back to Andrew, the warm spots we left in the metal shrinking as the heat dissipated into the cool air.

After some consideration, Andrew decided food was worth a try. Eating when nauseated was not something I was prone to do, so maybe his condition was improving. Or was he just desperate enough to try anything?

Even Carlos liked the idea—at least after we offered to pay. He suggested we wait for his friend, though. As a local (of which city remained a mystery), he would know the best options. For the next ten minutes, we waited, thinking things might change for the better.

When the friend showed, he told us everything was closed.

So much for that plan.

Ushered by Carlos, we climbed back into the pickup. As we pulled away from the curb, Andrew—still sitting shotgun—leaned his head against the seat and released a sigh.

Over the next few hours, the road did not improve.

"Hey, Scott?" Andrew's voice shook, a manifestation of his physical condition. At the same time though, it was calm.

I was sitting in the middle of the back bench, Scott on my right, Carlos' friend on my left. Scott leaned to talk around the seat.

"Yeah, buddy?"

Andrew's composure took an edge of politeness. "Would you, please, ask one more time if it's possible for us to stop?"

Scott's sigh swept across my cheek. The situation had become a growing frustration for everyone. It was worst for Andrew. His physical discomfort had grown with every curve and bump. Scott had been attempting to convince our drivers that we needed a break for the sake of Andrew. And Carlos and his friend, despite the delay each had caused, were now determined to make the trip as fast as possible. They were just shy of flat out refusing to stop—despite the occasional moan from the front seat.

This time Andrew followed up with a new tactic. "Let them know I would be willing to pay for their room in a hostel should we find one. Just…" Andrew let out a sigh of his own, drawn out, not of frustration, but of defeat. "Whatever it takes. Please. I'm not doing well up here."

"Alright," Scott said.

Thus began another round of negotiations. Scott engaged both our drivers in conversation, which lasted longer than any other attempt. There was a side discussion between our two drivers before they addressed Scott again.

His sigh was drenched in relief.

"Andrew, they need to be back tomorrow, so they won't stop for the night. They have agreed to stop for an hour though, in the next town, so we can all get some sleep."

Andrew only nodded. It wasn't what he wanted, but it was still something.

It made me glad for my diarrhea. Back on day two, my stomach issues had been horrible. And though they had persisted for several days, it was of some comfort to be on the road, even to operate the mototaxi. It didn't do much to help my recovery, but the road had been a distraction. Even when I had felt like garbage, covering ground had been a consolation. For Andrew though, the road was the source of his ailment. Progress along the route now meant worsening his condition.

The next town was small. We parked off a gravel road, on a slight uphill. Carlos set a timer. Then he held it out for everyone to see. One hour...go.

I still sat rear middle. Both front bucket seats reclined trapping my legs in a split position. I slouched as much as possible and dozed off.

Then I snapped awake, legs crawling. The tingle was strange—not a loss of circulation. The prickling was from restlessness, like my legs were hyperactive. In the limited space, my legs couldn't bend or straighten or stretch. But they still screamed for it. I rocked them side to side, and rolled my hips in the seat, its leather not loud enough to wake anyone. My eyes surveyed all the doors, behind any of which was relief.

Carlos's phone lounged on the dashboard, screen dark, the time remaining until my liberation unknown. So I tried to guess. I had slept, so there were probably only five or ten minutes left. I could last ten minutes—it wasn't worth waking everyone. But what if it was more? Half an hour—could I last that long? What if there were still forty-five minutes on the timer? No way I could make it. But I must have slept more than fifteen minutes...right?

Scott and Andrew were both asleep, Andrew giving the occasional moan. Hopefully the break was improving his condition. If not, it was at least a brief reprieve...one I didn't want to interrupt.

I set my jaw and decided to stick it out. I sat wide awake, massaging my legs, trying to promote circulation. Was that even the problem? Whatever...I had to do something to keep from counting upward. That could only slow the passage of time. My eyes fixed on the phone.

Now.

Now.

The alarm will go off...now!

How long I was scrunched up, I don't know. Without a doubt though, it was the longest part of that drive.

The timer struck zero. No alarm had ever sounded so beautiful.

People were too slow to stir. I needed out. Didn't they know? I had done my part, had stuck it out. I had sacrificed myself. I hadn't anticipated this lethargy, this wait before I could get out of the pickup and stretch. Scott was still coming around, but I couldn't wait any longer. I nudged him. "Scott, can you let me out?"

I made the request a second time before he opened the door. I slithered past the reclined front seat.

The air was frigid and wonderful. I walked up the hill, still convinced of a circulation problem. After two laps though, I was still stiff—the walking wasn't helping. More blood flow? I started skipping. This did the trick. I skipped up and down the road in front of the Hilux while our drivers collected themselves. I skipped while Andrew and Scott dug through Clifford's cargo bay, searching for another dose of Dramamine. I skipped while I shivered.

My legs calmer, I resumed walking. Scott joined me.

"You all right?"

"Yeah, my legs were just…" I shook my head. "I don't know. Not good. They were very restless at first, then achy, then there were shooting pains. It was weird."

"Very weird. Better now, though?"

I thought about my latest discovery, the one I had made while skipping. "Yes and no."

Scott's brow furrowed. "What do you mean?"

I hesitated. "Don't tell Andrew." Scott's face gave away to inquisitiveness at the hint of humor in my voice. "Take a look." I lifted my head over Scott's shoulder. He turned. "Hell of a place our drivers chose to stop, huh?"

"You said it."

We stood together in front of the building, eyeing the large sign above the door. It was a hostel. We had parked forty yards downhill from a hostel.

"You're right," Scott said. "Better not tell Andrew."

It was a few hours to dawn, and a few more to Urubamba. We were close to the end. Our destination nearly in sight, we crawled back into the Hilux.

Chapter 40
Green Machine

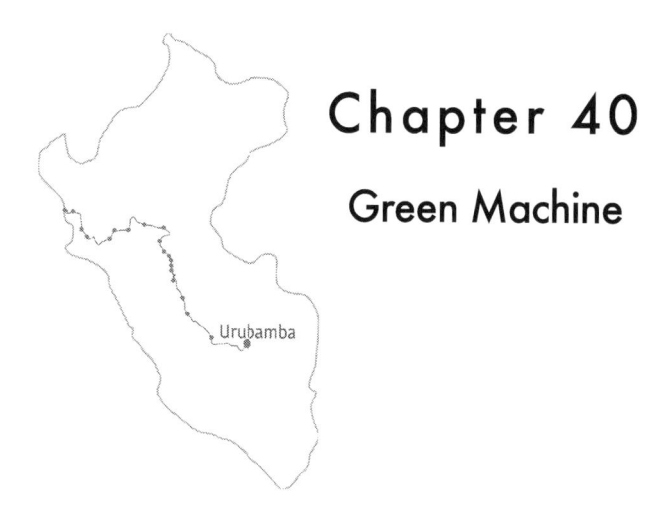

URUBAMBA is one of three villages between Cusco and Machu Picchu, one of the most-trafficked tourist routes of the country. Like most mountain villages and cities, we first spotted Urubamba from the top of a ridge, basking in the early morning light. This view slowed time, holding the finish line just beyond our reach. And though the twists and hairpins of the grade into the valley tried, they couldn't prevent our drivers from delivering us.

In town, we parked outside the restaurant that was the official finish line and fell from the cab of the Hilux onto our knees, kissing the ground. Then the five of us unloaded Clifford. He too took a tumble out of the Hilux, thankful to plant his tires.

Andrew and I did a quick walk around while Carlos and his friend examined the Hilux. They asked to be compensated for a small dent in the bed and a scratch on one of the tail lights. Scott pointed to the rear end of our mototaxi. One whole taillight was missing, marked only by the stubs of copper wiring sticking from the frame. Carlos laughed, shrugged, then extended a hand to Scott. They shook. Our drivers jumped back into the pickup and started off.

"Not much for taking breaks, are they?" Andrew said, one hand splayed across his stomach.

"No," I said, head shaking. "No, they're not."

The pickup disappeared down the street, a trail of dust dangling in its wake.

We turned to the restaurant, the Tim Cahill quote in my ears. "An adventure is never an adventure when it happens." I smirked. We had made it, despite the road conditions, a shoddy carburetor, and two failed electrical systems. We had survived sleep deprivation, food poisoning, and diarrhea (though mine still persisted). We had made it through construction zones, past armed roadblocks, and over Death Road. We had covered miles under Clifford's own power, but had also managed to get a tow from both a tuk-tuk and a mototaxi, had taken a box truck tour, and had gone for two very windy Hilux rides.

All that was left to do was cross the street and pass over the official finish line. That would transform every overheated stop into a chance to admire the view, every mechanic visit a chance to interact with the locals, and every damn set of *rompemuelles* a fun test of our suspension. Cross that line, and it would all solidify into an adventure.

We couldn't though—there was a gated wall in our way.

"The restaurant is still closed?"

"What time is it?"

"Not quite seven."

Our shadows were still long on the ground, but the sun was getting warm.

"Now what?"

"Should we wait?"

"We passed Sue and Dorian not too long ago. They should be here soon, don't you think?"

"Maybe."

"Let's take a look at the map."

I pulled a hand-drawn map of Urubamba from my bag, compliments of Duncan. Marked were some key locations.

"Should we try to get a room at this hotel?"

"May as well check it out."

After another party session on the kick-starter, we got the taxi going and headed down the road. The hotel lobby was also closed, so we took back to the streets, aimless, savoring the last moments with Clifford...until the engine started to sputter again. We hightailed it back to the restaurant, the familiar cascade of gasoline spewing from the carb and the sound of combustive death announcing our arrival.

Things at the restaurant had changed. The perimeter's tall, red brick wall now suspended banners, large words splayed across them: "Mototaxi Junket." And the wall's green wrought-iron gates were now open.

Even with the fuel valve off, gas vapors geysered from our carb as we wandered up to the gate, peeking around the red brick. The inside of the courtyard was...unexpected. Crisp blades of manicured green filled the ground. Tables hidden beneath white tablecloths and flanked with white chairs sat atop the grass beneath white canopies meant to limit the brilliance of it all beneath the noontime sun. Tucked along the inside of the wall was more vegetation, lush, colorful, and tamed. Stone pavers led to a building more glass than wood, with stout timbers supporting a thatched roof. Behind it, another building. It was larger, with tree trunk columns spaced across the veranda, holding the roof that extended past the stucco walls.

We exchanged a glance. This wasn't the Peru we had come to expect...or know. But there was no mistaking the banners, or the large sheet of paper mounted on a large easel that leaned next to the closest table. It was blank, except for the large heading scribbled across the top: "Sign In Sheet."

"Are we first?" Another glance at each other.

We stepped forward and grabbed the pen from the easel's tray. We signed our names beneath our team name and stepped back.

"We made it," Andrew said.

"Finally," I gasped.

"That kind of sucks we were first," Scott replied.

"Why's that?"

"Sue and Dorian were still going strong when we passed them."

"Maybe they'll have the satisfaction of being the first team to finish that didn't catch a ride," I suggested.

"Nope," Andrew replied. "Remember day one? They passed us getting a tow, before we even made it to Piura."

"Oh yeah," Scott and I chorused.

"Guys! You made it!" Oscar, our Peruvian liaison, came through the gate. "The restaurant called my hotel to say a team was here. I was beginning to wonder where everyone was." He clapped us on the shoulders. "Ready for some celebratory beers?"

Beers…at eight in the morning?

"Hell yes!"

While Oscar tracked down a bartender, I delivered our fare: Cindy. The plastic she was wrapped in shed some dust while I unrolled her, but she was still in one piece, with the pink boots, blue jeans, lime green gown, and voice box. Her hair was askew, but that could have just been the humidity.

I strolled up to Oscar standing at the bar. "I just have one question, Oscar." I sat Cindy next to him. "Why does she sing *Yankee Doodle*?"

He laughed. "Does she really?"

"Yeah," Andrew joined in, "Why sing an American song?"

Scott took a beer Oscar passed him. "And why is she wearing blue jeans under her dress?"

Oscar almost spewed his beer all across us, as though he were our carb. "And how'd you boys figure out what she's wearing under that green dress?" We exchanged an all-too-innocent glance. "Well, she seems to be in a fine state. You should see some of the Pink Fairies from past races. There were a few that were clearly violated."

"Violated?!" We all laughed, beers in hand, the morning sun on our faces.

Oscar motioned towards the mass of white. "Let's grab a table and I'll tell you about it."

We spent the morning swapping stories. Oscar had been one of the original event testers and had driven a mototaxi across Peru as well, and then into Bolivia, back when the race was longer and less tame. We were still chatting when Sue and Dorian arrived. They signed their names, shared a beer with us, then took off again for Machu Picchu.

Our weakened stomachs roused by the beer, we took our leave too. We went to a restaurant Oscar suggested to grab breakfast, then found a hostel and promptly passed out from exhaustion.

* * *

I dreamt of an oil container, abandoned roadside, tipped and leaking feces. The solution to pollution is dilution? No. Duncan had it right. The solution to pollution is "don't be an asshole."

We can live ignoring the fact that millions of little pieces of ourselves are dying every moment. Really, cell death is inconsequential to us—which is understandable. But that millions of little pieces of the planet are dying every moment is not inconsequential. Even so, we act as though it were, as though the tarnishing of the biosphere is inevitable, a certainty that we have no influence over. So why bother worrying about it?

Because of this elected ignorance, modern man's relationship with the planet has become an inconclusive negotiation for symbiosis. In case you don't recall, that's one definition of disease. And right now, mankind could be likened to planetary cancer. And even as our societal tumors choke at the arteries of life, we still choose ignorance.

We don't care about the production of greenhouse gasses and other harmful emissions. We burn forests and desertify grasslands. We thaw glaciers and chip away at the ice caps. We erode soils and empty aquifers. We let chemicals flow into our rivers. We replace marine life with plastics. We dig massive pits, chasing heavy metals. Then we dump our electronics into landfills, where we let those same heavy metals accumulate and toxify. We eliminate species daily. And we leave spent oil on the roadside.

I'm reminded of Cindy. "The Slut"? Not at all. Cindy didn't deserve that title, but it stuck. In part, because our behavior toward Cindy was degrading and belittling. We cut Cindy from her protective plastic, discarded her piñata; not for her benefit, but for ours. We wrapped her up and crammed her next to the bundle of tools in our cargo bay; not for her benefit, but for ours. We paraded her and posed her for photos, but that wasn't for her either.

Cindy's proportions might be a bit different than the planet's, but they are both fond of blue and green. And right now, everything we are doing to the planet is for our benefit, and ours alone. There is a key difference between Cindy and our planet though: our lives don't depend on Cindy.

This planet is a living organism, a giant green machine, and we are a part of it. This global organism is as susceptible to disease as any of us and, right now, the cancer is growing.

There is a bright side here, though. Don't forget what Cindy was always trying to remind us of: those Yankees that had owned their shortcomings. We could do the same. We could acknowledge and change our shitty behaviors; we could actively integrate new ideals into society; we could stop being assholes. Yes, there may be a clash of cultures in the beginning, but the conflict may highlight the best features of both. And when it does, we'll have an excellent recipe for heterosis, a hybrid-invigorated culture hell-bent on progress, development, and environmentalism.

Or not. We could just continue the same way we've been going.

To those casting a vote for that option, I would point to that other message we've been constantly hearing. Not the one from Cindy, but from her blue and green counterpart: Earth. Temperatures are rising; seas and oceans are creeping inland; storms and droughts are reaching extremes. Is this message falling on deaf ears? I would argue that it doesn't matter.

The planet's biosphere can be viewed through a planetary lens as a vast ecosystem, and like any ecosystem, this one is living. According to at least one theory, the process of living is a process of cognition, meaning this global system is going to self-regulate. What are the implications for humanity?

The planet *will* go on living. Life has persisted through countless disasters, several of a magnitude that human activity could never compare to. However, the question is if humanity will continue to be a part of that system. Will we achieve a symbiotic state with the planet, or will we be regulated out of existence?

It's up to us. If we wanted, we could take charge of that cognition. We could regulate. Just like the scientists that worked with nuclear bombs and their byproducts, we are smart and we are clever. And now that we have unwittingly created one hell of a problem for ourselves, we can look forward to the immense satisfaction we will feel when we actualize a solution.

And a good starting point for that solution: "don't be an asshole."

Chapter 41

The Finish Party

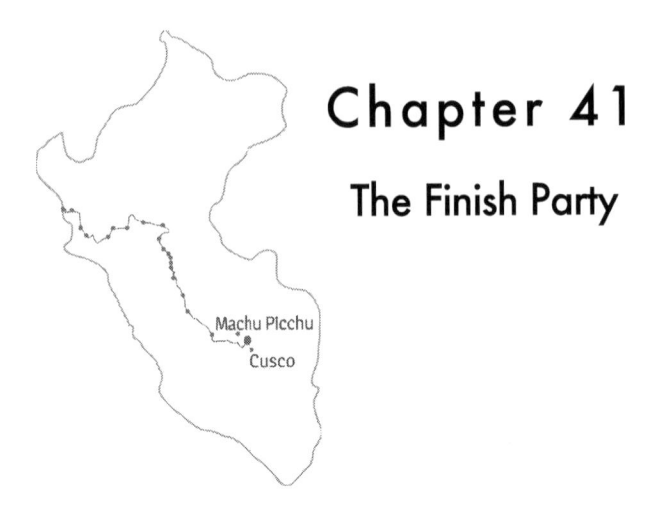

DURING THE NEXT TWO DAYS, the other teams arrived. Some coasted in on fumes, mototaxi bits missing. Several came as ours had—in the bed of a Hilux. When the Swiss team arrived, they had stories of smooth mototaxi sailing during the day and wild discotecas at night. And when our long-lost Texan friends finally arrived, we let out a long exhale. No one had heard from them in more than a week.

"You guys end up in the mountains?"

"No, heard about all the climbing. We went east instead."

"Good. We were worried you would go south thinking you were following us."

"Yeah, we're glad we didn't. Our crappy engine wouldn't have made it. It barely got us to Moyobamba."

"You find a mechanic there?"

Aaron and Josh laughed and exchanged a look. "Actually, we found a truck for the mototaxi and a plane for us. We've been in Cusco for a week! We picked up our mototaxi just this morning for the drive here."

It became obvious pretty quickly that everyone had been towed or trucked at some point (I'm pretty sure we were still the only team to get towed by a tuk-tuk, though). The South Africans had even, through a miscommunication, ended up on the trailer of a semi headed for Lima—the wrong direction. After they realized this, they caught another truck headed back toward Cusco and the finish line. All of this they shouted to us over the beers they had promised us after our tandem nighttime descent.

Something else that became clear was the divide between the quality of our taxis. Some teams had mototaxis that gave minimal trouble. The Swiss team hadn't even bothered to change their oil. Meanwhile, other taxis had undergone massive amounts of work. While discussing this, Oscar let slip that the organization had been considering the purchase of new mototaxis for our race, but had decided to postpone.

There was a chorus of alcohol-charged shouting at that bit of news, but we turned back to laughter before any rioting could start. The yelling was all in good fun—we could all appreciate the extra challenges and opportunities afforded us by our shitty mototaxis.

The day of the Finish Party, only three teams had not made an appearance. One hadn't been able to handle the stresses of the race and had broken the one actual rule—they had abandoned their mototaxi in the middle of nowhere to be retrieved later by Oscar...if he could find it. We didn't expect to see them.

The second was team *Rubber Duckies*. Pete was persistent. He had lost his bag on a rough stretch of road; it bounced right out of the sofa half of his taxi. Though he had backtracked, he didn't find it. Not long after though, Pete and another Junket team stayed in the same house for the night. The next morning, the other team left before Pete and had forgotten one of their bags. Pete hadn't managed to catch them and return it, so he was utilizing the clothing and gear.

The morning of the Finish Party, he was still a ways out. Amidst the hopes that he would make it, there remained some doubt. So the beer and Pisco Sours started to flow without him.

Before the banquet started though, a mototaxi rolled up outside the restaurant.

"It's Pete!"

We flooded from the courtyard to surround the yellow mototaxi with the giant rubber ducky strapped on top. Pete was dazed, his eyes stuck in a million-mile-stare after a long day on the road. People tried to push drinks into his hand as he dismounted, but his shoulders were locked in the position that combated the mototaxi's rightward pull. In a matter of minutes though, the celebrating brought Pete back to life and his hands clasped a drink. We guided him inside, ushering him to the easel.

When the banquet began, we loaded our plates with the local cuisine. One of the main dishes was *cuy* (guinea pig), served with little rodent claws and all. As we finished feasting, another exhibition of dancers began. It was another beautiful display of clashing cultures, a juxtaposition of traditions that threw each into high relief.

This beauty was lost though as soon as *we* were pulled onto the floor. We took turns spinning around, hand in hand with the local dancers: all the Brits, the Romanians, and the Swiss; the Kiwis in their orange jumpsuits; Barry and Gerald, parading their tiny Australian flag; Josh and Aaron, still handing out suckers; and the Scots, Shaun having successfully worn his kilt through the entire race and up to this moment, which meant flashing his junk when he spun fast enough.

And Andrew.

And Scott.

My own teammates. Witnesses to the adventurist in me, and me to the adventurists in them.

The only people missing were on that third team: Jan and Paddy. We checked their social media and saw that they were taking things at a more relaxed pace and were trying to make the most of their overland tour, stopping to see the sights and even making a side trip or two. I had looked forward to catching up with Paddy and swapping stories, but they were still days from Urubamba. There was no chance we would see them before leaving Peru.

After the eating and dancing, we made our way out to the white tables and cool air, where the drinking continued and where we scared off any other tourists, their clean and pressed clothes standing in contrast to our dirt and oil-stained wrinkles. And finally, after enough alcohol had been consumed, Cindy was pulled from her sitting position on the bar and paraded around the party, the subject of pictures and punch lines alike. She sang *Yankee Doodle* through it all.

Like I said in the beginning, the victim of this story is Cindy.

A Note from the Author

A NUMBER OF ORGANIZATIONS were referenced in the telling of this story, all of which are deserving of another mention.

The Adventurists are still hard at play, planning and hatching events in a vein similar to the Mototaxi Junket. If you've been inspired to participate—or just want to probe—you can find them at TheAdventurists.com.

Cool Earth—official charity of the Adventurists—is growing a protective barrier around the world's rainforests by empowering local communities. To learn more or to donate, visit them at CoolEarth.org.

World Bicycle Relief is mobilizing students, health care workers, and entrepreneurs in developing countries, helping people overcome distance with the help of a bicycle. Learn more or donate at WorldBicycleRelief.org.

And don't forget to see what has become of Brenden and Emma, the Aussie cyclists. Their tour may have reached a final destination, but their trip lives on through motivational and other speaking engagements. Find them at TotallyTandem.com.

About the Author

A CRAVING for new ideas and different perspectives has pulled Nathan Doneen into the world of travel.

After a rural upbringing fostered his love for the outdoors, Doneen earned degrees in Biology and Environmental Science. He currently works as a clinical chemist while he studies the craft of writing.

Want to see more or read more? For pictures of this trip and excerpts from Nathan's other books, visit NathanDoneen.com. Continue on to read the first two chapters of Nathan's *The Divide: A 2700 Mile Search for Answers*.

The Divide

A 2700 Mile Search For Answers

Chapter 1

Beginnings

"What the hell am I doing?"

My legs burned with a week's worth of laziness, and my lungs stung with the cold morning air. I sat next to my bike in the shadow of the mountains, gravel digging into my legs. Why had I ever considered this?

"You can still bail, Nathan. Megan can't be that far away yet. You have no idea what you're doing."

My first bike tour was off to a great start. Twenty minutes earlier, my friend Megan dropped me off at a trailhead at the south end of Banff, Alberta. I had assembled my bike and packed my gear. We asked two mountain bikers to snap a few photos before I set off. Locals. My gear gave away my intentions, and my chest swelled when they said neither of them had attempted the route and only knew one guy that had—he hadn't been able to finish. Riding high on my bike, my chin to the sky, I set off into the mountains where the sun had just touched their tops. I extended my arm and gave a final wave to Megan and the mountain bikers.

Now, 1.6 miles later, instead of riding my bike, I sat next to it trying to assess the damage. I had come around a blind corner and hit a trench carved into the trail by the rain. The impact, paired with my poor pannier-packing skills, caused each of the rear plastic pannier clips to snap. I was 1.6 miles in and not sure I could effectively carry my gear. That's a problem when you're riding the Great Divide Mountain Bike Route, the longest route in the world, following the Continental Divide through two Canadian provinces and five U.S. states, reaching as far south as the Mexican border.

"What the hell am I doing?"

* * *

I wasn't a mountain biker. So why was I even out there? It all started with a graduation card given to me a year earlier. I had been at home, skipping my own college graduation. It wasn't a big deal—I planned on going to graduate school anyway. Besides, I had gone to an award ceremony the night before that was ceremonious enough. In truth, graduation was another one of those events I feared would leave me empty.

I was in the living room when there was a knock on our front door. It was Amber, my ex-girlfriend. She didn't cross the threshold, but remained on our front steps, the hideous preformed concrete that had begun to crumble at the corners. She had stopped by on her way out of town for the summer to drop off a graduation card for me. This was unexpected, but not surprising. Before Amber and I started dating, she had started sending me letters and cards, homemade and handwritten, the kind of solid sentiment you tend to hold on to in the proverbial shoebox. But Amber and I had broken up more than a year before. "Friends" is too bold a word to describe what became of us, but we were more than just cordial and polite with each other. We hadn't ended in a bad way, but our closure hadn't been satisfactory. It had just been bad timing.

Now, after a year of friendly, impromptu conversations, here was Amber on the crumbling steps. Her freckles faded behind the rising burn in her cheeks, her hand holding the card extended. I fumbled it as she let go and turned to leave, uttering a quick goodbye. I watched her go, the card unopened, as the pale blue sky carried the sounds of graduation through the door, the source only a few blocks away on top of the red turf in our football stadium.

I closed the door and opened the card. The color in my own cheeks rose. I could always trust Amber to be honest. A second, then a third reading revealed the one word that was misplaced: "man." I was one of the "greatest men" she knew? I squinted at the word and closed the card, beads of sweat on my forehead.

I had never thought of myself as a man. The previous year had been difficult, but I didn't know if it qualified me as a man. I didn't feel like a man, but maybe I should have. Why didn't I?

Amber's card raised all kinds of questions. Questions without answers. And that word: "man"—it was the inciting incident of my journey, a journey that had begun several months before.

* * *

The previous September, I was home on my family's wheat farm, working with my dad and oldest brother. Harvest was always stressful, but even more so this year. It had taken longer than usual, and we were under pressure to finish before the weather turned. I also had to get back to school, which started the following week.

The day started like any other: me in a combine harvester in a field of peas. Meanwhile, my brother's combine suffered a serious breakdown that disabled him for the majority of the day. That afternoon, when it was running again, my dad and brother traded places.

Brandon, now in a grain truck, pulled out of our shop's driveway headed for the field. Running alongside him, our dog Axel. No dog has ever known freedom as Axel did. He never knew what a fence was, or a leash, or even a collar. He roamed free, played with coyotes, tailed us all day in the fields begging for the scraps from our lunch boxes, and as any free dog would, he chased cars. In fact, he became quite notorious for it. He would occupy the middle of our narrow country roads, waiting. Drivers that knew Axel did not flinch. He always waited until the last second, but he would always move. Despite his agility, he earned us more than one visit from the police. He never once got hit though. Cars, pick-ups, school buses, grain trucks, tractors, tractor-trailers; nothing. Until that day in September.

My brother, in the grain truck for the first time that harvest, pulled from our shop's drive—Axel chasing after him—when he got "that feeling." But his quick reflexes and evasive maneuver were not enough to spare Axel. Axel's body crumpled under the suspension. My brother locked up the brakes and jumped out. Behind him on the road, our dog of 15 years lifted his head through labored breathing to look at my brother, the gravel digging into his body.

"Tim, you copy?!"

"Yeah, I got you Brandon, go ahead."

"I need to know where your gun is right now!"

"... What ... what do you need my gun for?"

"I got Axel. It's not good."

I sat alone in my combine and heard the fate of Axel sealed over a CB radio, the fate of a life-long companion I had known since he was a puppy. I stopped the combine, a farming sin, but I couldn't see through my tears. Axel was lying on that road alone and afraid. I wanted to be by his side, but there was no time to get there. Now he would never again follow me through the fields; he would never again bring me a dirt clod to play fetch with; he would never again chase a car. What a crappy friend to let my dog die alone, without the ones he loved most. My brother ended Axel's suffering. His body was buried with a wheel tractor.

The day only got worse.

* * *

A week later, I was back at EWU in Cheney, Washington, home in the Biology Department. That quarter, I took my Senior Capstone, an animal physiology lecture paired with experimental research of our own design. That one class may as well have been a full-time job. I was fortunate enough to work with two of my friends in a group of five, which was no surprise—groups were assigned according to shared interests.

The majority of students in the class were biology majors of the "pre-" nature: pre-med, pre-vet, pre-dent. Of course the "outdoorsy" students interested in wildlife and ecology would be assigned to each other.

The experiment we designed focused on the effects a hormone had on freshwater crayfish. This was my first time doing physiological research, and it was fascinating trying to see pass the hard exterior and into the crayfishes' interior biochemistry. We decided to use a few measurements that would help us understand how outside stresses could change the internal processes of our critters. One involved provoking our crayfish—their response was then recorded.

This was a unique project compared to any research done in that class, in that quarter or previously and, in my opinion, had the most relevance. Why not perform an original study on an ecological problem common across the country? Our project was ambitious to say the least, but our group was looking for a challenge. Our experimental design had heads turning in the department, and we had to call in every favor our super-senior (5th-year senior) status could muster.

One favor came from Dr. Hancock, the man in charge of the aquatics lab, a basement level research lab that would make any plumber shit himself. The maze of water inlets, outlets, flow meters, valves, and drains was the perfect scientific backdrop to a cement room that smelled of seafood. Not only was the research of a graduate student taking place in this lab, but so was the research of Dr. Hancock himself. We persuaded him to give us a key to this lab. The paperwork he had to fill out to get a copy was justification enough to deny us the convenience of our own key, but we were convincing. When we got our key, the number of people who had access to that lab doubled.

Once our research proposal was approved by a review committee, we ordered our crayfish from a biological supply company. Our order was for 30, but orders of this nature always included extra specimens in case shipping was too much for some. We expected 35 crawdads would be shipped. Of those that survived, 24 would be part of the experiment.

The supply company shipped 50 crayfish.

They all survived.

* * *

"Please enter your password."

We had unpacked and found housing for all 50 crayfish, a number we were unprepared for. Once we reached that milestone, we called it quits. With the extra time at home, I ran our bins down to the recycling center a few blocks away. I was gone 15 minutes and found a new voicemail waiting for me when I got back.

"Hey Nathan, it's Jake. Listen man, I just got a call. We fucked up. Hancock is saying we need to get all of our stuff out of his lab ... today. I just got home, but I'm headed back to campus now. Give me a call if you can't make it. If not, I'll see you soon."

My heart clenched, not rhythmically the way it was meant to though. For the first time in weeks, I had felt good. One missed call and one voicemail later, I was red in the face, my heartbeat was in my ears, and my head was buried in my hands to catch the groan that came out. I grabbed my bag and headed for campus.

We were moved from the lowest point of the building, the aquatics lab, to the highest, most removed part of the Biology Department: the greenhouse. The direction of this move in no way reflected the change in our status, but the magnitude did. We went from being the golden students with the highly original, ambitious, interesting experiment to those students that almost ruined actual research.

In our attempt to house our 25 extra crayfish, we turned on a water supply valve we shouldn't have. The opened valve caused a pressure drop elsewhere in the system, the in-flow to the hot tub-sized aquaria that housed Dr. Hancock's fish. The out-flow, regulated by a different system, remained the same and caused a slow, steady drop of the water level in his aquaria. Luckily, I had sent Dr. Hancock an email to give him an update of what we had been up to. When he stepped in to check on our work, he discovered his fish in too little water. We had almost killed his fish and wasted months of time he had invested into his study. He wasn't pleased. He wanted us out.

After we relocated, we went searching for Dr. Hancock. I expected him to be livid. When we found him he was anything but. He played the classic "not angry, just disappointed" card. I would have preferred him to yell and let out his frustration at us. But he was calm, collected. I couldn't say the same about me. Standing in the white, windowless hallway outside his office, I pulled the lab key from my keychain and held it out to him, as requested. The loss of the key was a big blow, but what it represented was even more devastating: the loss of Dr. Hancock's respect.

Chapter 2

JUNE 2013

RESPECT.

Here I was losing it again, crouched over my bike at mile 1.6.

The air had lost its brisk edge, and my breath was once again invisible. Sweat glazed my palms and my heart raced as I tried to get moving again, not for the purpose of progress, but so I could leave behind the disdainful stares of the mountain peaks that looked down on me as the rising sun woke them.

My panniers lay on the ground while I adjusted the rear cargo rack when the cyclists from the parking lot came around that blind corner. They flew past without hesitation, not stopping to check on me. I sighed as they disappeared down the trail. I'm not sure I could have handled the embarrassment of admitting to these cyclists I had no idea what I was doing— cyclists that had had the slightest hint of reverence in their voices when we spoke just 30 minutes before. I could barely handle the chuckle I thought echoed back up the trail from their direction.

I adjusted the cargo rack and packing arrangement and used zip ties to secure what was left of the two broken pannier clips. They held, but how long would they last? The next bike shop was back in the States, some 300 miles away. Banff was right behind me, 1.6 miles backwards.

"This is crucial Nathan. This is going to set the tone of the whole trip."

Go back? Or press on?

Before I set out, I decided to avoid going backwards at all cost. It was the opposite of progress, but it was only 1.6 miles back to the trailhead. Maybe a total of 2.5 to the bike shop? I could solve the problem, or I could take my chances. I could go backwards or move forwards with a debilitated setup.

"This is a crucial decision."

The next 20 miles went much smoother than the first 1.6. I did stop and tighten every bolt of the cargo rack assembly after it was shook to pieces, but the sun filled valley made the day perfect for a ride. I cringed at my decision not to return to Banff, but only before I cracked a wide grin. The broken panniers might become a bigger problem, or they just might become a great story to tell my friends. No, a few pieces of broken plastic would not stop me. They would not force me to turn around. They would not weaken my resolve. Why should they? People have done greater things than this, in the face of adversity greater than any broken pannier clip. If anything, my resolve was strengthened.

Cycling along Spray Lake, I saw my first cyclist. Already? I guessed it would have taken longer to run into someone else riding the route, at least more than three hours on the first day. My pace was quicker than his, and it wasn't long before I caught him. His name was Freddie, and he was from Switzerland. Although he said he was impressed with my light load, he wasn't as thrilled about having me for company. He claimed he was stopping for a break after just a few minutes of riding with me. A break Freddie? Only three miles from where you camped the night before? I didn't want to be a nuisance, so I left Freddie sitting along the shade-less talus bank of the reservoir.

Several hundred yards farther, I crossed a bridge and glanced up a deep canyon to find the source of a thunder. I turned my bike around and left it on the side of the trail while I hiked up a small hill. This would have been a much better rest location, Freddie. The angular fractures of the canyon walls had been smoothed where the water flowed. Water that was robin's egg blue appeared from nowhere, fell five feet into a small pool, and continued down another 25-foot fall, the blues abandoned for the white spray that vanished into the shadows of the canyon below.

* * *

A smattering of rain began as I climbed away from the banks of Spray Lake. The rain's light drumming on my waterproof material was joined by the rattle of my gear as another pannier clip broke as well as one of the repair zip-ties. I pushed up the remainder of the hill and stopped on level ground to assess the situation. Had I made the wrong decision to not return to Banff? Only 30 miles in and suffering from my gear situation was daunting. Knowing I still had more than 250 miles before I would have the chance to find replacements was unfathomable.

Zip-ties were not a viable solution to my pannier problem. I snacked on some Pop-Tarts and mulled things over while I decided on a course of action. In my gear, I had 50 feet of cord and a carabiner to suspend my food at night to prevent animals from snooping, especially bears. During the day though, these items had no purpose—until now. A variety of knots and friction hitches transformed the cordage and carabiner into the main support for the panniers. Was it pretty? Not a chance. Was it functional? I hoped.

As I arranged the cord on my panniers, a familiar face crept up over the crest of the hill. Freddie stopped, but still straddled his bike.

"Is everything all right?"

"Yeah, it's just my pannier clips are breaking. I think the panniers are too full for how hard some of these hits are, so I'm reinforcing them."

I was using the carabiner to tighten the cord when Freddie reached into his handlebar bag. I looked up at the click of his camera shutter. At least my panniers would make a good story for someone. What I would give for a copy of those pictures now. Freddie continued on as I finished securing my panniers. It was 5 minutes after that I was moving again, now with wobbly panniers, but without the fear of them falling off.

The light sprinkle continued as I emerged from the trail's tree cover onto a wide road. The sun was fully consumed by the clouds and the mountains began to disappear beneath the slate gray as well. I urged forward, trying to catch Freddie and trying to outrun the coming weather. I coasted down a hill and automatically applied the brakes as my next obstacle came into sight.

"You've got to be kidding me."

This was not the first time I had seen a moose. This was not the first time I had been this close to a moose. However, this was the first time a moose had been in my way. She was standing in the middle of a bridge only wide enough to accommodate one vehicle at a time on its wood planks. I wanted to appreciate my first wildlife encounter, but the long valley was disappearing in the waves of rain the wind carried towards me. This was not the ideal time to stop.

I pulled on my rain jacket as the first wave reached me. The rain, pushed sideways by the wind, raised the skin of my exposed legs; the wind circled me and whipped the fabric of my clothing; the moose didn't move. If she was bothered by the sudden weather change, she didn't show any sign of it. She remained where I found her, inhibiting my progress.

A pickup sat on the other side of the road. Where was the driver? It was apparent the driver, like the moose, was unperturbed by the rain. After a few minutes without any sign of the driver, I pushed my bike to the back end of the pickup where its orientation to the wind created a small rain shadow.

The moose milled around on the bridge for another fifteen minutes. My backside started to complain about the pointed gravel sapping the heat from my body; my joints whined about the cold air; water dripped from my helmet. Then a few things happened at once. My small section of sheltered road became inundated with runoff making its way down the road; a car approached the bridge opposite the side I was on; and the moose, jarred back to awareness by the car's horn, left the bridge and disappeared behind the tree line. I waved a shivering limb at the driver to offer my thanks and picked up my bike. Within seconds of leaving the rain shadow, I was drenched.

* * *

During the delay, I learned from my map that across the bridge was a turn that would take me to a lodge. It wouldn't hurt to stop in and see if I could wait out the rain, so I made the turn. I nestled my bike in a corner of the lodge, under an eve and found the door. I stepped inside and was greeted by Chris.

"Hi there. It looks wet out there."

"Just a little."

"Maybe more than a little. You must be a racer?"

"No, but I am doing a tour on the same route. I was just wondering if I could wait out the rain here?"

"Yeah, of course. Let me show you in."

Chris showed me where to hang my gear, still dripping with water, and led me to the lodge's dining room where I was offered coffee and tea. Chris knew all about the bike route and was a big fan of the race, which had been through only three days before me.

The race, the Tour Divide, was an annual collection of adventure cyclists that rode the whole route solo and unsupported. Racers could choose between an independent time trial or the Grand Depart, the official start. Racers carried GPS locators that were linked to the race's website. If you knew a racer's name, they could be located at any time.

Chris updated me on the racers and their locations, then returned to work leaving me with a mug of tea cupped in my soggy hands. Its warmth spread through my fingers while my eyes traced the red line that traversed the map laid out in front of me.

The 2,700-mile route was broken into seven maps and all were bisected by the red line that marked the official route. This was the line I would be following for the next several weeks. My goal was to average 80 miles a day. To reach that goal on day one meant crossing Elk Pass. I looked up from my map and through the large windows of the lodge. Rain blotted out the valley. Maybe Elk Pass would have to wait.

"Hi there. I just wanted to let you know that our guests will be served an afternoon snack in about an hour. You are more then welcome to join everyone if you would like."

"That sounds wonderful."

"Or, if you are hungry now, I can heat up some of the leftovers from last night's dinner for you."

"Really?! That would be amazing. What's your name?"

"I'm Shari-Lynn."

Shari-Lynn was Chris's wife and they managed the lodge together. I was taken aback by the kindness I received from Chris and Shari-Lynn. With the warmth returned to my hands, I pulled out my journal and wrote an entry about them.

"Here you are," Shari-Lynn said as she placed a bowl of steaming food in front of me. She leaned in with a lowered voice and said, "We don't serve our guests food outside of scheduled meals and snacks, so if anyone asks, you work here, ok?"

I held back a chuckle. "Of course. Again, thank you so much."

With a smile, she returned to her upright posture. "And don't forget to finish chopping that wood when the rain clears up," Shari-Lynn said with a wink.

* * *

Two hours later, I returned to the bike with improved spirits. I pulled my bike from the corner, began to walk down the drive, and turned back for one last look. Would I remember this place? Would my feelings of gratitude for the lodge, Chris, and Shari-Lynn persist? They were immensely important to me today, but where would I be in four, five, six weeks? With the hope my memory was longer than the mountain's, I set out into a landscape lost to the fact it had just experienced a heavy rain. Blue hues dominated the sky, accented by the white wisps of clouds and sharp snowcaps. Had it just rained?

With my renewed vigor, I put Elk Pass in my sights, the first Continental Divide crossing of several. I found the parking lot where the climb began and started up what the map called a "virtual wall." There was no argument to be made about that. The hike alone made my legs throb and lungs burn while the sound of my breathing drowned out all other noise—forget riding up it. After a short descent and second steep climb, the trail emerged from the trees and into a clear-cut where a set of power lines crossed the range. The sun was warm still, but not warm enough to evaporate the rain that had fallen earlier. Riding through this mud was difficult. I walked most of this segment but fought my exhaustion long enough to find the top of Elk Pass.

There was no celebrating when I crossed through the gate that marked the top. The long day of riding paired with my pannier problems left me tired and unconcerned with my first crossing. Was it monumental? No, it was just another pedal stroke underfoot, a landmark on the map that could now be crossed off. What's next? What landmark would I use to track my progress tomorrow? That was what the route would become: goal after goal after goal. Always looking forward. Progress now, reflection later.

I removed my sunglasses and zipped my jacket as I rode into the mountain's shadow. Was it time to unpack my warm sleeping bag yet? The map showed a cabin available along the route, on a first come, first served basis. This was my goal for the night; if it wasn't available I would camp along the road.

It wasn't.

Clothes hung from the porch. My line-of-sight extended as I coasted past. Against the cabin was a bicycle, then a picnic table, then a stove, then the cyclist. It was none other than Freddie. I had caught him.

I remembered his early break and kept coasting, sure he didn't want my company. He turned at the sound of the gravel beneath my tires and we waved to each other.

I had never considered myself to be that competitive, but the sight of Freddie stirred something in me. With a new burst of energy, I kept going. Every mile I covered would be that much more I had done in my first day than Freddie had done in his first two.

Ten miles down the road was a campsite nestled alongside the Elk River. A fire ring was situated near a picnic table, the remnants of beer cans among the ashes, the brands unknown to me. There was also a small outhouse at the end of a short trail, its paint faded and peeling and its hinges in need of oil. The river water was fresh, icy, and fast flowing. The small bits of dry wood I gathered helped to warm my legs after a quick rinse in the water. The small flames were hypnotizing as they tasted the aluminum cans. The popping of the wood became less frequent and gave way to another sound: the crackle of gravel. A cyclist came down the road, passed my camp, and had crossed the bridge to the far side of the river before he saw me. When he turned around, I walked out to the road to greet him.

What a light load! A full suspension bike with a frame bag, a seat bag, and small handlebar bag. I was still inspecting his bike when the rider removed his hand from an insulated glove and extended it.

"Are you racing?" I said.

"Yup."

"Did you start today?"

"No."

"Did you start with the race?" This guy looked way too experienced to have started with the Grand Depart three days earlier. But he didn't start today?

"I actually started in May ... down in Mexico. I headed out of Banff this morning and am heading back to Mexico."

Who was this cowboy? None other than Billy Rice, a veteran of the Tour Divide bike race. No one had ever attempted a yo-yo style ride of the route. Billy decided he would be the first.

"Are you a rookie?" Billy said, meaning if it was my first time on the route.

"Yeah, this is my first bike tour actually."

"What kind of pace are you aiming for?"

"I'm hoping to average about 80 miles a day."

"Yeah, that's a pretty moderate pace, you should be able to do that."

Moderate? Not for me, Billy. Thanks for the vote of confidence though, and the advice. Billy told me about places to rest, towns to resupply, sections of the route that were challenging. The guy had one foot on his bike pedal the whole time we were talking, yet he took the time to impart a bit of wisdom to me. I was grateful to listen.

"And be careful with your gear in camp," he said, pointing to my suspended bags. "I've seen a ton of bears this year. A couple today even."

With a final handshake, Billy remounted his bike and leaned on his aerobars, head ducked and hands gloved, the final light of the day failing. That would be my only encounter with Billy Rice, but not the last I would hear of him.